TREATING DEPRESSION WITH HYPNOSIS

Integrating Cognitive-Behavioral and Strategic Approaches

Michael D. Yapko, Ph.D.

BRUNNER-ROUTLEDGE
ALERE · FLAMMAM
Taylor & Francis Group

USA	Publishing Office:	BRUNNER-ROUTLEDGE
		A member of the Taylor & Francis Group
		325 Chestnut Street
		Philadelphia, PA 19106
		Tel: (215) 625-8900
		Fax: (215) 625-2940
	Distribution Center:	BRUNNER-ROUTLEDGE
		A member of the Taylor & Francis Group
		7625 Empire Drive
		Florence, KY 41042
		Tel: 1-800-634-7064
		Fax: 1-800-248-4724
UK		BRUNNER-ROUTLEDGE
		A member of the Taylor & Francis Group
		27 Church Road
		Hove
		E. Sussex, BN3 2FA
		Tel: +44 (0) 1273 207411
		Fax: +44 (0) 1273 205612

TREATING DEPRESSION WITH HYPNOSIS: Integrating Cognitive-Behavioral and Strategic Approaches

1 2 3 4 5 6 7 8 9 0

Printed by George H. Buchanan, Co., Philadelphia, PA, 2001
Cover design by Nancy Abbott.
Cover photo by Myles McGuinness/superstock ©.

A CIP catalog record for this book is available from the British Library.
⊗ The paper in this publication meets the requirements of the ANSI Standard Z39.48-1984 (Permanence of Paper).

Library of Congress Cataloging-in-Publication Data
Yapko, Michael D.
    Treating depression with hypnosis : integrating cognitive-behavioral and strategic approaches / Michael D. Yapko
        p. cm
        Includes index.
        ISBN: 1-58391-304-1
        1. Depression, Mental–Treatment. 2. Hypnotism–Therapeutic use. I. Title.

RC537 .Y357 2001
616.85'270651–dc21   2001022313

ISBN 1-58391-304-1

*To Madeline and Jerry Harris with much love,
gratitude and respect. You can ask (loudly),
"For what?", but you already know the answer . . .*

A Complete List of Books by Michael D. Yapko, Ph.D.

Psychological 911: Depression, 2001, Yapko Publications

Hand-Me-Down Blues: How to Stop Depression From Spreading in
    Families, 1999, St. Martin's Press

Breaking the Patterns of Depression, 1997, Random House/Doubleday

Essentials of Hypnosis, 1995, Brunner/Mazel

Suggestions of Abuse: True and False Memories of Childhood Sexual
    Trauma, 1994, Simon & Schuster

Hypnosis and the Treatment of Depressions, 1992, Brunner/Mazel

Trancework: An Introduction to the Practice of Clinical Hypnosis, 2nd
    Edition, 1990, Brunner/Mazel

Brief Therapy Approaches to Treating Anxiety and Depression (Ed.),
    1989, Brunner/Mazel

When Living Hurts: Directives for Treating Depression, 1988, Brunner/
    Mazel

Contents

List of tables

Foreword

Dr. Yapko has had a long association with the Milton H. Erickson Foundation in Phoenix and has published many professional articles and books. This has given his work much exposure with the risk of criticism, especially from peers who can become dangerously demanding of a perfection they only envision from afar. However he has earned the admiration and respect of students and colleagues, of clients and research subjects alike because of his integrity and genuineness. Added to these human qualities are his solid training, senior expertise and, especially, clarity of thought that make him a disciplined thinker, a convincing teacher, and a clear writer.

This book, his fifth on depression with its many manifestations and consequences for the individual, the family, and society, is true to Yapko's uniquely innovative, caring, and effective hypnotic approach. Recognizing with balance the limited value of medications, he insists in a truly caring method to deal with depression and thus devises hypnotic techniques respectfully individualistic for each client. He makes hypnosis a meaningful healing experience for the depressed individual. This method provides them with a powerful, subjective healing experience.

With unusual courage in these times of pharmacodomination, he insists that depression arises primarily from psychological and social factors and teaches the clinician not to be seduced by the lure of magical neurochemical cures. Though he does not delve in this volume directly into the causes for depression, he gives enough hints to conclude that this emotional epidemic in our country may be linked to the absence of the spiritual in our lives. In fact, in a personal communication with me he stated that "There's more to depression than materialism, of course, but it's undeniably true that *cultural emphasis imparts perspectives that place people at risk*" (my highlighting).

One of the peculiarly prevalent goals in American culture is *controllability*, which shows itself in the effort to have a perfect world. This "heaven on earth" will comfort us by the abundance of material conveniences that fulfill all our needs and solve every one of our problems. Even the angels that made their presence felt in recent years as *spiritual* are mostly materialistic self-centered caricatures of the non-material.

Like it or not, this is our society, reflecting these values even in its approach to mental health. For instance, among Cohen's risk *factors for depression*, cited in Chapter 3 of this book, is "economic deprivation." Curiously enough, greed, instant gratification, and materialism are not considered risk factors for depression. We may have to ask if these values can satisfy our existence. The increasing numbers of depressed people in an abundant society like ours make us wonder. And the fact that in 1990 America had the highest suicide rate for young men in the world (see S. J. Blumenthal on suicide over the life cycle), hints at a negative answer to the question. Because it seems that materialism cannot fulfill our existential yearnings, I believe it deserves to be listed as one of the risk factors for depression.

By not passing on spiritual values to the younger generations, our nation may be planting the seeds of depression for their future. Consequently, one explanation for the increase of depression in our culture might be that we are denying and disregarding our spirit; that we are trying to find happiness "in the wrong place." In all the excerpts of his hypnotic work, Yapko shows his way of opening new options, possibilities, vistas, often transcending the rigid "shoulds" and expectations of the world in which we live. Spiritual awareness recognizes that human life is more than its material aspects and experiences, more than possessions, power, speed, and external success. Life is also, and very importantly, transcendence, service to others to the point of sacrifice, communion with nature and all other human beings, recognition of our limitations as individuals interdependent of each other. The fruits of this view of life are inner peace, appreciation, contentment, creativity, and joy expressed in respect, justice, and caring for all.

The concept of spirituality linked to depression also has interesting corollaries for psychotherapists, the ones Yapko daringly challenges to be *validated*, rather than the treatments they employ. In this he agrees with Seligman's *effectiveness studies* that gave preeminence to the relationship between therapist and client in contrast with the *efficacy studies* demanded by managed care that require *empirically supported treatment*, disregarding the human interaction. From this perspective, we can ask whether a therapist whose values are mostly materialistic can be as effective dealing with depression as one who has accepted the spiritual dimension of human existence and lives accordingly.

The cure of depression is vitally dependent on changing one's way of thinking, one's beliefs and expectations of others and life, in its daily details and in general. The new hypnosis Yapko teaches and practices is especially important in this regard because it reaches into the person's individual unconscious belief system, values, and ideals that damage the entire thinking process. This new hypnosis teaches all of us to define and choose our thoughts and to emphasize the positive aspects of life. As this book reminds us, depression feeds itself by the adherence to many self-limiting and self-defeating beliefs, attributions, and interpretations of the world. Yapko helps depressives realize that they use negative self-hypnosis on themselves and guides them out of this cognitive trap. Thus, he helps them capture the positive in the negative, leading them to a self-liberation through hypnosis. He shows in detail, especially in the final chapters, the relaxed

subtlety of his work with depressives; "being hypnotic," as he calls it, helping them discover and use new inner strengths for their own wellbeing.

A good book is one that makes us think, ask questions, view things from
different angles; one that teaches us something new. This is what *Treating
Depression With Hypnosis* did for me. It engaged me. It gave me a fresh
view of psychotherapy and hypnotherapy, even after 40 years in the field.
Its emphasis on the relationship between clinician and patient, its honesty
and directness, its accumulated evidence against many of the myths we
have accepted as a profession, made me realize that we still have much to
learn about depression and the wonderful ways in which hypnosis works
to alleviate it. With hypnosis, we reverse depression so that humans can
enjoy the experience and the mystery of being alive. The joy of living can
and should replace the painfully depressive job of living. Yapko's well tested,
new approach to hypnosis is a powerful tool to effect this replacement.
And this book is a giant step towards that goal.

Daniel Araoz, Ed.D., FAPA, FaCoP, FAFamP (ABPP), ABPH
Professor, Mental Health Counseling, C. W. Post Campus,
Long Island University, Nassau County, New York

Introduction

In 1999, the World Health Organization (WHO), the international monitor of global health concerns, issued a devastating proclamation regarding the prevalence of depression: Depression is currently the world's *fourth* most debilitating human condition, behind heart disease, cancer, and traffic accidents. Worse was WHO's dire prediction that by the year 2020, less than a mere two decades from now, depression will have risen to become the *second* most common cause of human suffering worldwide (Murray & Lopez, 1997).

How can this be? Isn't this a disorder we in the mental health profession supposedly know how to effectively treat? What about all the "miracle drugs" we continue to hear about that promise to make people "better than well"? With the United States alone consuming 75% of the world's Prozac, and spending billions of dollars each year on antidepressant medications (Breggin, 1999), surely the rate of depression in America must have dropped a point or two, right? Wrong. In fact, the rate of depression in the U.S. is on the rise *in every age group* (Klerman & Weissman, 1989). Depression is spreading, and the less-than-effective response of the National Institute of Mental Health (NIMH), the leading force in shaping mental health policy in America (and all those who follow America's lead), is to simply try to tell more people about the "disease of depression" while throwing ever more money at drug research. NIMH apparently hopes more doctors will cast their nets into our country's troubled waters in order to find more people with symptoms to medicate once they've succumbed to the "suggestion" that "depression is a disease just like diabetes" (Mondimore, 1993).

What kind of strategic response to a huge and still-growing social problem is *that*? Spending more billions on developing more drugs as if drugs will magically provide the solution is *already* an ineffective response to the rising rates of depression. Doing *more* of what isn't working is not atypical of human nature, of course, but in this context is deeply troublesome. Borrowing on James Hillman and Michael Ventura's blunt book title, *We've Had a Hundred Years of Psychotherapy and the World's Getting Worse*, I could call this introduction, "We've Got Lots of Antidepressants and Depression's Getting Worse."

Lest one form the wrong conclusion, I'm not against the use of antidepressant medications. I'm not that extreme, and I value the data which show that medications have a great potential to help depression sufferers. People who know me and read my work consider me quite balanced in my perspectives, so much so that I was even asked to write the authoritative section on treating depression in the 1997 *Encyclopedia Britannica Medical and Health Annual* (Yapko, 1996). But, we have amassed a fantastic array of excellent research to show that depression is far more about psychological and social contributing factors than only biological ones. Unfortunately, these complex factors are not as easy to address nor are they as attractively simplistic to describe in comparison to proclaiming that "it's all in your genes" or "it's all about neurotransmitter deficiencies."

We should not tell the desperate public we purport to serve that better drugs will continue to be developed to eventually "conquer depression" (Schrof & Schultz, 1999, p. 62). That's an absolute falsehood and it fuels false hopes, a basis for making depression *worse* when the hopes don't materialize. When depression is spreading so quickly, and the social transmission of depression has been studied and affirmed as *more potent than genetic transmission* (Joiner, Coyne, & Blalock, 1999), suggesting there will one day be a drug to stop its spread is a little bit like saying there will one day be a drug that will cure other mostly social problems with a strong biological component to them, such as drug abuse (Can drug abuse really be eliminated in a culture that not only tolerates drugs, but exalts them?). Meanwhile, those people who need to be active in pursuing their recovery from depression are being told, even if only indirectly, that they can be passive and "wait for the drug to work." It is in the medically sanctioned training of such passivity that a greater damage is being perpetuated. We can do better than that.

In this book, as you can already tell, I will be blunt. Consider it a sign of the sense of urgency I feel to poke my mental health colleagues in the ribs. I want to disrupt our interdependent hypnotic state, apparently induced by superb medical hypnotists who rhythmically chanted, "Prozac . . . Zoloft . . . Luvox . . . Serzone . . . It's biochemical . . . It's genetic . . . Paxil . . . Celexa . . . Go deeper and deeper into neurochemistry . . . Effexor . . . " It is essential that we encourage a wider view of depression than the exclusively medical one. The best data we have consistently show that medication is vaulable, but not by itself.

Thus I want to emphasize the value of and *necessity* for psychotherapy in treating depression. I'm not an advocate of psychotherapy for depression for subjective or arbitrary reasons. I'm an advocate of psychotherapy because the treatment data highlight this simple but key point: *Depressed individuals generally fare better in psychotherapy than they do in drug treatment* (Antonuccio, Danton, & DeNelsky, 1995). They *feel better* in the treatment process, they usually have *lower relapse* rates, they consistently have the *same or higher success rates*, and they routinely report a *higher level of overall functioning*, even beyond the remission of depressive symptoms (Antonuccio, Danton, & DeNelsky, 1994). Realistically, no amount of medication can teach coping or problem-solving skills, or enhance one's social skills, all factors in reducing depression. Medications are valuable, and so is psychotherapy, each in different ways that work synergistically to the client's benefit.

Wherever psychotherapy is best applied, so is the use of clinical hypnosis, since the two are fundamentally inseparable. Current research simply affirms what I wrote more than a decade ago in my hypnosis textbook, *Trancework: An Introduction to the Practice of Clinical Hypnosis* (Brunner/Mazel, 1990). I described hypnosis in the clinical context, where one person strives to change another in some helpful way, as a model of social influence. I suggested that social forces such as expectancy, power, obedience to authority, prestige, interpersonal attraction, conformity, and prescribed social roles were far more relevant to understanding *therapeutic* interactions involving hypnosis than studying individualistic phenomena such as brain waves following an induction or someone's responses to arbitrary measures of suggestibility. (There are still those clinicians and researchers who would disagree, of course, thinking the response to a suggestibility test item will somehow predict therapeutic success more than the specific "real-life" components of the actual therapy, but there is plenty of good reason to doubt that for reasons described in this book.)

In 1992, my book *Hypnosis and the Treatment of Depressions* (Brunner/Mazel) came out. Remarkably, but perhaps not in light of common mythology about hypnosis, it was the first book ever written about the application of clinical hypnosis to the client population of depression sufferers. In it, I described the horror stories of hypnosis precipitating hysteria, psychosis, and suicide that had littered the hypnosis literature in regards to treating depression up to that point. I explained why, in terms of current understandings of both depression and hypnosis, the fears about using hypnosis with depressives were entirely unwarranted. I advocated some simple ideas: We treat people, not labels. We can strive to amplify our clients' strengths, not just diminish weaknesses. We can teach specific skills to people that will help them manage their moods—and their lives—better. And, we can be client-centered rather than technique-oriented.

This last point is still an especially challenging idea to many seemingly knowledgeable clinicians whose idea of hypnosis is that it *is* merely a technique. It isn't. Hypnosis encompasses a wide variety of concepts and methods that share the common denominator of appreciating that people generally have more abilities than they consciously realize. Hypnosis helps make those abilities more well-defined and more readily accessible. It is an applied "positive psychology."

The key point, however, is that hypnosis is embedded within the larger context of a therapeutic relationship. Its essence is defined by the larger context, not just by the words of the hypnotist. The words mean *nothing* if the relationship between the clinician and the client don't support their integration and utilization.

Hypnosis and the Treatment of Depressions seemed to catalyze some significant changes in the field of clinical hypnosis. The ideas and methods I presented were apparently compelling enough to warrant kind invitations to present my work at major hypnosis meetings around the world. Clinical hypnosis societies in Argentina, Australia, Belgium, Canada, Chile, Denmark, England, France, Germany, Iceland, Mexico, New Zealand, South Africa, all over the United States, and in nearly a dozen other countries have all organized clinical trainings to learn more about depression and ways hypnosis can be integrated into sensible, empirically supported, short-term treatment strategies. Depression had *rarely* been a topic at hypnosis conferences before 1992, but now it is featured routinely. Depression had been taught by some hypnosis societies as a universal contraindication for the use of hypnosis, even failing their students at exam time who neglected to mention this "fact." Many of these same societies have now updated their curricula to include hypnosis as a viable treatment for depression. Beyond hypnosis societies, many psychological and even psychiatric societies have also shown an interest in hypnosis as a treatment tool for depression.

About this book

This book is a follow-up and extension of my earlier work. In the time since *Hypnosis and the Treatment of Depressions,* I have written three more books on depression: *Breaking the Patterns of Depression* (Doubleday, 1997), *Hand-Me-Down Blues: How to Stop Depression from Spreading in Families* (St. Martins, 1999), and *Psychological 911: Depression* (Yapko Publications, 2001). These books were for the general public, the first focusing on ways an individual could learn the skills needed to overcome depression, the second focusing on depression in the larger family context (since depression is known to affect more than just individuals), and the third on providing straightforward information in a simple question-and-answer format. But, with this book, I'm back to writing for my professional colleagues again.

Much has happened in the fields of depression and clinical hypnosis in the interim, and there is now more to say about the vital role hypnosis can play in enhancing psychotherapy. Thus, the focus in this book is on structuring and delivering hypnotic interventions for major depression, with a substantial use of concepts and techniques from cognitive-behavioral and strategic approaches as a foundation. I have included current research data on depression to emphasize our still-growing knowledge of the disorder, and I have provided many detailed examples of hypnotic strategies at work in the clinical context, with an emphasis on addressing the unique and practical demands associated with clinical practice.

There are two main sections to this book, the first being the "Conceptual Framework." This section encompasses the first three chapters. In Chapter 1, I summarize much of what we currently know about depression, from the extent of the harm it causes to the things we've learned in exploring methods of treatment. In Chapter 2, I describe much of what we currently know about hypnosis as a treatment tool, addressing its potential to enhance the efficacy of therapy. In Chapter 3, I begin the transition into the practical issues associated with applying hypnosis in the context of psychotherapy, addressing the choosing of targets in treatment and the formation of well-designed interventions.

The second and larger section of the book focuses on "Clinical Applications." In Chapter 4, I present the issue of how people deal with ambiguities in life as a potential depressive risk factor and then present a step-by-step hypnotic strategy for teaching the skills of recognizing and tolerating ambiguity. In Chapter 5 I focus on the future, highlighting the power of expectations, positive or negative, in shaping moods and quality of life. This chapter includes a description and a sample of a strategy employing hypnosis for enhancing positive expectations. In Chapter 6, I focus on perceptions of controllability, since hopelessness is so closely tied to depression. A strategy using hypnosis to encourage action and a greater clarity about what is and is not controllable is included in this chapter. In Chapter 7, I describe the role of coping styles in increasing or decreasing the risk for depression, emphasizing the value of being a skilled problem-solver in allaying depression. A session transcript, including commentary and analysis, is provided as a means for teaching a strategy for effective problem-solving. Chapter 8 also provides a session transcript with commentary and analysis, illustrating well the value of hypnosis and multiple level interventions with a depressed man who also has a history of serious physical and emotional abuse. The ninth and final chapter considers the issue of prevention, challenging clinicians to better use the information we have to develop effective prevention strategies.

Throughout the book, my enthusiasm for hypnosis will undoubtedly be evident. I still find hypnosis an intriguing domain of psychological inquiry after all these years, and I believe that as powerful a tool as it is, we have only scratched the surface of its applicability.

I have the idealistic wish that we can prevent WHO's prediction from coming true. To do that, clinicians will need to think critically and not just blindly endorse simplistic drug solutions that may actually delay more multi-dimensional interventions. Clinicians must actively rediscover the many ways psychotherapy can promote the best in people so they won't keep living *down* to our lowest expectations. The capacity for hypnosis to help people get absorbed in a particular frame of mind is well established. Whether that frame of mind serves to free people from lives of despair—or unwittingly traps them in it—is largely up to us as clinicians.

I hope this book helps us choose wisely.

Michael D. Yapko, Ph.D.
Solana Beach, California
www.yapko.com

Acknowledgments

There are many people I'd like to thank publicly for their support and assistance with this project. Directly and indirectly, their contributions to my work and my life are invaluable.

My wife, Diane, gets top billing now and always. She never ceases to amaze and delight and inspire me. Her love and support mean the world to me, and in this year of our 25th wedding anniversary, I know and appreciate how lucky I am to have Diane as my life partner.

My mom, Gerda Yapko, and my brother, Brian Yapko, are forever looking out for me. Their love, concern and advice are wonderful bonds between us. My dad, Benjamin Yapko, would have been proud of us all.

Diane's folks, Madeline and Jerry Harris, are my folks, too. You won't find better role models anywhere for living life lovingly, generously, and with class. My brothers-in-law, Ken and Mitchell Harris, and their families, are wonderfully adept at sending their love and support over a long distance, a gift I value greatly.

My best friends are the Horowitz family: Megan, Wendy, and Richard. We have lovingly shared our lives together for more than three decades, practically living life together as an integrated family unit. Sharing all the best and worst that happens in life with them has been a privilege. The Hugbug is still the best.

I have received valuable support, feedback, and inspiration along the way from quite a few friends and colleagues I'd like to thank: Brian Alman, Daniel Araoz, Norma and Phil Barretta, Aaron Beck, George Burns, Lisa Butler, Omar Chogriz, Jay Haley, Ross Halpin, Ernest Hilgard, William Kroger, Stephen Lankton, Steven Lynn, Camillo Loriedo, Martin Seligman, Peter Sheehan, Rick Whiteside and Frances Steinberg, and Jeffrey Zeig. Thank you also to my many workshop sponsors, friends, and colleagues, all who have helped me present my ideas—and further develop them—to audiences around the world. And, finally, thank you to my clients, who have taught me the most about what hypnosis and therapy is really all about.

CONCEPTUAL
FRAMEWORK

Paving the therapy road with good intentions 1

The eyes of depression

Depression is an urgent and widespread problem. Currently, nearly 20 million Americans are known to be suffering with the disorder (National Institute of Mental Health, 1999). Each afflicted individual directly affects others (family, friends), multiplying the number of people touched by depression to many tens of millions. Realistically, we are *all* affected by depression, even if only indirectly, by having to share in the hurtful consequences of the many antisocial behaviors (such as child abuse and drug abuse) that often have their origin in badly managed depression (Weissbourd, 1996). For those of us who are clinicians, though, depression is far more immediate in its effects than statistics regarding prevalence alone might indicate. To look with compassion into the eyes of someone suffering the pain, anguish, despair, and hopelessness of depression can be a profoundly moving experience. To be in the position of authority, by virtue of one's very profession, of having to argue against a client's desire to commit suicide or, far more frequently, to have to push people feeling defeated by life to do even the simple things they might do to help themselves, is the hard work of treating depressed individuals. Depression is categorized as a mood disorder by the mental health profession, but it is so much more than that on so many different levels. Depression can be a terribly debilitating condition that tends to exact a very high price from people—nothing less all-encompassing than the quality of one's life.

The primary purposes of this book are twofold: First, to highlight some of what we already know about the nature of major depression and what works in its treatment, and second, to draw attention to ways clinical hypnosis can further enhance the treatment process. Given the costliness of depression, the value of *any* tool that can enhance recovery is substantial.

The costs of depression

The price of depression is exorbitant on many levels. One study placed the *financial* cost of depression to the U.S. economy at more than $40 billion,

3

stemming from days off from work, poor job performance (tasks done poorly or needing to be redone), psychotherapeutic care, and even the loss of potential earnings from suicides (Greenberg, Stiglin, Finkelstein, & Berndt, 1993).

The *emotional* cost is more meaningful for clinicians to consider, given the terrible waste of human potential when one leads a life filled with despair, distress, grief, or apathy. Life is too short to spend part or all of it emotionally impaired.

The *physical* cost of depression is only now starting to be recognized. A large and growing body of evidence informs us that depression affects more than one's mood—it also affects one's physiology in detrimental ways (Buchanan, Rubenstein, & Seligman, 1999). One study showed that heart attack patients who became depressed were at much higher risk for subsequent heart attacks than those who did not become depressed (Glassman & Shapiro, 1998). Another study showed that depressed patients have longer average hospital stays and more complications during recovery than nondepressed patients (Frasure-Smith, Lesperance, & Talajik, 1993). A third study showed that a depressed person is at a higher risk for a heart attack than a nondepressed person (Everson et al., 1996). Depression clearly poses serious health risks.

The *social* cost of depression is incalculable: Family conflict, poor parenting, divorce, friendships and colleaguial relationships destroyed through antagonism or neglect, and socially irresponsible behavior (such as drunk driving, drug abuse, and child abuse) are just some of the terribly damaging effects of depression on human relationships (Hammen, 1999).

Given the reach of depression into our pockets, our personal relationships, our communities, and our very lives, addressing it in timely and effective ways is an especially urgent challenge we as healthcare professionals face. Our mission is to respond as directly and forcefully as we can to the rising rates of depression, and to use our advanced knowledge in new and bolder ways for the benefit of all those who suffer that we purport to serve. In order to do that, we will need to shift some of our focus away from what has distracted us in order to better notice some of what we have learned about depression that currently receives too little attention. An unfortunate result of under-representing some important aspects of what we've learned is the diminished capacity for responding to depression effectively. The rising rates of depression indicate this concern is legitimate. We can do better in helping diminish depression in peoples' lives, but not by simply doing more of what we're already doing when the evidence is clear that what we're doing isn't working very well.

Amplifying and de-amplifying awareness

Perhaps the very first lesson one learns in studying clinical hypnosis is that when one focuses on something, one amplifies it in one's awareness, in effect, associating oneself to it (Zeig, 1980b). Conversely, diverting one's focus away from some stimulus reduces its prominence in one's awareness, in effect, dissociating oneself from it. Much of what one learns as a clinician applying hypnosis in clinical contexts centers on discovering the consequences in answering this practical question: What do I want to try to (hypnotically) *associate the client to* and/or *dissociate the client from*? A key aspect of treatment planning is knowing which aspects of experience the client would likely benefit from engaging with (associating to) and which he or she would likely benefit from disengaging (dissociating) from (Lynn, Kirsch, Neufeld, & Rhue, 1996).

Manipulating or influencing the awareness of other people, to one degree or another, is an inevitable component of conducting not only psychotherapy, but of conducting *any* human transaction. Each comment one makes or question one asks draws a respondent's attention to some specific aspect of experience, for better or worse. The mental health profession has been learning the hard way of late that therapy is not an entirely benign process, and that the potential to help also holds an equal potential to harm (Yapko, 1994). What we draw people's attention to—or divert it away from—can have profound consequences for the quality of their subjective experience. Focusing people on what's wrong with them—or what's *right* about them—generates quite different feelings in someone.

On amplifying biology as the problem and drugs as the solution

The drive in the mental health profession at this time is to increase the amount of attention paid to the biology of depression. Depression is often described as a biological disease, and drugs are popularly promoted in the professional and public arenas as the treatments of choice. There is typically only a passing mention of the potential benefits of psychotherapy in these arenas. The increased focus on genetics and biochemistry has amplified a general awareness for the presumed role of specific neurotransmitters in both the etiology and course of depression. In fact, the release of Prozac as the first of a new generation of antidepressants more than a dozen years ago brought the terms "serotonin deficiency" and "biochemical imbalance" into widespread usage (Kramer, 1993).

Prior to the release of Prozac, the first psychoactive drug to achieve the status of a "star" with its many magazine cover stories and television news magazine features, pharmaceutical companies advertised antidepressive medications only to physicians in medical journals. But, with the new generation of antidepressants also came a new generation of expensive but highly lucrative drug marketing strategies. Ads in magazines and on television appealing to the public to proactively ask their doctors for the drug, rather than waiting for their doctors to prescribe it, helped propel Prozac into the position of being the fastest and best-selling psychoactive drug in pharmaceutical history. The rationale for taking Prozac—or *any* antidepressant drug—was an appealingly uncomplicated one: that depression is caused by a neurochemical imbalance that is correctable with the drug.

While this statement may be simple and compelling, it can too easily mislead people because it is only partially accurate. People seem to lose sight of the fact that *everything* has a biochemical correlate, and that experience shapes biochemistry at least as much as biochemistry shapes experience (Azar, 1997). To think of depression only as a unidirectional phenomenon in which "bad chemistry causes depression" is simply incorrect. To then try and "chemically adjust" people to what may well be depressing circumstances is generally a misdirected effort, and likewise may account for the higher relapse rates associated with medications compared to psychotherapy (Fava, Rafanelli, Grandi, Conti, & Belluardo, 1998).

Many more antidepressant drugs have been released since Prozac, making Prozac old news; at least two dozen more new drugs are currently in line awaiting FDA approval, which is expected to be given, and then they will be available in a relatively short period of time (NewsRx.com, 2000). The amount of money involved in selling the "drug solution" is beyond most people's grasp: More than $5 *billion* a year is spent just on advertising antidepressants, and just the combined sales of only three antidepressant medications—Prozac, Zoloft, and Paxil—exceeded $5.5 billion in 1997 (Breggin, 1999). One can safely assume the numbers have risen in the interim.

Who benefits the most from promoting the neurochemical aspect of depression seems clear. What seems most unfortunate, however, is the zeal with which the mental health profession has wholeheartedly endorsed an exclusively biological viewpoint. Consider the following:

- In June, 1999, the White House held its first ever conference on mental health, at the urging of Tipper Gore, the then vice-president's wife. Having publicly acknowledged her own battle with depression, she put the national spotlight on mental health issues. The conference featured prominent National Institute of Mental Health and other researchers in an effort to promote greater public awareness both for the prevalence of mental health problems and the advances made in treatment. A primary goal, Americans were told, was to find ways to better identify more of the people who suffer mental disorders of all types, and get them the treatment they require. In effect, however, the White House strategy was simply to look harder to find more people suffering emotional disorders to medicate for what researchers said was their brain disease (The White House, 1999).
- The American Psychological Association (APA) continues to lobby, apparently quite successfully, for the right to prescribe drugs just as physicians do. The ultimate effect of reinforcing the focus on drugs as the primary intervention for disorders like depression remains to

be seen, but what exactly does it say when the psychological community is set on redefining itself as drug advocates? Instead of striving to provide a counterbalance to the "drugs as the solution" message, the APA has instead chosen to reinforce it (DeLeon & Wiggins, 1996).

- The National Depressive and Manic-Depressive Association (NDMDA) conducted a 1999 survey which revealed that the great majority of people taking antidepressants are *not* satisfied with the drugs, nor are they satisfied with the doctors that prescribe them, typically complaining their doctors don't listen to them. (Why listen if all you have to do is write someone a prescription?) The NDMDA's conclusion to their study? We need more and better drugs (Reuters Health Information, 1999).

The enthusiasm for antidepressant medications rises with every magazine ad or author's claim for the miracles they perform, with every celebrity's endorsement, and with every doctor's prescription written. Is this enthusiasm justified? Or are we focusing people on biology and thereby amplifying its importance to the exclusion of other, perhaps even more important, variables affecting the etiology and course of depression? For that matter, what do we really know about depression?

Some of what we know about depression

Depression has been and continues to be heavily researched. The amount of data generated by clinicians and researchers has been impressive by any standards, and has led to some firm conclusions:

- Depression has *many* contributing factors, not a single cause. The three primary domains of the contributing factors are biological, psychological, and social. Hence, the so-called "biopsychosocial model" predominates (Cronkite & Moose, 1995; Thase & Glick, 1995).
- Depression has many underlying risk factors and comorbid conditions associated with it (Stevens, Merikangas, & Merikangas, 1995). Numerous medical and psychological conditions are found to commonly coexist with depression, requiring sharp differential diagnosis and comprehensive treatment planning (American Psychiatric Association, 1994).
- Depression can be managed in the majority of sufferers with medication, psychotherapy or both (Yapko, 1997). While no one antidepressant has been shown to be superior in efficacy to another, therapeutic efficacy studies show some psychotherapies outperform others in treating depression. These include cognitive, behavioral, and interpersonal approaches (Antonuccio et al., 1995).

- Medication has some treatment advantages, such as a faster rate of symptom remission and greater effectiveness in treating the vegetative symptoms, such as sleep and appetite disturbances (DeBattista & Schatzberg, 1995). Medication also has some disadvantages, such as reinforcing client passivity (a most detrimental cornerstone of depression), uncertain dosing and effectiveness, potentially negative side-effects, habituation, and "poop-out" (i.e., the drug may eventually stop working), and higher initial rates of relapse (Dubovsky, 1997; Altamura & Percudani, 1993).

- Psychotherapy also has some treatment advantages and disadvantages. The advantages are therapy's focus on skill-building and the associated reduced relapse rate; the value of the therapeutic relationship; the greater degree of personal empowerment; the increased capacity for individualized, rather than standardized, treatment; and the potential to not just perform a "mop-up" of pre-existing problems but to teach the skills of *prevention* (Seligman, 1991; Yapko, 1999). (Medication is, by definition, relegated to a lesser role of mere reactivity to existing depression, but psychotherapy can—and *should*—proactively focus on teaching prevention skills.) The disadvantages of psychotherapy are the greater reliance on the level of clinician competence (experience and judgment); the greater time lag between the initiation of treatment and the remission of symptoms compared to medications; the lesser effect in reducing vegetative symptoms; and the potential detrimental side-effects of exposure to a particular theoretical or philosophical stance (Mondimore, 1993; Thase & Glick 1995).

- The extraordinary ongoing success of the Human Genome Project has highlighted the oversimplification of the earlier model describing the relationship between genetics and disorders, called by at least one researcher by its acronym, the "OGOD" model. The acronym stands for "One Gene—One Disease," and the now largely disproven assumption was that each disease had a specific gene directly responsible for its development (Dubovsky, 1997). Of more than two thousand genes mapped, and nearly a thousand cloned, the OGOD model has only held true in about a dozen cases (including Huntington's disease and cystic fibrosis) (Begley, 1996). The U.S. Surgeon General, Dr. David Satcher, stated the salient point accurately and succinctly in his well-received report dated December 13, 1999: "No single gene appears to be responsible for any mental disorder. Rather, small variations in multiple genes contribute to a disruption in healthy brain function." No "depression gene" has been found, but what has been found is that no depression gene *will* be found. Genetic vulnerabilities or predispositions exist, but they operate in association with environmental variables that may increase or decrease their likelihood of expression (Siever & Frucht, 1997). In the specific case of depression, the genetic contribution has been shown by research to be mild, with environmental factors (both so-cial and psychological) appearing to have the greater influence in its onset (Kaelber, Moul, & Farmer, 1995).

• Serotonin and other brain chemicals are not unidirectional in caus-ing emotional disorders. In other words, it is not simply a biochemi-cal anomaly which inevitably leads to depression. The relationship between neurochemicals and experience is bidirectional, meaning environmental triggers influence neurochemistry *at least* as much as neurochemistry influences experience (Azar, 1997). It is reasonable to think of psychotherapy as a means for directly and/or indirectly affecting neurotransmitter levels in the brain (Schwartz, 1996).

There are many, many other important things known about depres-sion, of course, but the above statements reflect a high level of general consensus among depression experts and thus are foundation enough to justify this book. The enormous value of psychotherapy in treating depression is very well established; wherever psychotherapy has proven benefit, the positive value of hypnosis is assured, since the two are in-evitably intertwined.

We can walk AND chew gum

To promote drugs as the solution for a problem that is inaccurately por-trayed as entirely biological—or, conversely, to promote exclusively psycho-logical interventions for a condition that may well be rooted in medical problems such as diseases or hormonal anomalies—is simply untenable in light of the massive amount of evidence indicating the multidimensional nature of depression. The incongruity of telling people they are victims of biology while trying to empower them, should be a painfully obvious mixed message, one that can be reduced by expanding our target areas for inter-vention. It is equally incongruous to tell people they can "control it all" when biology establishes some non-negotiable parameters of human expe-rience. We can credibly hold a biological *and* psychological *and* social view of depression.

Some of what we know about treating depression with psychotherapy

This book is about the value of psychotherapy in treating depression, espe-cially highlighting the added benefits of employing clinical hypnosis in the treatment process. In this section, some of the key findings about the use of psychotherapy with depressed clients will be presented.

In 1993, the Agency for Health Care Policy and Research (AHCPR), a component of the U.S. Public Health Service, released its clinical practice guidelines for treating depression (Depression Guideline Panel, 1993). After reviewing thousands of research studies on therapeutic efficacy and using the best studies as the foundation for their clinical recommendations, the guidelines reflected a substantial level of agreement among depression experts as to what constitutes reasonable and effective treatment of depression (American Psychiatric Association, 1993). In 1998, the guidelines were updated to incorporate subsequent research, and were widely disseminated to health professionals (Schulberg, Katon, Simon, & Rush).

Four important insights about depression were incorporated into the AHCPR guidelines: 1) Three psychotherapies were shown to be the most effective: Cognitive, behavioral, and interpersonal psychotherapies. These are identified as the psychotherapies of choice, and any or all can be applied *according to the client's symptom profile* (not the clinician's preferred orientation); 2) Psychotherapy should be an *active* process in the way it is conducted, involving active exchanges between clinician and client which would typically involve providing psychoeducation, the development of skill-building strategies, the use of homework assignments, and the use of the therapy relationship as both a foundation and a vehicle for exploring relevant ideas and perspectives; 3) Therapy should not only focus on problem-solving, but the teaching of problem-solving skills, especially as they relate to symptom resolution, the guidelines' suggested focus of treatment; 4) Effective therapy need not have a historical focus. On the contrary, the most effective therapies are goal-oriented, skill-building approaches. *None* of them focus on attaining historical data to explain the origins of depression. Rather, they focus on developing solutions to problems and coping skills for managing symptoms. This sharply distinguishes an *event-driven* perspective (the view that depression has its origin in specific historical events that must be identified and "worked through") from a *process-driven* perspective (the view that depression has its roots in ongoing ways of negatively or erroneously interpreting various life experiences). Recognizing that depression arises for *many* reasons of a process-driven nature accentuates the realization that *by the time depression strikes most individuals, the risk factors* (such as perceptual style, cognitive style, and level of social and problem-solving skills) *had already been well in place.* Thus, time spent in therapy looking for *the* cause of depression, as if there were a single one, is generally not time well spent (Yapko, 1997).

The illusion of empirically supported treatments

The current zeitgeist of the mental health profession is to place great emphasis on the value of clinical research, directly challenging clinicians to develop greater objectivity about their work and to use only those treatments with a proven value. Given how silly much of what has been termed "therapy" has been in the past, it is a welcome evolutionary step to seek greater objectivity about the therapy process.

There is a "but," however. As much as researchers strive to validate the techniques of therapy, even scripting session-by-session treatment protocols to follow, their foundational premise is only partially valid. The assumption is that what is therapeutic lies entirely in the therapy techniques (or, for that matter, in the medication), while ignoring the personal, interpersonal, and contextual variables that contribute to therapy. This is not reasonable in light of the evidence to the contrary.

There is simply no substitute for clinical judgment—the ability of the clinician to recognize and observe salient client data, and respond spontaneously and appropriately with accurate and helpful input. It is interesting to note that clients responding to exit surveys regarding their experience of therapy almost invariably report on the value of the therapeutic alliance and only rarely on the specific techniques the clinician employed (Ablon & Jones, 1999). That doesn't mean the techniques were unimportant, of course, just that the value of techniques was perceived as secondary to the interpersonal context in which they were used. That is a powerful "strike one" against a singularly technique orientation.

Psychotherapy has always been and always will be primarily art, not science. The complicating factors of comorbid conditions (largely ignored in efficacy studies which typically exclude those individuals who have any diagnoses beyond an Axis I Major Depression), the rise of spontaneous significant life events (such as the death of a parent), and variable personality characteristics across clients make treatment protocols undesirable as anything more than a loose outline of treatment. "Strike two" against rigidly structured treatment protocols.

The same problem of rigidity exists, of course, in the use of clinical hypnosis. There are scripted approaches to hypnosis that have proliferated over the years, as if somehow those specific words organized in that specific sequence delivered in a prescribed demeanor were responsible for the treatment result. Clinicians trained in more traditional methods of hypnosis all but ignore the individual differences in information processing and response styles, instead responding with ritualized procedures of induction and suggestion formation. Hypnosis can't be ritualized yet simultaneously remain responsive to individual needs and variations. Any clinician who wants to apply hypnosis meaningfully and with the greatest likelihood of success will have to consider the same personal, interpersonal, and contextual variables as in formulating meaningful psychotherapy (Haley, 1973; Yapko, 1990).

It is an illusion to believe that all the power of therapy is in the technique and not in the relationship between the client and clinician, or in their mutual expectations, or in their individual and shared beliefs, or in the many other such variables that can either make or break a therapy. *Perhaps it would be far more valuable to empirically validate therapists than therapies.*

The reality of empirically supported psychotherapies for depression

The value of having researched empirically supported treatments for depression is that there is now much that has come to be known about what helps the majority of depression sufferers. Despite the inability to globally address unique aspects of individual cases, there are clearly some common denominators that many depressed individuals share. How they respond to interventions addressing these shared features is highly instructive. Thus, the proven value of cognitive, behavioral, and interpersonal psychotherapies in treatment cannot be ignored or minimized. Collectively, they highlight the value of therapy that emphasizes *skill-building* in the service of a *goal-orientation* employing *active and strategic intervention strategies*.

Another valuable aspect of the empirical research into therapeutic efficacy concerns the division of the therapy process into distinct phases: acute, continuation, and maintenance. How each therapy fares in addressing the immediate symptoms, the ongoing progress of therapy, and the possibility of relapses is vital information to have in making informed treatment decisions. The AHCPR guidelines provide valuable data regarding the efficacy of both medications and psychotherapy in each of the stages of treatment. The data make it clear that each of the psychotherapies match or exceed medication-only approaches. The power of psychotherapy to reduce symptoms, lower the risk for relapse, and even function as a preventive tool is well supported in the literature (Clarkin, Pilkonis, & Magrude, 1996; Giles, 1993; Persons, Thase, & Christoph, 1996).

Is clinical hypnosis an empirically supported treatment?

Many clinicians who employ clinical hypnosis have come to believe that hypnosis is not a therapy in its own right, such as cognitive therapy or interpersonal therapy (American Psychological Association, 1993; Yapko, 1995). Rather, they suggest that hypnosis may best be viewed as a vehicle or tool for delivering information, amplifying client responsiveness, and facilitating learning on experiential (multidimensional) levels (Yapko, 1992). While hypnosis may share some traits with established therapies, it seems obvious that there are some important differences as well that justify its being considered more than a mere catalyst for other therapies.

Therapeutic efficacy research involving hypnosis specifically for depression has, to this point, been essentially non-existent. Practitioners of hypnosis are generally not researchers, and clinical researchers have generally focused on evaluating specific forms of therapy, and not therapeutic adjuncts such as hypnosis. Further complicating matters is the history of hypnosis in relation to depression in particular. Prior to my book *Hypnosis and the Treatment of Depressions*, it was widely believed (and apparently still is in some areas) that depression was a specific contraindication for the use of hypnosis (Crasilneck & Hall, 1985; Spiegel & Spiegel, 1987). No research had even been attempted to either validate or invalidate that conventional wisdom.

Another reason hypnosis has been excluded from efficacy research concerns the very nature of depression itself. "Depression" is a global construct clinicians employ merely for the convenience of having a common clinically descriptive language. In fact, depression is comprised of many specific patterns of perception, attribution-formation, and multidimensional symptoms that are adequately (but not entirely correctly) listed in DSM-IV. The value of the global term "depression" is reduced when considering its variations in individual appearances.

Hypnosis has been evaluated for its therapeutic merits in a number of arenas. The research shows that treatments which also employ hypnosis compared to the same treatments not employing hypnosis have a significantly more favorable outcome (Kirsch, Montgomery, & Sapirstein, 1995; Lynn, Kirsch, Barabasz, Cardena, & Patterson, 2000). More will be said about these studies in the next chapter.

It is an extrapolation of available data to suggest that hypnosis can enhance treatment results for depression. Undoubtedly, that will be a valid concern to those who only want therapeutic efficacy data specific to depression. But, until such research data become available, we can rely on the strong clinical evidence that, when integrated with other established therapies, hypnosis can be helpful in addressing and resolving many of the most troublesome components of depression. These will be discussed in detail in the next chapter. Suffice it to say here that there is a strong body of clinical evidence and a growing body of empirical evidence that hypnosis can contribute significantly to positive treatment results directly and indirectly related to depression.

Re-thinking our priorities

In this final section of the chapter, it bears repeating that we are dealing with a dangerous, widespread, and still-growing problem called depression. Too many in the mental health profession have been lulled into a comfortable complacency, believing that drugs are already solving the problem of depression. If only that were true. However, there is ample reason to believe that not only are drugs *not* solving the problem, but may actually be contributing to it through their encouraging a mild sort of "magical thinking" that works against striving to develop the very skills already known to reduce and even prevent depression.

Despite the sophisticated research into the nature of depression and the qualities of effective psychotherapies, we still largely treat depression as an individual—and even more reductionistically, a biological—disorder.

We tend to all but ignore the social context in which depression arises and proliferates, virtually guaranteeing the eventual realization of the World Health Organization's dire prediction presented earlier. We can't ignore the powerful evidence of depression as largely a social problem (found in the excellent research on gender differences and cultural differences, for example) without revealing that we're *choosing* to ignore or warp vital information. It's like the old joke of the drunk looking for his keys under a street light where he can see things better even though he lost them in the dark somewhere down the block.

Will we encourage people to "chemically adapt" themselves to a faster and more complex world? Or will we help people become proactive agents of therapeutic change in their own lives? The position we as health professionals take will have profound consequences for us all, and sooner rather than later.

Applying hypnosis in psychotherapy 2

Hypnosis has played a significant role in the evolution of psychotherapy from its very inception. Although exploring the history of hypnosis is a fascinating venture, it is well beyond the scope of this book. Knowing, however, that hypnosis has played a primary role in the development of many important concepts and techniques of psychotherapy helps put recent developments in the field into a more meaningful perspective (Spanos & Chaves, 1991; Watkins, 1987).

Until relatively recently, hypnosis had long been considered a form of therapy in its own right. Practitioners often referred to themselves, and many still do, as "hypnotherapists," a nomenclature indicating a therapy practice revolving around the use of formal hypnotic procedures (Frischholz, 1998; Strauss, 1993). The underlying assumption was that hypnosis was itself a curative method, as if merely by being exposed to an induction and a presumably therapeutic array of suggestions, the goals of therapy could be accomplished. Hypnosis was viewed as the healing agent in the process, and considerable attention was paid to developing more diverse and effective ways of generating and using the hypnotic state. By emphasizing the hypnotic state as the key to the therapy, hypnosis eventually came to be viewed as a separate and distinct approach to treatment (Weitzenhoffer, 1989; Yapko, 1992). After all, few, if any, other schools of therapy emphasized the necessity or value of first inducing the hypnotic state before attempting meaningful intervention.

Clinicians either used hypnosis as a deliberate method of intervention or they did not, and the distinction between practitioners who did hypnosis and those who did not was unambiguous. Unless one was favorably exposed to hypnosis in the course of clinical training (perhaps through academic coursework) or clinical practice (perhaps through consultation or supervision), hypnosis would remain merely an intellectual curiosity for most clinicians but be relegated to the position of a secondary ("alternative") treatment at best. Hypnosis just didn't seem to be a serious treatment methodology due to its ritualistic methods and the ease with which it could be used as cheap entertainment in smoky night clubs.

In my book *Trancework: An Introduction to the Practice of Clinical Hypnosis* (1990), and then again in *Hypnosis and the Treatment of Depressions* (1992), I promoted the view of clinical hypnosis as largely (but not entirely) a process of social influence. Recognizing that hypnosis done in the therapy context is, by definition, an interpersonal process, it seems obvious that the dynamics of interpersonal processes will inevitably be present in doing hypnosis with a client. To mislead oneself into believing that hypnosis is an entirely or even primarily intrapersonal phenomenon means underestimating and perhaps even misapplying the interpersonal variables evident in the therapy context. Intrapersonal factors such as expectancy and capacity for focusing affect the hypnotic interaction, as do contextual factors, such as environmental conditions. Skilled use of hypnosis considers all three domains (intrapersonal, interpersonal, and contextual) in formulating interventions.

To expand the view of hypnosis to not only encompass but *highlight* interpersonal factors suggests that hypnosis may not be so distinct as a treatment after all (Coe & Sarbin, 1991; Spanos & Chaves, 1989). Seeing the patterns of social influence evident in *any* psychotherapy reinforces the notion that hypnosis is *not* a therapy in and of itself, but is embedded within a larger social context or interpersonal relationship that is defined as therapeutic (Lankton & Lankton, 1983; Spanos & Coe, 1992). To see hypnosis in this much broader view obviates the need for the rituals of hypnosis and instead focuses on the role of potentially influential suggestions, present in all therapies. This view blurs the lines separating hypnosis from therapy in general. Suddenly, hypnosis seems far more relevant to all forms of clinical practice.

Wanting to determine the hypnotizability of an individual, or wanting to identify the neurophysiology of hypnosis remains a primary goal for many hypnosis researchers. From a purely clinical point of view, these are interesting lines of inquiry, but are not critical to successful clinical outcomes. There is still disagreement amongst professionals as to what hypnosis is, and we try and understand such abstract phenomena in terms we already think we understand (Hilgard, 1991). These two factors alone should cause us to rethink where we want to focus our research attention. I take an unequivocal position that what matters most in generating therapeutic responsiveness *in the clinical context* is not some arbitrary measure of hypnotizability, a position sure to annoy some colleagues, nor is it something measurable in a brain scan. I am convinced it's the way personal and contextual variables are managed in the therapeutic alliance. For hypnosis research to be more relevant, I believe it will need to better address practical issues, such as why some people respond to stories ("metaphors") heard in hypnosis with life transforming changes; why someone hears a suggestion several times and all but ignores it and hears it yet another time and finds it fresh and powerful; why a countdown induction yields no significant response from an individual but a suggestion to recall an experience of having been comfortable someplace yields a dramatic response, or why so many things become possible in one approach that were not possible with another approach. We generally prize cognitive flexibility in our clients, and we claim we want to acknowledge their uniqueness as individuals.

Should we then strive to ignore the fact that much of what we find in our clients is simply a product of what we go looking for?

To see hypnosis as a process of influence encompassing many contributing factors parallels the process of therapy. A clinician is placed in a prescribed role, as is the client. The roles clearly define key aspects of the interaction such that the clinician can introduce hypnosis as a concept, a set of techniques, or even a method of magic ("your unconscious can heal you") if so desired. The client's beliefs and expectations will be influenced to *some* extent by the degree of expertise and credibility assigned to the clinician by the client, as well as other such interpersonal factors (Spanos, 1991; Wagstaff, 1991).

How we define hypnosis matters, although to a limited extent. Hypnosis is a subjectively experienced and practiced phenomenon, and so definitions can vary widely. The American Psychological Association's Division of Psychological Hypnosis issued a formal definition of hypnosis in 1985. It was generally well received. Their definition is as follows:

> Hypnosis is a procedure during which a health professional or researcher suggests that a client, patient, or subject experience changes in sensations, perceptions, thoughts, or behavior.

To its credit, the definition encompasses personal, interpersonal, and situational variables affecting hypnotic responsiveness. But, as expected given the inherent difficulties in defining hypnosis, none of these variables is specified or described.

In 1999, APA's Division of Psychological Hypnosis went a step further in addressing the issue raised here about hypnosis as a specific form of therapy. It stated unequivocally that:

> Hypnosis is not a type of therapy like psychoanalysis or behavior therapy. Instead, it is a procedure that can be used to facilitate therapy. Because it is not a treatment in and of itself, training in hypnosis is not sufficient for the conduct of therapy. (p. 5)

The recognition that hypnosis is embedded in the larger context of psychotherapy is a welcome notion for those who have publicly taken the position (and often the accompanying criticism) that suggestion is inherent in the therapy process and cannot be well separated into an independent treatment modality. Hypnosis involves much more than suggestion, of course, yet suggestion must be recognized as one of the inevitable and irreducible interpersonal components of both therapy in general and hypnosis in particular. The artistry of both effective hypnosis and psychotherapy lies in the clinician's ability to know what to suggest and when and how to suggest it. Thus, the specific technique one uses matters only to the extent that the larger context in which it is applied (utilizing personal, interpersonal, and contextual variables), supports it (T. Barber, 2000). Technique is only part of the therapy picture, as research has shown.

If and when hypnosis is validated as an approach in the treatment of some specific client population under consideration, it is because the researchers will have addressed the question, "Is a particular therapy approach enhanced when hypnosis is integrated into the treatment process?" But, even though the answer may be (and so far consistently is) yes, *so what*? Knowing that hypnosis enhances treatment outcomes doesn't address how any one practitioner might use—or ignore—the information, or how one clinician using hypnosis might apply it methodologically in comparison to another. After all, the differences in how various professionals see and apply hypnosis are quite sharp despite each applying the label "hypnosis" to their work.

States, traits, and clients don't care

The historical debate over whether hypnosis is a "state" or "trait" continues even now (Kihlstrom 1997). One side is represented by the belief that the single most important determinant of the outcome of the hypnotic interaction is the client's *hypnotizability* (Evans, 2000). The ability to respond to hypnotic interventions is assumed to be a product of many personal variables, including one's neurological makeup, personality structure, and symptom profile. Hypnotizability remains difficult to measure, despite continuing efforts by researchers to define and measure it. The relationship between hypnotizability measures and clinical outcomes is an area of active research predicated on the notion that hypnotic interventions will likely be more effective on those who are more easily or highly hypnotizable than those who are less so, as measured by standardized tests of hypnotizability. Thus, from this perspective, client hypnotizability is important to measure formally, and the decision as to whether, and even how, to implement hypnosis is the byproduct (Brown, 1992).

The other side of the issue is represented by the notion that the single greatest factor in the viability of hypnosis as an intervention tool is *expectancy* (Coe, 1993; Kirsch, 2000). Expectancy refers to that quality of the client's belief system that leads him or her to believe that the procedure implemented by the clinician will produce a therapeutic result. Positive expectancy involves multiple perceptions. The clinician is seen as credible and benevolent, the procedure seems to have a plausible or even compelling rationale, and the therapy context itself seems to support its application. Thus, by the client being instructed in the value and the methods of hypnosis, whether directly or indirectly, an expectation is established that the associated procedures will have some potentially therapeutic benefit.

Clearly, both sides of the debate—hypnosis as a trait or state—have valid points. Despite this, there is a deep division within the field on this and related issues. The polarity that exists within the field of professionals aligning with one perspective over the other is puzzling, given the substantial supportive evidence for both views.

As described in *Trancework*, and emphasized here, hypnotic responsiveness in the client is determined by the interactions between three general domains: personal characteristics, interpersonal factors, and contextual variables. All of these must be well managed in the clinical context in order for therapeutic success to occur. To attend to only one aspect and ignore or understate the others is a likely path to poor clinical outcome. Thus, to focus on hypnotizability of the client as the primary factor influencing treatment outcome is to miss the obvious: How someone responds to a formal test of hypnotizability has had too little predictive ability for one's degree of responsiveness to specific interventions. Simply put, how a client responds to suggestions for an arm levitation in a suggestibility test will indicate little as to how that same client will respond to suggestions for symptom reduction.

Hypnotic responses are largely context-specific, and so even a positive responsiveness to hypnosis in one session does not predict a similar response for the next session. Furthermore, focusing on the client's hypnotizability suggests that the client's innate ability to respond matters more than the specific technique or approach one employs. With this perspective, truly meaningless techniques can be employed, such as the traditional countdown method of induction. What relationship does counting numbers have to entering hypnosis *unless* it is defined as hypnotic and unless one has the expectation that such a procedure can induce hypnosis? Otherwise, one may as well name cities in France with the instruction that "with each city named your relaxation intensifies." The countdown technique, indeed *any* hypnotic technique, is activated only through the client's willingness to engage with it (J. Barber, 1991; T. Barber, 2000).

On the other hand, focusing on expectancy to the exclusion of other factors of potential therapeutic effectiveness can also be limiting. Someone can have positive expectations yet generate no meaningful therapeutic results for a variety of reasons. For every client who began therapy with high hopes that went unfulfilled, the point is clear that positive expectations are not enough. These expectations must be realistic and they must occur within a larger therapeutic framework that is able to convert the promise of expectancy into the reality of a goal accomplished. Thus, technique *does* matter, and whether the technique employed holds the key to imparting the salient therapeutic information or skill in relation to the problem is at the heart of therapeutic effectiveness. When therapy is unsuccessful—or worse, goes badly—it may be because of the poor fit between the techniques chosen, the clinician's style, the problem and client characteristics that led to a particular treatment choice, and the larger context in which they were applied. Expectancy matters, but even positive, well-defined expectations can become a source of problems rather than a source of solutions if they are unrealistic.

Clearly, the magic of therapeutic effectiveness is not simply in conducting rituals of hypnosis. It seems equally clear that hypnosis isn't innately therapeutic. As is also true of therapy—whatever has the potential to help has an equal potential to hurt.

Suggestions for how to think about hypnosis

How clinicians conceptualize hypnosis, with all its inherent ambiguity, determines to a great extent how they will apply it. In *Hypnosis and the Treatment of Depressions*, I provided a detailed review of all those views of hypnosis that had led to the entirely indefensible view of hypnosis as dangerous and specifically contraindicated for depression sufferers. In light of subsequent research and a growing recognition that hypnosis can be a valuable treatment tool for managing depression when skillfully applied, the topic clearly warrants much greater consideration.

What does hypnosis do?

Hypnosis amplifies and/or de-amplifies experience. Perhaps the most basic principle underlying hypnosis is that when you focus on something, you amplify it in your awareness. As a corollary, when you focus on some specific stimulus, you reduce or de-amplify your awareness for other coexisting stimuli. Another way of saying it is that through hypnosis you will *associate to*—relate more directly or closely—a portion of experience and you will *dissociate from*—relate less directly to and more distantly from—other aspects of experience. Clinically, the practical decisions that go into formulating a specific treatment plan involve addressing some variation of the question, "What should the hypnosis (or therapy) session amplify in the client's experience and how and what should the amplified awareness be associated to?"

Does hypnosis cure people?

Theorists argue about how to differentiate hypnosis from suggestion, and they debate about suggestibility as distinct from hypnotizability (Hilgard, 1991; Kirsch, 1997). From a clinician's pragmatic viewpoint, the use of suggestions to encourage the development of desirable therapeutic responses is at the heart of hypnosis and therapy. Hypnosis doesn't cure people—in fact, hypnosis cures *nothing*. What is potentially therapeutic or curative is what happens *during* hypnosis, specifically the new and beneficial associations clients make that enable them to relate to or manage some portion of their experience differently and more self-beneficially. Thus, the artistry of applying hypnosis is in having the ability to organize ideas, present information, suggest perspectives, motivate a willingness to experiment with new ideas and behaviors, explore new possibilities, and challenge one's own self-imposed limits (Erickson & Rossi, 1981). Some clinicians are more adept at applying the skills of communication and the dynamics of interpersonal influence than others. Some advocate the position that the ability to respond is entirely in the client's domain, somehow ignoring the reality that some people elicit far more positive reactions in people than do others. It can help to know why.

Hypnosis and amplifying client resources

Besides the obvious role of suggestion in *any* therapy, what is unique to hypnosis as a tool is its ability to gain access to and mobilize helpful resources within the client that he or she has that are largely unrecognized and unused. For example, if I were to ask you to make your left arm numb from the elbow down in the next ten seconds, could you do it? Probably not. But, after you are exposed to and choose to absorb yourself in a hypnotic process (induction procedure and a series of suggestions to facilitate responsiveness), you can be given the same suggestion and probably develop a numbness in your arm quite readily. Why? Truthfully, no one really knows (including those who pretend they do). But, clearly the ability to generate an anesthesia in response to a suggestion is a capacity many people, perhaps most people, have. People typically have no conscious awareness for how to produce the response, yet they can produce it in this ambiguously defined experience called hypnosis (Chaves, 1993; Eimer, 2000).

If people have such sophisticated personal resources, why don't they use them? The best answer, it seems, is that the resources are dissociated. The clinician's job is to build the bridges to them that can make them accessible. Thus, the most compelling reason to use hypnosis is to help empower people to discover and use more of their personal resources, and to step outside the often painfully narrow (symptomatic) self-defining boundaries of their subjective experience. All the remaining chapters in this book describe hypnotic and strategic ways to do this, as empowerment is an essential goal in the treatment of depression sufferers (Yapko, 1997).

Why use hypnosis for treating depression?

Ernest Hilgard, Ph.D., one of the true giants in the field, once described hypnosis to me as "believed-in imagination." That is a very astute framing, I believe, capturing both the flesh and spirit of hypnosis. To go a step further, though, we could also say that anyone's view of life is similarly a product of "believed-in imagination." For one person to project onto the ambiguous stimulus of life a belief that "life is wondrous and joyful" while another projects "life is a miserable burden to endure" represents two different "believed-in imaginations" that have specific and measurable consequences for each individual.

The body of literature about the relationship between the quality of one's projections and one's mood is huge: It is well established that the positive, optimistic person is likely to suffer less depression. Likewise, such a person will also benefit: (a) *physically* by likely suffering less serious illness and greater rates of recovery; (b) in terms of *productivity*, having higher levels of focus, persistence, and frustration tolerance; and, (c) in terms of greater *sociability* and likeability, enjoying the many benefits associated with more close and positive relationships (Seligman, 1989, 1990; Yapko, 1999).

The overlap between depression as a problem and hypnosis as a means for addressing it centers on the "believed-in imaginations" of the depressed client. Believing "life is unfair," or "I'm no good," or "I'll never be able to do that," are just a very few of the many, many self-limiting and self-injurious beliefs that depressives may form and come to hold as true. Thus, it is no coincidence that cognitive-behavioral therapies, which challenge depressed individuals to learn how to identify and self-correct their cognitive distortions and behave more effectively, have been shown to be highly effective approaches (Clarkin et al., 1996; Greenberger & Padesky, 1995).

These, and other strategically effective therapies as well, tend to challenge the client's "believed-in imaginations" and encourage them to widen their self-limiting boundaries. Each does so in a different way from hypnosis when practiced independently, but each can easily be integrated with hypnosis. In fact, much of what is presented in the remaining chapters is what I would characterize as cognitive-behavioral therapy performed within a hypnotic and strategic framework. The added value of mobilizing the hidden or undeveloped resources of the client through the use of hypnosis makes for both a powerful catalyst in treatment and also a more multidimensional treatment. Beyond cognitive or behavioral dimensions of experience, hypnosis can also be used to influence physiology, affect, relationships, symbolic and spiritual meanings, specific contextual response cues, and even historical narratives (Yapko, 1995; Zeig, 1980a).

Does hypnosis work?

A variety of therapeutic efficacy studies have been published attesting to the added value of hypnosis to established treatments, especially cognitive-behavioral approaches. No studies have yet been done specific to the use of hypnosis with depressed populations. Depression is a global term, however. In fact, depression is comprised of many different components, including cognitive patterns (such as attributional style), behavioral patterns (such as avoidant coping styles) and relational patterns (such as hypercriticalness). Many of these components have been addressed successfully with hypnosis (Kirsch, 1996; Lynn et al., 2000; Schoenberger, 2000). Likewise, depression can differ so markedly in levels of severity and range of symptoms that to treat depression as if it was a well-defined clinical entity is not entirely reasonable. In fact, this is the basis for some analysts criticizing the relevance of some research, such as when depression researchers have used less-than-realistic exclusion criteria in their research populations. For example, depression research subjects have typically been excluded from treatment protocols when they have any comorbid conditions, such as an anxiety disorder, substance abuse, or a personality disorder (Schuyler, 1998). In the real world, however, seeing a depressive *without* a comorbid condition is statistically unlikely. (The most common comorbid condition is an anxiety disorder, affecting about 70% of depressives. However, alcoholism, drug abuse, personality disorders, and medical conditions are also routinely associated with depression; Stevens et al., 1995.) The variant nature of depression is why I have previously talked about depressions (in the plural) rather than as a singular, well-defined clinical entity.

How has hypnosis fared in the literature in addressing some of the components and/or the comorbid conditions of depression? Relevant research has been done in a variety of areas, but more good research is needed. Doing such research is difficult, however. This is, in part, because such research requires incorporating many of the limitations into the treatment process that I actively encourage clinicians to avoid: (a) It requires making hypnosis a formal procedure to employ, despite many hypnosis experts agreeing formal hypnotic procedure is unnecessary for hypnotic responses to occur (Hilgard, 1965); (b) It requires establishing a standardized application of a formal treatment protocol, sacrificing the ability to deviate from the treatment manual and incorporate spontaneous clinical judgments and possibly fruitful diversions into unplanned areas. (This issue was at the heart of the often emotionally charged discussions several years ago about *Consumer Reports'* therapy Client Satisfaction Survey; Seligman, 1995); (c) It requires a standardizing of hypnotic approaches, precluding the ability to tailor approaches to the specific needs of an individual client (Yapko, 1990). I have already criticized such procedures for indirectly reinforcing the notion that the active therapeutic agent is in the technique itself, and not in either the therapeutic relationship or the larger therapy context itself.

Limitations aside, there has been a considerable body of literature already amassed attesting to the value of hypnosis as a tool of empowerment, especially important in diminishing depression. In fact, clinical reports in professional books and scientific journals describing symptom improvement in various disorders following the use of hypnosis routinely report a diminution of depression when describing positive results in treating pain, anxiety, and other physical and psychological symptoms (Crawford & Barabasz, 1993; Lynch, 1999; Montgomery, DuHamel, & Redd, 2000; Moore & Burrows, 1991; Schoenberger, Kirsch, Gearan, Montgomery, & Pastyrnak, 1997).

There will likely be criticism for encouraging the use of hypnosis in treating depression when there is little or no empirical basis yet for doing so. What has been established empirically, though, is highly relevant and reasonable to extrapolate: The more skilled the use of therapy, the more focused the intervention, the more dimensions of experience addressed in treatment, the more skilled the practitioner in creating a meaningful context for learning new skills and forming new associations, and the more the client is empowered to take charge of his or her life, the better the therapeutic result for the depressed client. What *is* established empirically is that hypnosis does all of these things and more.

Now, for the sake of the tens of millions suffering depression who need all the help they can get, we can start to focus on *how*.

Practical considerations in hypnotic treatment design

3

Knowing that depression is a serious and growing problem, and that hypnosis offers the potential to enhance the effectiveness of psychotherapy (especially cognitive-behavioral therapies, a treatment of choice for depression), we can now focus more specifically on developing practical hypnotic and strategic approaches to treatment. This chapter considers the practical foundational principles for introducing hypnosis into the therapeutic context.

Not all hypnosis is the same

Hypnosis can be used in many ways. It can be used to delineate individual differences, as when studying varying responses to a stimulus, such as a standardized induction. Hypnosis can also be used to explore the malleability of human perceptions, facilitate physical healing or alter physiology, explore consciousness, and even to develop one's spirituality. Each specific application of hypnosis has its own unique attributes. Current hypnosis research is busily trying to clarify the relationship between hypnotic procedures and the influence of variables associated with the context in which they are performed (T. Barber, 2000; Evans, 2000). This is vital research if we are to better understand how to skillfully use hypnosis as a tool in treatment.

In my opinion, no context is as complicated and burdened with confounding variables as the clinical context. When hypnosis is performed for the specific purpose of leading another person to change in some measurable and meaningful way, the interpersonal nature of the context is obvious. All its intricacies should not be underestimated when designing and delivering hypnotic interventions.

For many years, the conventional wisdom in the field was that hypnosis was innately benign—it couldn't really harm anyone. Leaders in the field offered such simplistic opinions as, to paraphrase, "Under hypnosis, a person will not do what he or she wouldn't ordinarily do" (Kroger, 1977), and, "All hypnosis is self-hypnosis" (Cheek & Lecron, 1968). Hypnosis was viewed as entirely within the client, and the clinician merely a "guide." We have since learned that that is not entirely true, and we now seem to better understand that anything that has the potential to help has an equal potential to harm (MacHovec, 1986). If the clinician using hypnosis is merely a guide, it is important to appreciate that he or she has the potential to be a hazardous one.

Doing hypnosis versus being hypnotic

There are many practitioners of hypnosis who know how to perform hypnotic techniques. However, I believe there is an important distinction to make between *doing* hypnosis and *being* hypnotic. Someone reading a script to a client may be doing hypnosis, but I don't believe he or she could be considered hypnotic. It's a distinction between moving a client through an arbitrary procedure that has no inherent meaningfulness, such as an utterly arbitrary method like a "countdown induction method" (what's meaningful or absorbing about counting numbers—unless you're an accountant?), versus stimulating meaningful associations in a client through individualized suggestions that acknowledge and incorporate his or her uniqueness.

Clinicians unanimously agree that each person is unique, then typically disregard the uniqueness at the level of clinical intervention by performing standardized (i.e., non-individualized) procedures. Being hypnotic means engaging purposefully with people, accepting the responsibility for being an agent of influence and change, and striving to use the capacity for influence intelligently and sensitively. Being hypnotic means knowing that the capacity for being absorbing, engaging, and influential doesn't only happen when formal induction takes place. Being hypnotic simply means incorporating hypnotic principles into one's very way of being, and is revealed through each interaction.

The skills needed to be an effective clinician, in contrast to those needed to merely perform an induction, are substantial. These include a broad knowledge of current clinical literature, an ability to relate to the client and form a therapeutic alliance, and an ability to organize and direct a well-structured intervention. These are all complex skills which require significant investments of time and effort to develop.

Doing art and doing science

I'm ambivalent about the field being subjected to research protocols to determine the efficacy of various treatments. On one hand, it's invaluable to know whether there is even a shred of objective evidence for the positive value of a specific form of treatment. On the other hand, too many people seem to think that the value of a treatment is inherent in the treatment protocol. This largely ignores the fact that therapy always has been and always will involve a large component of artistry in the process that no amount of standardized protocols will eliminate. If treatment can be standardized, as it has been with hypnotic scripts, one might well ask why we should train clinicians if all we really need are script readers.

Who we are as people is the foundation onto which the veneer of our clinical training is later glued. Consider for a moment why you practice the style of therapy you do. What does it say about you as a person that you maintain your individual philosophy of treatment, are attracted to and strive to practice well a particular style of therapy, and practice in such a way as to even try to lead your clients to believe as you do, however directly or indirectly you may do that?

This is hardly a new concept. We've known for a very long time that we get attracted to and practice therapy, including our hypnotic interventions, on the basis of what we subjectively find appealing. Someone goes to a hypnosis workshop and learns about and experiences an "inner sage" technique, for example, and thinks it was an inspiring experience. So, he or she goes back to work with a new enthusiasm and starts doing "inner sage" techniques with almost every client. Or, someone goes to a conference on the controversial "XYZ Disorder" and then starts seeing it in clients never previously known to have "it."

Therefore, it may be best to avoid using oneself as the reference point for relating to the client. Our personal backgrounds and interests should not be the primary basis for designing and delivering our interventions, hypnotic or otherwise. For example, having a deep and abiding interest in psychoanalytic approaches is not a legitimate basis for using such methods with depression sufferers, given the data that show it is generally a poor treatment alternative for the disorder. (That is not a global indictment against analytic approaches, but a specific conclusion that they are less effective than other approaches for depression; Depression Guideline Panel, 1993). Symptom characteristics and client attributes should be the basis for interventions, not whatever arbitrary framework we happen to adopt because it somehow pleases us. The clinician's experience and frame of reference may have little relation to that of the needs or interests of the client, and professionalism involves adapting oneself to the client's needs.

The ambiguity of a particular person's symptoms invites projections from clinicians: "I think you're depressed because your thinking is distorted and you need to learn to identify and self-correct your cognitive distortions," or, "I think your depression is caused by too low a concentration of serotonin in your brain." The same problem can be interpreted and treated from many viewpoints. It seems important, to me at least, to distinguish between facts and inferences in designing treatments.

The art of design

How do we get from the client's presentation of symptoms to the design and delivery of a useful clinical intervention? In line with my above point about ambiguity, it would be best to try to minimize the tendency to inter-pret the meaning of the symptoms. To diagnose a depression is not the same as declaring that it has a specific meaning. Aaron Beck, M.D., was right to have questioned more than three decades ago whether instead of depression being the outgrowth of some deeper intrapsychic conflict, de-pression might itself be the problem and the symptoms of depression be the most appropriate targets for treatment (Beck, Rush, Shaw, & Emery, 1979). This provided us a foundation for a clever "divide and conquer" strategy that works quite well, as efficacy studies repeatedly show us. Now, more than a quarter century later, we can recognize that each of the treat-ments that has been deemed "empirically supported" for treating depres-sion is short-term and focuses on the goals of skill-building and symptom resolution (Schulberg, Katon, Simon, & Rush, 1998).

I like that part of where the efficacy research has taken us. I've always thought therapy should be goal-oriented, even when surrounded by thera-pists who said, "It's the journey that matters, not the destination." Only clinicians ever seem to say that, though. Clients never do. Clients want *results*, and they typically want them right away.

Hypnosis and the targets of treatment

Having professed a philosophical position of wanting to minimize inter-preting the meaning of people's symptoms, the practical question natu-rally arises as to how to organize treatment without doing that.

I am in the fortunate position of regularly traveling all over the world, including all over the United States, conducting clinical trainings. Most of these are large workshops, but some of these trainings are small-group supervisions. I routinely encounter clinicians who will accept as goals from their clients statements such as, " I just want to feel better," or "I just want to have a good relationship." These are such global complaints as to be nothing more than mere wishes, not well-defined targets for clinical inter-vention. If a clinician is unclear as to what he or she is specifically needing to address, the intervention will likely go nowhere. Yet, somehow a culture of magical thinking has arisen around hypnosis, promoted by those who are attracted to the rather idealistic (and self-flattering) notion of an orga-nized and benevolent unconscious mind: Clinicians are told to "trust your unconscious" to (magically) develop an appropriate intervention, while the client is told to "trust your unconscious" to (magically) learn what is rel-evant (Gilligan, 1987; Grinder & Bandler, 1981).

I don't advocate taking a "trust your unconscious" approach. I think there should be specific goals in treatment and well-defined steps toward reaching them. In my opinion, the times hypnosis in particular and therapy in general work best are when there is a target to be hit and a well-defined means for doing so.

Where to begin?

In real world circumstances, unlike participants in traditional therapeutic efficacy studies, clients have multiple problems, even multiple diagnoses. Clinical judgment, an artistic evolutionary development, requires making a decision about where to begin. Not all problems are equal, of course. Some symptoms are generalized throughout the client's life, and some are specific to particular situations. Some are merely annoying, some are clearly dangerous. Some are relatively easy to resolve, some are refractory.

The first priority, of course, is what is urgent, and urgency is governed by hazard potential. Suicidal ideation, drug abuse, and reckless behavior that endangers one's self or others, are just a few examples of when clinicians must establish an order of priority that they might not otherwise choose if the client's symptoms posed no immediate danger.

Building therapeutic momentum and response sets

Where to begin, though, if no symptoms or issues are in urgent need of immediate attention? Generally, it is best to begin where one can generate some rapid symptom relief in order to address the low frustration tolerance typical of depressed individuals and to build a positive momentum in treatment. One of the most underemployed but useful constructs in applying hypnosis is called the "response set" (Erickson & Rossi, 1979; Lynn & Sherman, 2000). In fact, if asked what single characteristic I think most distinguishes the best hypnosis practitioners from the rest, I'd say it's how much deliberate attention they pay to building response sets.

Building a response set means building a momentum of responsiveness. For example, if I offer someone four consecutive statements I know he or she will agree with, what is that person's most likely response to my next statement? For example, if I say, "Each person is unique as an individual . . . Human experience is often complex . . . People frequently have more resources than they realize . . . Sometimes it feels good just to sit and relax . . . "—all agreeable statements—where does the momentum of responses carry the client? Most likely into the realm of agreement for the next statement.

In the practice of clinical hypnosis, then, effectively utilizing this principle means structuring interventions to go from general to specific. Thus, before I give someone a specific suggestion to develop an age regression, for example, I would first offer a series of general suggestions about memory that I know he or she would agree with, such as "Each person is capable of remembering many different experiences . . . some memories are much more vivid than others . . .", which gradually lead the client in the direction of later remembering or even reliving (i.e., revivifying) a specific memory.

Response sets can only be effectively designed and delivered when the session's goal is relatively clear. If one can't clearly state the hypnosis session's goal or primary therapeutic message in 25 words or less, then it may be best not to do the session (unless the goal is to simply "go fishing," which may occasionally be a reasonable choice). An unfocused session which yields little can too easily demotivate the client for participating in further hypnosis sessions.

Symptoms as intervention targets

Depression's symptoms

DSM-IV lists a depressed mood most of the day or a loss of interest in or lack of pleasure from things normally experienced as interesting or pleasurable as the foundational symptoms of depression. Additionally, DSM-IV indicates the depressed client may experience significant appetite disturbance and an associated weight change, sleep disturbance, agitation, fatigue, feelings of worthlessness, excessive or inappropriate guilt, diminished concentration, and thoughts of death or suicide and even making suicide attempts (American Psychiatric Association, 1994).

A major cross-cultural study published in the *Journal of the American Medical Association* affirmed most of DSM-IV's list of symptoms as among the most common symptoms of depression found across cultures (Weissman et al., 1996). Most frequent of all symptoms were the symptoms of insomnia (but, interestingly, not hypersomnia) and feeling fatigued most of the time.

Insomnia: Sleep disturbances and hypnosis

Depression is a global term describing a complex experience characterized by specific symptoms on multiple dimensions (physiological, cognitive, behavioral, affective, and interpersonal). The symptoms are themselves the product of ongoing or patterned ways of organizing perceptions and processing experience. For example, consider the symptom of insomnia. Insomnia is typically (but not always) a consequence of the typical depressive pattern of rumination. Insomnia can take three general forms: 1) primary—difficulty initially falling asleep; 2) middle—falling asleep relatively easily, but awakening only a few hours later and then having difficulty falling asleep again; and, 3) terminal—the so-called "early morning awakening" that causes people to awaken several hours before needing to and being unable to fall back to sleep. Terminal insomnia, so-named because it interferes with the terminal (end) phase of sleep, is the most common among depression sufferers (Thase & Howland, 1995).

Having asked literally hundreds of individuals who declare themselves "good sleepers" what they tend to think about when they go to sleep, their answer is consistently "nothing." That doesn't mean literally nothing, but it means the content of what they think about is so minimal in its complexity and level of emotional arousal that sleep comes easily. Asking hundreds of people with sleep problems what they tend to think about when trying to go to sleep, their answer is some variation of *"everything"*: problems to be solved, people to call, obligations to fulfill, significant events to either plan or rehash, and on and on. The level of emotional arousal is sufficiently high, the agitation so immediate, that the person's mind races and sleep becomes nearly impossible.

Such simple observations about what "good sleepers" do in comparison to "poor sleepers" provide us with clear targets at which to aim hypnotic interventions. The use of hypnosis to teach the ability to direct one's thoughts rather than merely react to them is a well established dynamic and a principal reason for using hypnosis in *any* context (Lynn et al., 1996; Yapko, 1990). Reducing the stressful wanderings of an agitated mind and relaxing the body while simultaneously teaching the empowering ability to create and follow a line of pleasant thoughts that are soothing, restful, and associate positive images and feelings to sleep creates the possibility of improved sleep.

The reductions in rumination and anxiety can contribute to better sleep, but even more important interventions are taking place indirectly just by teaching relaxation skills and self-hypnotic inductions. The depressed person is again being told that he or she can assert some control over his or her internal experience rather than merely be its victim. Furthermore, the depressed person, who typically has a global cognitive style (a style of thought in which one sees the "big picture" at the expense of the salient details), is also beginning to learn how to compartmentalize his or her experience, and the importance of doing so. In other words, to fall asleep more easily without experiencing agitating ruminations, *the individual must learn to establish boundaries separating problem-solving time and personal reflection time from his or her sleep time*. To enhance that boundary, the clinician may encourage the person to set aside specific periods during the day for problem-solving and reflection, reinforcing the critical teaching that bedtime is not the time to solve problems or contemplate one's life. To do so is to impair both the quantity and quality of sleep. Realistically, the depressed client who is prone to rumination is not very likely to stop being ruminative entirely, but a realistic goal remains to reduce ruminations when it's time to sleep. More will be said on ruminative coping styles in Chapter 7, particularly in regards to reducing the frequency, severity, and length of depressive episodes.

Targeting insomnia with hypnosis has special importance. For reasons currently unknown, there is a correlation between insomnia and later relapses (Kravitz & Newman, 1995). If someone suffers a depressive episode and experiences a sleep disturbance, if the sleep disturbance remits when the depressive episode ends, the person is at a lower risk for later relapses. If, however, the depression lifts and the person's disturbed sleep does *not* return to normal, the person is at a higher risk for later relapses. Thus, assessing the client's sleep is important for clinicians to do. Actively intervening with hypnosis to enhance sleep (through suggestions both for relaxation and diminished rumination) can have a profound impact on both the course of depression as well as the risk for later relapses.

The relationship between insomnia and fatigue, another frequent symptom of depression, seems obvious. When someone sleeps poorly, how can he or she feel an adequate level of energy? Furthermore, when someone has a global cognitive style that may lead him or her to see all problems as piled together in an insurmountable mountain of woes, how can he or she feel energized to want to move through them? Thus, addressing insomnia and simultaneously addressing any global thinking that may contribute to the client's sense of being overwhelmed and exhausted (just by thinking of all the problems to be faced) become vital aspects of treatment. How many people become depressed simply from unrelenting fatigue: an ongoing sense of never getting caught up, always having too much to do and not enough time to do it, routinely feeling sleep- and fun-deprived, and regularly living from frantic moment to frantic moment? (Bell, 1997).

I believe this is one of the major contributors to the rising rates of depression. In asking thousands of professionals attending my clinical trainings each year, "How many of you feel your pace of life is slower now than in the past?", it is most uncommon to get affirmative replies. Beyond my informal survey of my audience, the data describing the ever-quickening pace of life for most of us are abundant and should lead us to ask, "What happens to all those people running on life's treadmill when they can no longer keep up?" The answer, it seems, is that many of them become depressed. They work harder, work longer hours, juggle more responsibilities, connect less frequently with family and friends for social support and recreation, and expend more and more effort just to try and maintain. Fatigue sets in, despair sets in, life becomes burdensome and overwhelming, and depression may then surface. I doubt any clinician reading this hasn't struggled with these issues personally, and certainly has had to admonish clients to "slow down" and "stop and smell the roses" many, many times.

No amount of medication will help people learn to "slow down," to curtail their ruminations, and to establish stronger boundaries between work and personal lives, and between problem-solving times and sleep times. These are life skills that must be learned with clinicians serving as teachers. Hypnosis can be an effective vehicle for teaching such skills. The symptoms a client presents point the clinician in the direction he or she must go if the client is to be empowered to get some control back and reduce or eliminate the symptom. *For as long as a client feels victimized by symptoms, recovery from depression is extremely unlikely* (Beck, 1987). This is particularly true when the client is "doing this to himself or herself" with no insight as to how or why.

Using insomnia as just one example of depressive symptoms that must be targets, it is clear that by the time a symptom has formed, the associated risk factors had likely already been well in place long before. Comprehensive treatment must take the risk factors into account as well.

Risk factors as intervention targets

A risk factor is any factor that increases the probability of a particular disease or disorder occurring. There are numerous psychosocial risk factors for depression, including:

Stressful life circumstances
Marital conflict
Physical or sexual abuse (past or present)
Economic deprivation
Social skills deficits
Problem-solving skills deficits
Self-management skills deficits
Dysfunctional ways of thinking, perceiving
Comorbid mental conditions (e.g., anxiety) (Cohen, 1994)

The goals of therapy include not only reducing or eliminating symptoms, but also reducing or eliminating risk factors for successive episodes. Depression is often described as a "recurrent disease," and statistics bear out an ever higher probability of later episodes the more episodes one has (Glass, 1999). My view, however, isn't that depression is innately recurrent in nature—I believe *life* is recurrent. Each person faces loss, disappointment, rejection, humiliation, and other such painful life experiences many times over the course of a lifetime. If depression is one's response to such episodes, then depression will predictably recur with the same regularity of life experiences recurring. Helping someone "chemically adjust" to such negative episodes in life almost guarantees later relapses, whereas teaching clients to identify and reduce their risk factors for recurrences holds greater potential to reduce them (Tolman, 1995).

The risk factors I'm referring to here are the patterned ways each person evolves for interpreting and responding to life experiences. In the next chapter, I describe the ambiguous nature of most of life experiences, meaning the absence of a clear meaning or definitive answer to the events and questions of life. Each person must struggle with finding ways to think about and relate to the demands of life, from answering the cosmic questions ("Why are we here?") to the more mundane but equally ambiguous ones ("Do you want Chinese or Italian food for dinner tonight?"). I will describe how hypnosis can play a role in teaching a comfortable means for dealing with the ambiguities of life.

The patterns of thought, information processing, and relating to others may continue to evolve over the course of a lifetime, but are established early in life. Their consistency over time allows for much of personal experience and even general human experience to be predictable. Personality is largely a stable phenomenon, an enduring way of relating to self, others, and life (Philipchalk & McConnell, 1994).

Thus, the risk factors to be targeted in treatment, along with their associated symptoms, represent some of the deeper applications of hypnosis and psychotherapy. To ignore underlying risk factors and focus only on the client's symptoms is a relatively superficial intervention, addressing only the problem's content but not its structure. (The content refers to the details—the *what*—of the problem, while the structure refers to the process—the *how*—of how the symptom is produced.) Using the previous section's example of insomnia as a target, insomnia is the symptom. But, unless the individual's ruminative coping style is altered, and unless the global style is addressed by teaching better compartmentalization (boundary) skills to separate problem-solving time from sleep time, the mere teaching of relaxation skills is unlikely to be of enough help to the person.

Key risk factors to address in regards to my emphasis on addressing underlying structures include such self-organizing factors as: (a) Cognitive style (Abstract or concrete? Global or linear? Attributional style?); (b) Response style (Self or other-directed? Open or guarded?); (c) Attentional style (Focused or diffuse? Focused on saliency or irrelevance?); and, (d) Perceptual style (Focuses on similarities or differences between experiences? Magnifies or diminishes events or perceptions?) (Yapko, 1988).

By identifying these and other patterns of self-organization, the clinician is in a stronger position to aim interventions at more meaningful risk factor targets. Perhaps the most well researched of such risk factor patterns is "attributional style," the characteristic ways a person explains life events to himself, herself, or others. Attributional style encompasses such dimensions as *personalization* ("Are negative events due to me or others?"), *permanence* ("Are negative events temporary or transient?"), and *pervasiveness* ("Do negative events adversely affect all things in my life or just some things?") (Billings & Moos, 1985; Sacco & Beck, 1995). Without intervention, one's attributional style is an enduring way of organizing subjective perceptions. The typical depressive pattern of seeing negative events in life as personal, permanent, and pervasive (so-called "internal," "stable," and "global" attributions), represents a high level of risk for depressive episodes whenever life gets painful (Seligman, 1989). Thus, a risk factor level of intervention would strive to teach the person to make *realistic* attributions context by context, rather than maintaining a negative attributional style pattern that increases the risk for depression.

Risk factors for depression may be addressed singly or in combination. The therapeutic goal, of course, is to introduce variability and accuracy according to situational cues into the pattern. Thus, instead of the person interpreting things in a rigid, consistent manner (e.g., routinely taking things personally, even when they're not personal), the person would learn to distinguish when it is and isn't personal, and how to respond to specific contexts flexibly and appropriately.

lying adaptability that "every pattern is valuable somewhere, but no pattern is valuable everywhere."

Diminish weakness or amplify strength?

It represents a significant philosophical shift in performing psychotherapy to focus on the relationship between patterns and contexts rather than analyzing "psychopathology." This book focuses the reader on the tremendous value of what key figures like Milton Erickson and Virginia Satir taught decades ago, and what former American Psychological Association President and renowned depression researcher Martin Seligman currently advocates—the need for clinicians and researchers to identify and build on human (including client) strengths (Myers, 2000; Seligman & Csikszentmihalyi, 2000). Depressed clients don't have to be viewed as "sick" or "diseased" in order for clinicians to help them. Teaching coping and problem-solving skills is far more appropriate in treatment than is analyzing psychopathology. The efficacy data simply affirm that when people are empowered, and when they learn the skills for living better, they are likely to recover (Lewinsohn, Munos, Youngren, & Zeiss, 1986; Schulberg & Rush, 1994).

Getting started using hypnosis

Having interviewed the client and gotten a symptom description and history, medical history, and having assessed the psychosocial factors operating in this person's life, the clinician might well have enough information to formulate a meaningful hypnotic intervention, even in the very first therapy session. Some clinicians claim one should have a strong rapport and therapeutic alliance *before* doing hypnosis early in the treatment process (Frauman, Lynn, & Brentar, 1993). I wouldn't disagree, but I believe that position is too limited. I would suggest instead that one can often use the hypnosis itself as a means to build the necessary rapport and therapeutic alliance with a client. In fact, I demonstrate this very process with a client named Mike, in Chapter 8.

When someone is in distress, feeling hopeless and overwhelmed, it seems both cruel and entirely unnecessary to say, "give me more of your history" and "I'll start helping you next time." Why shouldn't the client begin to get some help right away? Given the typically low frustration tolerance of the depressed individual, who wants and hopes for some immediate relief, why not provide some when this is one of the things hypnosis does best? The ability of hypnosis to provide anxiety reduction to lower agitation, and to reduce ruminations are some of the best reasons to use hypnosis early on in treatment as a means for demonstrating to the client that his or her symptoms are malleable.

Relating to the context

Recognizing the patterns of depression may lead clinicians to an awareness that the client's problems are largely problems of context. The symptomatic person is applying some behavioral or perceptual pattern in a situation where the result is detrimental. *Why* the person would apply an
ineffective or self-limiting strategy invites theorizing and projection. Typically, though, it's all the person knows—it's what he or she has learned to
do through socialization.

The client is immersed in subjective reality and is typically unaware of
his or her own "blind spots"—namely, the person doesn't know he or she
has a global cognitive style, for example. He or she only knows that "*everything* is so overwhelming." The clinician recognizes such statements as evidence of a global cognitive style and may therefore decide to teach the skill
of breaking big, overwhelming problems into smaller, more manageable
ones.

But, is a global cognitive style a "bad" thing? No, it isn't a unilaterally
negative pattern but in *some* contexts it will be harmful for the problems it
creates. To be global in one's thinking about a movie, for example, might
well prevent picking apart any plot and character inconsistencies that would
prevent its enjoyment. However, to be global in trying to manage one's
finances spells disaster, since every detail counts in the context of managing money. So, a global style can benefit someone in one circumstance, yet
be troublesome in another. Context determines the value of any pattern,
not the pattern itself. *Any pattern has the potential to be helpful or harmful,
depending on the context in which it is applied.*

The heart of therapy, therefore, is in teaching clients to identify which
subjective patterns will work best in a given context and then use one's
interventions to deliberately associate them to those patterns. It requires
people to read situations accurately in order to know what the situation
requires (e.g., an impersonal response) and what specific resources one
has to meet those demands (e.g., an effective strategy for reminding oneself the criticism isn't personal based on clear criteria).

This is precisely what people *don't* do, however, to their own detriment. They want to self-disclose ("Let me tell you what I think of this job")
but they don't read the context well in order to recognize this isn't a safe
place for self-disclosure (i.e., it'll get back to the boss and likely be pun-
ished).

"Relating to the context" means adapting to situations flexibly. Facilitating flexibility in clients while simultaneously encouraging them to be
more observant (therefore less internally and more externally oriented)
and critical in their thinking are primary goals of each of those therapies
that enjoy the greatest amount of empirical support for their effectiveness
in treating depression. Hypnosis can help magnify the key learning under-

The first session is an especially critical one for reasons of therapy mortality. A mortality in psychotherapy refers to the client who comes in once (or twice) and doesn't come back. Sometimes the client doesn't come back because he or she got what was wanted. But, other times the client doesn't come back because he or she quickly concluded that therapy won't be helpful because all the clinician did in the first session was ask for history. Clinicians have had a range of interesting attributions (all external in structure) for this phenomenon: "He wasn't ready"; "She must enjoy her depression"; "He's getting secondary gains for being depressed"; "She finds therapy too threatening"; and so on. It would help matters if clinicians were less quick to blame the client for those times when therapy goes awry. It may be easier to say the client's expectations for a first session were unrealistic, but it may be more therapeutic to offer meaningful help even in a first session.

Gathering lots of history may make clinicians (and HMOs) feel better, but it doesn't do much for the client. The depressed client typically feels hopeless ("nothing will help"), hopeful ("maybe this shrink can help"), impatient ("I better get some relief fast"), and even suspicious ("this shrink better not try to hook me into drugs or years of therapy"). The clinician's responsibility, even in the very first session, is to facilitate hope and meet the need for at least some relief as quickly as possible. Hypnosis can help do both, in specific ways which will be discussed and modeled in Chapter 5.

Introducing hypnosis to the client

One can interview a client and then twenty or thirty minutes into the session say something such as the following as a lead-in to hypnosis:

> "I've been listening to you now for the last half hour or so, describing your symptoms and problems, and how *absorbed* you have been in just trying to manage. I've been impressed by your suffering and despair, and it's obvious to me that *you want things to change*. Having been so *focused on and absorbed in* all the most hurtful thoughts and feelings, it seems obvious to me how valuable it would be to you to *start to consider and get absorbed* in *different thoughts and feelings* that can help you feel better. You came here knowing it would be important to *get absorbed in a different way of looking at things,* and to help you start to get absorbed in a different way of thinking and feeling you can just let your eyes close and focus yourself on some of the possibilities I want to describe to you. . . . "

And thus the hypnosis session begins. I cannot think of a single instance in nearly a quarter century of practice in which a client refused to participate or was even reluctant to join the process. Clients are typically looking for direction and feedback, knowing *something* has to change, but they are typically unclear as to what. When you read the transcript in Chapter 8 of a session done with a man who has no background in hypnotic approaches, who does not know me or my reputation at all, who does not know what to expect from me or what he will be asked to do, you will see the response that is typical: A variation of "I'll do anything that you, the professional and expert in matters such as these, tell me to do if you think it will help." That drive to get better is what leads desperate clients to even participate in what prove to be useless or even anti-therapeutic practices. People just want to feel better.

Choosing one's hypnotic style

The last section of this chapter briefly addresses the issue of hypnotic style. It's an important issue, because the issue is still being hotly debated as to whether hypnosis is a "state" or a "trait." Thus, whether hypnosis is seen as an intrapersonal or interpersonal phenomenon dictates to a significant extent one's approach and methods.

It is recommended that one choose a style based on the client, not some preferred theory. In the same way the AHCPR Depression Treatment Guidelines say that "cognitive, behavioral or interpersonal therapy may be sensibly used *according to patient profile,*" hypnosis guidelines must likewise say that any hypnotic approach can be sensibly used *according to patient profile*. The idea is *not* to be a cognitive therapist, or a behavioral therapist, or an interpersonal therapist, or an Ericksonian therapist, or a (fill-in-the-blank) therapist, and then treat all depressed clients according to that model. The idea is to be fluent in *all* those approaches, and to draw upon their methods as client symptoms and needs dictate. Arguing over whether direct or indirect suggestions are superior is a colossal waste of time when we should already have reached the understanding that *no* suggestion, direct or indirect, is powerful or useful until a client *chooses* to respond to it. The divisiveness in the field over this and other such academic questions that are entirely of no interest to the client seeking treatment is something we cannot be proud of if we want to be socially relevant. We continue to argue about such points, and meanwhile depression keeps infecting more lives.

Therapy is more art than science, a condition unlikely to ever change as long as therapy remains an interpersonal process involving clinical judgement and social skill. Hypnosis is even more artistry than science, utilizing subjectively created hypnotic phenomena such as regression or dissociation that arise from suggestive influences within the hypnotic relationship.

It is no coincidence that I choose to land on the side that strives to improve the artistry of clinicians using hypnosis. More data won't help us be better humans doing clinical work. There is simply no substitute for having the range to formulate direct *and* indirect suggestions, positive *and* negative suggestions, process *and* content suggestions, and authoritarian *and* permissive suggestions. Having the range, the flexibility, to impart information and perspective in a variety of ways is what artistry is about. Disavowing client uniqueness by summarily believing that "if he or she is hypnotizable, it won't matter how you phrase a suggestion," allows ineffective suggestions to be attributed to client limitations. It makes some clinicians feel better to do that, apparently, but I'd caution against anyone really believing it.

Does hynotizability matter? Of course, but not nearly as much as the *interplay* between client skills and clinician styles of presentation. Believing the client can respond to some degree, and expecting to and striving to find a channel for meaningful shared communication, is a great way to initiate hypnotic interventions.

CLINICAL APPLICATIONS ||

Ambiguity and the vulnerability of believing 4

Having studied and practiced clinical hypnosis full-time for over a quarter century, I have come to appreciate some of the paradoxes inherent in doing hypnosis in the clinical context. In applying hypnosis with clients who are striving to change some aspects of their lives, one cannot underestimate how fragile people are and, paradoxically, how powerful they are. Nor can one ignore how utterly vacant someone can be, usually right before, paradoxically, he or she demonstrates a remarkable resourcefulness. People can be mindlessly ritualistic and then, paradoxically, dazzle you with their creativity. These and many other seeming paradoxes of human nature are amplified in hypnosis (Haley, 1973).

My view of human nature has been profoundly influenced by my clinical work with clients. I have certainly learned the importance and power of people's beliefs. Many years ago, William Kroger, M.D., a pioneer in hypnosis in the 20th Century who frequently taught and eventually cofounded the American Society of Clinical Hypnosis together with Milton H. Erickson, M.D., defined hypnosis for me as "the induction of conviction" (Yapko, 1987, p. 4). I think he was right about that. And, I think it was perceptive on Kroger's part to frame hypnosis in terms of belief systems.

It is an entirely human phenomenon to have minds that can be so easily manipulated, under the right conditions, by our own innate need to believe. Whether discovered in ancient archaeological digs or pulled out of today's headlines, the very human need to believe is instantly evident as the force controlling human behavior and even human evolution. How have your beliefs shaped your life? What have they led you to do, and led you to avoid doing? What beliefs have you held that ultimately were proved wrong, and when they were, what did that spark in you? A crisis of faith, an evolutionary leap in consciousness, or nothing at all?

Depression is closely connected to beliefs. So much of what we as clinicians do in treatment is find creative and respectful ways of challenging the depressed client's worldview, namely, the specific beliefs they hold (e.g., "Life is no damn good") that can cause or exacerbate depression. And, we challenge the mechanisms by which such beliefs are formed (Kovacs & Beck, 1985).

Focusing on "why" someone would hold an erroneous, self-limiting, even depressing belief is an unnecessary question to ask. The question is as global as this answer: the vulnerabilities associated with the need to believe. Why do we have a need to believe? In large part, to make sense out of randomness and nonsense, and thereby have a sense, however illusory, of having some control over our experience (Seligman, 1993).

Ambiguity

Ambiguity may well be the most powerful and pervasive risk factor for depression of all known risk factors. Ambiguity in this context refers to the lack of clear meaning associated with one's various life experiences. Events occur, we observe them occur, but what we most often don't know is what, if anything, they mean. The great majority of events in life do not have a clear and inherent meaning, leaving each of us the task of having to establish for ourselves our own subjective interpretation of what the meaning or significance is of the event. This is the process of "projection"—projecting meaning onto ambiguous stimuli. In response to any life event, however minor or major, the formation of an idiosyncratic meaning represents the heart of a belief system, whether self-reinforced (e.g., "I believe it no matter what others might think") or culturally reinforced (e.g., "Any true American would believe this"). Beliefs are multidimensional, encompassing feelings, physiology, and behavior, as well as the obvious cognitive components, and all will need to be addressed in a comprehensive intervention.

Like the well-known Rorschach inkblot test requiring respondents to project personal meanings onto ambiguous inkblots, we all do the same throughout life. Thus, life can be described as an "experiential Rorschach," and what this book is about—and what therapy is about—is dealing with the consequences of the projections one makes. The consequences in terms of mood are the most relevant for this book—the optimism and good feelings that come from an expansive projection that says, "Life is an adventure, a wondrous opportunity to experience all the glories of living," or the despair and anguish that come from a hurtful projection that says, "Life is a bitch, and then you die" (Peterson, 2000).

Depression is largely (not entirely) about projections that hurt. In the face of ambiguity, the depressed person forms perceptions, attributions, beliefs (pick one) that are painful in some way. Once the person adopts and integrates his or her depressogenic perceptions (attributions, beliefs), a personal conviction has been induced—but in an anti-therapeutic direction. Hypnotic patterns—the induction of conviction—clearly have the potential to harm.

Cognitive therapy (CT) in particular has flourished as the most well-studied and most systematic form of psychotherapy. Aaron T. Beck, M.D. and Albert Ellis, Ph.D., in particular, spawned a revolution in the field of psychotherapy by shifting the focus away from *what* someone thinks (the content) to *how* someone thinks (the process). Whether assessing the specific *cognitive distortions* in the context of Beck's Cognitive Therapy (1997), or *irrational beliefs* in the context of Ellis' (1997) Rational Emotive Behavior Therapy (REBT), the underlying mechanism for the development of depression is in the inability to distinguish inferences (projections) from facts. *Why* are there cognitive distortions or irrational beliefs to have to correct in CT or REBT? Why can't people willingly and with self-awareness sidestep the vulnerability of their own beliefs?

Let's consider as an example a so-called cognitive distortion, "jumping to conclusions," the error of reaching a conclusion despite the lack of supportive evidence. Why jump to conclusions, if not merely to *have* a conclusion? But the corollary question is, why have the need for a conclusion? What is it about ambiguity that is so compelling in the force it generates to produce an answer, even if it is a wrong or hurtful one? How much human misery could be alleviated by a refined and perceptive means for simply saying, "I don't know" and leaving it at that? Consider these questions:

Is there a God?
Is there life after death?
Why do innocent babies die of terrible diseases?
Is reincarnation true?
What capacity does the unconscious have for healing sickness?
Is there such a thing as fate?
Why isn't life fair?

You can answer these and a million more such "cosmic" questions however you might like to, but whatever answer you have settled on is merely your belief. These are and will remain open questions that no amount of analysis, either scientific or philosophical, will definitively answer. Believe what you want, but if these could be answered definitively, they would be answered, and would be in no need of the continuous exploration and re-exploration each question still engenders.

What quality of life, including a quality of mood, does your—or anybody's—answer create? What would happen if people were able to simply say, "I don't know" in response to such questions? At the very least, the level of struggle both intrapersonally and interpersonally would be greatly reduced. There would be fewer people feeling the need to kill or hurt other people for their having the "wrong" (i.e., different) politics, religion, skin color, sexual orientation, age, or gender. People would develop a greater tolerance for personal beliefs, arbitrary as they might be, that enhance someone's sense of personal and social responsibility. People would be more aware of the distinction between fact and inference, and strive to develop more facts when possible, and more acceptance of diversity in projections ("creativity") when no such facts either do now or will ever exist.

Recognizing and tolerating ambiguity

It is no coincidence that one of the most basic goals in treating therapy clients in general, and depressed clients in particular, is to teach them how to *recognize* and *tolerate ambiguity*. It is a therapeutic goal that even *precedes* identifying specific cognitive distortions or irrational beliefs in the client. Before teaching someone to avoid jumping to conclusions (or personalizing, or thinking dichotomously, for example), that person would have to be comfortable having no conclusions (i.e., a reduced drive to have an answer). Thus, by addressing the issue of ambiguity in therapy, and making it a primary target of a specific hypnotic intervention, the larger goals of therapy such as teaching skills in rational thinking are well facilitated (Sacco & Beck, 1995). For as long as an individual is unable to tolerate uncertainty, he or she will be motivated to continue forming projections onto life experience with little or no insight into the process, and thus suffer the mood consequences when they are accepted as "true." Simply put, the essence of depression is that *people think things, and then mistake their thoughts, beliefs, and perceptions for "truth."* The sophisticated skills of identifying and then self-correcting one's cognitive distortions are vital skills for *any* human being, depressed or not, to learn and master if one is to create a better world for oneself (and the rest of us).

Less globally and wishfully, the positive value of cognitive therapy in particular has been well documented in the literature, and is clearly a treatment of choice for depression (Dobson, 1989). Cognitive skills can be learned more easily with hypnosis as a vehicle of experiential learning, and what little efficacy research there is bears that out. Further, cognitive skills can be more easily learned when the basic human need to believe something—*anything*—can be reduced and, metaphorically, surrounded with warning signs that flash the message, "Warning: Vulnerability to Symptoms Ahead, Proceed With Caution." People simply have to learn that their beliefs represent, paradoxically, both their potential strengths and weaknesses. Clinicians want their clients to learn how to stay connected to ("associate") those beliefs that serve them well by enhancing their outlook on life, improving their physical health, increasing their productivity, and enhancing their relationships. Likewise, clinicians want their clients to learn how to disconnect from ("dissociate") any beliefs that impair functioning on any of those dimensions.

Flexibility

What hurts or helps changes over time, though. The beliefs that help make one strong (e.g., "Never give up!") can easily become the very beliefs that are the basis for emotional pain and even depression when circumstances change and now make such beliefs unrealistic and self-damaging. Thus, the goal of therapy is not just to teach how to let go of or self-correct specific dysfunctional attitudes or beliefs, but how to *recognize the changes in context that now require a modification, coupled with the flexibility to actually achieve the modification*. To achieve this, one would have to be relativistic in one's thinking—the opposite of believing in "absolute" truths, namely, beliefs that do not and will not vary according to context. It is difficult to be relativistic when cultures and families often promote a belief in absolutes: "Trust your intuition" . . . "All things happen for a reason" . . . "Keep your feelings to yourself" . . . "Be fully present in the moment." Even in the hypnosis culture, the absolutes exist: "Always have the client sign a hypnosis release form" . . . "Always assess hypnotizability" . . . "Never tell the client the meaning of the metaphor" . . . "Hypnosis is all about the skill of the client, not the techniques of the hypnotist" . . . "Always have the client sit with both feet on the floor before beginning an induction" . . . "Never use hypnosis with depressed clients."

Is it any coincidence that the field generates divisive polarities in views and practices of hypnosis? The disdain many traditional practitioners of hypnosis have for "Ericksonian hypnosis" practitioners, and vice-versa, is irrational and unjustifiable. Each approach can work well with some clients but not others. Isn't that the basis for striving to use what works for an individual rather than striving to remain loyal to one model by devaluing another when either one can be shown to have aspects to it that don't work universally well for everyone? So how did debates emerge that it's "better" to be direct than indirect, or vice-versa? Better for *who*? Certainly not the client, who doesn't make suggestion structure an issue other than by simply being responsive to one type or another. Some will respond well to direct approaches, some won't.

Culturally, people get caught up in the same polarized (dichotomous) thinking as clinicians. For example, we tell clients, "Be fully present in the moment," then complain about how impulsive they are! Why don't we teach them more relativistic thinking, such as, "Be fully present in the moment *sometimes*"? But the larger point is that when clients don't have the ability to adapt their thoughts, feelings, and behaviors context-by-context, the rigid nature of their patterns will *sometimes* yield distress and symptoms.

Teaching the ability to discriminate

In line with this chapter's focus on ambiguity and the vulnerability of beliefs, a primary task of the clinician is to teach "discrimination strategies." A discrimination strategy is an internal strategy the client can use to distinguish when it's "this" and when it's "that." Using the example above of absolutes, if we want to teach someone who is often inappropriately impulsive to "be fully present in the moment *sometimes*," we would first have to provide him or her with a means for positively valuing "being in the moment" and, likewise, a positive countervalue for "transcending the moment."

Next we would need to teach the person how to read a given situation in order to determine whether this is a situation requiring "being in the moment" as an effective response. How is "an effective response" evaluated? How would you as a clinician delineate a strategy for determining whether an effective response would be to "be in the moment" or to "transcend the moment?" Pause and think of your response.

You might appreciate that it will be hard for you to think of a useful strategy if you haven't had one (perhaps because you've never really thought about it, or perhaps because you have been absolute in your advocating the need to "be fully present in the moment"). But, if you have recognized that there are times to be present in the moment and there are times *not* to be present in the moment, then you are already leaning in the direction of appreciating that either focal point can be helpful, depending both on what the goals are and what is appropriate for the context. Taking the time to watch a lovely sunset is a good time to be "present in the moment," but getting a root canal is a good time to "transcend the moment."

Pick any of the absolutes about life mentioned earlier ("Trust your intuition" . . . "All things happen for a reason," etc.) and find the exceptions. Pick any of the absolutes about hypnosis mentioned earlier ("Always assess hypnotizability" . . . "Never do hypnosis with depressed clients") and find the exceptions. When you can explain to someone how you know in one context it's "this," but in another context it's "that," you'll know you're a step or two closer to being an effective clinician, teacher, parent, friend, colleague, and human being.

Discrimination strategies

So much of human misery could be alleviated by teaching people to sidestep the vulnerabilities associated with being a believer. Much of that misery arises because people aren't content to just believe. They also often feel compelled to attack those who don't believe similarly, or exert pressure on them to change their beliefs in the direction of their own. Social psychology as a science has done outstanding research on the dynamics of conformity, interpersonal attraction, and prejudice, all of which are highly relevant to therapeutic intervention (Aronson, 1999). (In fact, I would suggest that the literature of social psychology is, in many ways, more relevant to doing clinical work than is the literature of clinical psychology.) For example, consider what happened in the so-called "recovered memory debate." I took a moderate position of saying sometimes recovered memories can be accurate and sometimes they can be confabulations, and without external evidence there is no way to distinguish the two (Yapko, 1994). That is a relativistic statement. But to absolutists who believe the memories are *always* reliable (e.g., "always believe the victim") or are *never* reliable (e.g., "never trust a memory that surfaced in therapy"), a moderate position which allows for either possibility actually seems extreme and so is attacked. Similarly, when I took the position that hypnosis can be helpful in treating depression sufferers (Yapko, 1992), a relativistic position, some absolutists who said "*Never* do hypnosis with depressed clients" went on the attack.

I use these personal examples here to illustrate a point. Absolute thinking is, by definition, global. It is the antithesis to linear, critical, or compartmentalized thinking. By discouraging the ability to think critically, context by context, clinicians can inadvertently contribute to their client's depression by advocating one-size-fits-all formulas that, in some contexts, are guaranteed to harm the client. The therapeutic goal, therefore, is to use hypnosis to help teach discrimination strategies.

Consider the following six examples out of dozens I could list of discriminations a person would need to make skillfully if he or she is to manage related situations well.

How do you distinguish . . .

1. what you are and are not in control of?
2. when you can and cannot "trust your guts"?
3. when rejection is and is not personal?
4. whether your expectations are or are not realistic?
5. whether someone can or cannot meet your needs in a relationship?
6. when to "hold on" and when to "let go"?

In each of these situations requiring a "clean" (i.e., well delineated) strategy for making an important discrimination, one can easily see how an inability to make the necessary discrimination might prove harmful. For example, consider the first one addressing the issue of controllability. Martin Seligman's "Learned Helplessness" model of depression provided valuable insight into how inaccurate perceptions involving a perceived lack of control in aversive situations could lead to depression in some people (Abramson, Seligman, & Teasdale, 1985). *Over*estimating the degree of control one has in a circumstance can likewise lead to depression when the person's inflated belief is shattered through experience. Clearly, the ability to distinguish degrees of controllability accurately is a central task in treating depression sufferers (Peterson, Maier, & Seligman, 1993).

The key therapeutic issue is how to teach depressed clients to "step outside themselves" long enough to consider how good the "goodness of fit" is between their beliefs and the context at hand. We can teach clients to ask themselves, "Is this context one that will be managed more successfully by doing *this*, or by doing *that*?" Or, "Will I feel better about (myself, my job, my marriage, my kids, my body, my health, . . .) by doing *this* or by doing *that*?"

To exemplify the point, let's plug some specifics into these statements. "Is this context one that will be managed more successfully by *focusing on my needs* or by *focusing on my partner's needs*?" "Will I feel better about myself by *getting the task done* or by *putting it off until later*?" "Will this client respond better if I use a *permissive suggestion style* or an *authoritarian one*?" "Will hypnosis help this anxious depressed person *relax* or will it *delay addressing an important issue*?"

None of these sample questions can be answered only internally without external feedback, or only in the moment without anticipating consequences. Key elements of teaching discrimination strategies are (a) teaching the client to look for external evidence when possible and (b) to consider the likely consequences in as much detail as possible. When people don't discriminate well, it's typically because they don't go outside themselves for additional information or perspective, and/or they do what's familiar and comfortable without ample consideration of the probable consequences. Thus, in this chapter, I am addressing the need to go outside oneself in order to seek information that may alleviate some of the anxiety associated with ambiguity, and in the next chapter I will focus on an orientation to the future, which can enhance one's ability to take probable consequences into account when deciding on a course of action.

The keys in teaching discrimination strategies are in helping the client recognize there is an ambiguity present in the situation that requires a conscious, deliberate decision to be made. The client learns he or she cannot automatically self-disclose, for example, but instead can recognize that self-disclosure may help or may harm an interaction, and therefore he or she must evaluate the available situational cues in order to determine what is likely to be the better choice.

Clinicians can't teach clients what they don't know. The more extreme a clinician's position on *anything*, the less able he or she will be to teach about exceptions to "the rule." Ask a cognitive therapist "When *isn't* cognitive therapy a good choice?" and you'll find out how well he or she understands the limits of the model. Ask an Ericksonian practitioner of hypnosis "When *isn't* metaphor a good choice?" and you'll find out his or her potential to recognize limitations of metaphors and how well he or she can identify the factors that distinguish effective from ineffective (or even iatrogenic) applications. Nothing is good (safe, effective, meaningful, therapeutic . . .) everywhere, but most things are good *somewhere*. The key to effective living, as far as I can tell, is in knowing what to do, which parts of self/life to engage with, and when.

Hypnotically facilitating the ability to recognize and tolerate ambiguity

There is perhaps no single more important *preventive* intervention than teaching people to recognize when a situation is ambiguous and, therefore, when they are most at risk for making potentially depressing projections. By better recognizing the probability of forming a depressing projection, the informed client can push himself or herself to generate multiple viewpoints and initiate a search for objective information to either rule these explanations in or out. I will explore the concept of prevention in detail in the final chapter, but in this section I want to affirm the value of multi-level interventions that cannot only reduce the frequency and severity of depressive episodes, but can even reduce or prevent the likelihood of later ones.

When an individual faces an ambiguous event, especially a negative one, and asks the sensible question, "Why did this happen?", the risk is in adopting a self-damaging or self-limiting explanation that has no objective basis. The rigid patterns of attributional or explanatory styles are the patterns for making meaning of life events. When people consistently explain events to themselves (or others) in ways that are hurtful, depression is a predictable consequence.

The primary therapeutic goals, therefore, are to: (a) learn how to quickly recognize ambiguity in situations; (b) be on guard against one's own tendency to interpret such events in some patterned way that may not be objectively true; and (c) develop a tolerance for ambiguity that permits comfort with not knowing.

Not knowing is a spur to finding out. Not knowing is *not* an indication of stupidity or incompetence, it's a statement about the limits of one's knowledge. Not knowing what's "right" or what's "true" in a given context can either be empowering or victimizing, depending on one's perspective. As well-trained professionals, we learn to turn ignorance into opportunities for meaningful research, and we learn to distinguish between speculations and established facts. The temptation we all face is to assert that we know more than we really do, derived from the very same discomfort with uncertainty.

An uncertain posture towards the client

The therapeutic value of uncertainty is most evident, I believe, when a clinician approaches a particular client with a clear and present sense of not knowing. When the clinician can acknowledge he or she doesn't know what the best induction is for the client, or what the best suggestion style will be for the client, or which ideas the client will find the most interesting or relevant, or what the client will discover about himself or herself that allows meaningful change to take place, or just when and where the client will apply new skills to his or her benefit, the clinician must take a more respectful approach to the client, a respectfulness borne of uncertainty.

The astute reader will see a permissive and personalized induction evident in the preceding paragraph. The induction might go something like this:

> Now I don't know what the most comfortable position is for you to sit
> in, but you can find a position for your body that feels good to you . . . and
> I don't know at just what moment you'll choose to let your eyes close,

but whenever you decide you'd like to let them close, you can close your eyes . . . and you know your internal experience better than I ever will, and so what you find to be the most comforting imagery is for you to decide upon . . . and when you discover what you find so soothing about those images . . . you might well discover how easy it is for you to relax comfortably . . . and listen easily . . . to the ideas I'll be presenting to you . . . and which ideas you'll find the most helpful, I really can't predict . . . it's for you to discover and use these ideas . . . and I will be interested to hear later what will occur to you in the next few minutes that will help you grow confident that you can develop some new skills . . .

The induction above is gentle, respectful, responsive to the individual's uniqueness, and is organized around "not knowing." It is a substantially different approach to induction than, "Here's my technique of (counting numbers, naming body parts, or whatever) and find a way to adapt yourself to it since *I know* the technique 'works.'"

Modeling a degree of comfort with uncertainty is the analog message to the words of such an induction. It models an "expert" as being able to say, in essence, "I know a great deal about hypnosis, but I don't know you and your unique way of experiencing it." It models an openness to discovery—the clinician's willingness to discover the client's unique talents, and the client's openness to discovering hidden personal resources or discovering the ability to learn and apply new skills.

Being the "expert" with the depth of knowledge and breadth of skill is an essential role for the clinician. We get paid to know, not to plead ignorance. But, that is a global appraisal of our role, not a critical analysis involving a sharp discrimination between when is "knowing" valuable and when is "not knowing" valuable?

It's valuable to "know" how to diagnose correctly when faced with a client presenting symptoms and patterns of depression. It's valuable to "know" when identifying specific experiential deficits (gaps or misinformation in the person's knowledge or base of experience), what the deficits are and how to therapeutically address them. It's valuable to "know" the research and the various treatment options available, and how to implement them sensibly and flexibly.

It's valuable to "not know" what abilities the client has to experience hypnosis meaningfully. It's valuable to "not know" what latent resources the client has that you will happily discover along with him or her. It's valuable to "not know" ways the client may use your ideas and information in ways that go beyond what you had intended. It's valuable to "not know" the client's ability to transform his or her own life.

Milton H. Erickson, M.D., used to say, paraphrased, that "the therapist is simply the weather," meaning the therapist merely provides an atmosphere conducive to the process of discovery in the client (Zeig, 1980b). That is a modest and respectful way of saying therapists shouldn't place unnecessary limits on their clients any more than clients should place unnecessary limits on themselves.

Treating clients, especially with hypnosis, from a position of uncertainty about their abilities would prevent many of the problems generated in therapy when the clinician's certainty proves wrong. For example, some "mind-body healing" enthusiasts are "certain" we can heal ourselves of serious diseases, such as cancer. What is a cancer patient to conclude, therefore, when not only did his or her cancer *not* go into remission, but metastasized? The patient may well conclude, as too many have told me over the years, that the clinician might have been right when he or she said, "Maybe you have an unconscious wish to die." Telling such patients, "You can heal yourself" is not entirely true or respectful. Telling such patients, "I am aware that some people have experienced remissions for any of a variety of reasons, singly or in combination. How much can your use of hypnosis contribute to a remission in your case? I don't know, and neither do you, and what we can do together is explore the possibilities. . . . "

Some will say the clinician needs an air of certainty to build hope. But as I will elaborate in the next chapter, hope must be realistic. False hope can be terribly damaging. It requires a sophisticated discrimination strategy to distinguish realistic from unrealistic hope.

Getting the clinician clear about recognizing and tolerating ambiguity in the client is one side of the coin. Getting the client to recognize and tolerate ambiguity in his or her own life is the other.

Structuring hypnosis sessions for recognizing and tolerating ambiguity

The goals of teaching clients to recognize ambiguity and to develop a tolerance for it is the principal means by which three clinically important things occur: 1) The client learns that his or her projections are potentially hazardous and therefore require extra scrutiny before accepting them; 2) The client learns to identify, evaluate, and self-correct his or her self-injurious projections; and, 3) The client learns to think preventively, consciously choosing not to follow a line of thought when he or she doesn't like where it's going.

Table 1, below, outlines a generic, process-oriented structure for a formal hypnosis session designed to encourage recognizing and tolerating ambiguity.

In calling the above strategy's structure "generic," I am stating unambiguously that not only will the content of the clinician's verbalizations vary according to the unique attributes of each individual client, but the steps themselves may vary according to what needs more or less amplification in the client's experience. One client might respond better to direct suggestions for greater comfort with uncertainty, while another client may

TABLE 1. A Generic Structure for Hypnotically Facilitating the Ability to Recognize and Tolerate Ambiguity

- Orient client to hypnosis
- Induction process
  - Build a response set regarding uncertainty
- Introduce the process of projection
  - Suggestions/metaphors regarding projections
- Introduce the value of knowing
  - Suggestions/metaphors regarding "knowing"
- Introduce the value of not knowing
  - Suggestions/metaphors regarding "not knowing"
- Reframing "not knowing" as desirable in some contexts
  - Suggestions for identifying when "not knowing" is desirable
- Post-hypnotic suggestions for integration
- Closure
- Disengagement

better respond to metaphors about brilliant people who are adept at publicly stating "I don't know" in response to questions supposedly in their area of expertise. As always, it is a matter of clinical judgement as to what a particular client is likely to respond to best. The more feedback from the client a clinician uses in formulating an approach, the more likely the interaction can be tailored appropriately.

Describing the strategy

Every hypnosis session has an identifiable structure, just as every psychotherapy session has a structure. From first greeting the client to saying goodbye at session's end, there is a sequence for how a session progresses. Sequences will vary, of course, with the goals and methods of specific sessions, but there are sequences nonetheless. I find it most helpful to have structured sequences for conducting hypnosis sessions, a progression of ideas and suggestions that move the client in the direction of the session's goals. Fortunately, we as a field have moved past asking the paralyzing question, "Is it right to influence the client?" and have reached the more mature understanding that influence is inevitable as an inherent part of the interaction. The goal is to influence the client respectfully and in a manner consistent with the client's therapeutic goals.

The first step is to *orient the client to hypnosis*. Any time formal (overt) hypnosis is to be employed, there needs to be a statement (or two or three) that encourages the client to prepare himself or herself for the hypnotic process to begin. A common tactic is to simply ask, " Have you experienced hypnosis before?" as a means for getting the client "on the track" of thinking about hypnosis.

The *induction process* is whatever means a clinician uses to absorb and direct the client's attention. Inductions can be structured (e.g., countdowns) or conversational (e.g., "Can you recall how good it feels to close your eyes and get absorbed in relaxing images?"). The chief function of an induction is to facilitate dissociation in the client, so the actual method employed is a secondary consideration. The primary consideration is the client's ability to relate well to it and get absorbed in it, *whatever* it is.

The *building of a response set* is the means for establishing a momentum in client responsiveness. To expect the client, following an induction, to instantly be able to relate to and absorb new ideas isn't usually realistic. Most clients need time to progressively develop their hypnotic responsiveness over the course of a session, and the goal of this step is deliberately assisting in that process. An example of the most commonly used response set is the so-called "yes set," a means for building agreement and receptivity in the client to further suggestions. The client may be offered a series of truisms (suggestions so obviously true there is no legitimate basis for rejecting them) with which he or she naturally will agree, establishing a momentum in the direction of more easily agreeing with whatever else the clinician might say (Erickson & Rossi, 1979). In the context of this strategy where the goal is to increase awareness and acceptance of uncertainty, a response set might include such suggestions as, "There are many different things I could say intending to help you relax . . . and I don't know which of them would be the most valuable in helping you get deeply comfortable . . . and you don't know exactly what I'm going to talk about that will be helpful to you . . . and you don't know quite yet how you'll come to think differently about yourself . . . and you don't really know at just what moment you'll find yourself so wonderfully comfortable with the possibilities you'll discover here . . . " In each suggestion, uncertainty is amplified but also associated to positive possibilities.

Hopefully, receptivity is now well established and the clinician can *introduce the process of projection* to the client. Direct and/or indirect suggestions can be employed in the service of getting across the concept that ambiguity invites projection. Suggestions to illustrate the process (in personal and/or impersonal terms according to client responsiveness) are used to teach the client that forming projections is normal (thereby depathologizing the client) but self-monitoring will be necessary because these projections are not always accurate. For example, one might say:

> I'm sure you've had the experience of calling someone . . . getting his or her answering machine . . . and leaving a message . . . and when the person doesn't call back in a time frame you think reasonable . . . you might wonder what it means . . . whether the person is busy . . . whether the answering machine worked properly . . . whether the person is avoiding you for some reason . . . or any of many possible reasons . . . and how do you know what the real reason is? . . . But it's human nature to speculate about what things that happen mean . . . and the real skill is knowing when you're speculating . . . and when you have evidence to affirm your interpretation . . . after all . . . you don't want to react to something on the basis of an incorrect interpretation . . .

Introducing the value of knowing is a validation of the human need to believe, the human need to understand. Another step in depathologizing the client, the goal at this stage is to affirm to the client that scientific and social progress originates in the desire to know, but the distinction between truly knowing versus merely projecting can begin to emerge. So, following the above example of no return phone call, one could say:

> . . . and all the speculations about why the person didn't call back . . . are normal . . . and reflect our desire to make sense out of things that don't seem to make much sense . . . and whether you want to understand something like why someone doesn't call back, or something much more complex like how the universe works . . . it's one of human beings' greatest strengths . . . that they strive to understand . . . and make sense of the things that go on around us . . .

In the next step, *the value of not knowing is introduced*. The goal at this stage is to depathologize "not knowing." Suggestions are offered to highlight that there are unanswerable questions in life that no amount of analysis will ever answer, and that not having an answer is not only acceptable, but may at times be the best possible outcome. The client, hopefully, begins to absorb the notion that "not knowing" is often preferable to "knowing" something that is merely made up. In line with the phone call example, one could continue by saying:

> . . . and the fact that you can generate so many different explanations for why someone doesn't call back . . . gives you an opportunity to realize you don't know why he or she didn't call back . . . you can make lots of guesses . . . but you really don't know for sure . . . and when you don't know how to explain something . . . it's perfectly alright to say you don't know . . . after all, no one really expects you to know why someone else doesn't return a phone call . . . it's a gift of honesty and clear thinking when someone says, "I don't know" instead of making up an answer that might well be wrong . . . there are so many times in life you'd rather be given no answer than a wrong one . . .

In the next step, involving *reframing*, the client is taught a strategy, an internal mechanism of sorts, that he or she can use to discriminate what is known from what is inferred. Such a strategy might be something as simple as the direct suggestion:

> Before you reach a conclusion, *any* conclusion . . . ask yourself, 'How do I know?' and if your answer is 'I just feel it's so' or 'I just think so,' . . . then know you are forming a conclusion with no apparent objective data . . . That doesn't mean you are wrong, necessarily, but it increases the chances considerably . . . So, you can remind yourself to go the next step and ask yourself, 'Are there any objective data to support this?', and maybe there will be or maybe there won't be, but you'll notice the quality of your ideas and conclusions getting better and better over time.

The function of the *post-hypnotic suggestion* is to associate new learnings to desired contexts. Post-hypnotic suggestions are a routine part of hypnotic intervention, for without them, new learnings would be unlikely to generalize to the relevant contexts of the client's life. So, a clinician might offer a post-hypnotic suggestion such as:

> And each time throughout the day you encounter a situation where the meaning isn't clear to you, or can even anticipate such an event before it happens, you can recognize there are many different ways to interpret the event . . . and you can instantly remind yourself *you don't know what it means* just yet . . . but can entertain a variety of interpretations . . . and can ask yourself directly how you will know which one—if any—it is . . . and it will lead you to look deeper and you can do so comfortably . . . knowing you can look for evidence for your views if it exists . . . and comfortably knowing you can adopt any perspective that might feel good to you . . . when one interpretation is merely as plausible as another. . . .

A session's *closure* can be suggested permissively, encouraging the client to "do whatever processing you need or want to do to bring this session to a comfortable close." *Disengagement* can also be done permissively, encouraging the client to "re-orient yourself at a gradual rate that is comfortable for you, and when you're ready to fully re-orient you can do so and allow your eyes to open."

Watching it work: The case of Bob

In 1998, while a presenter at the international conference on brief therapy called "Brief Therapy: Lasting Impressions," sponsored by The Milton H. Erickson Foundation, and held in New York City, I conducted a clinical demonstration with a man named Bob, whom I'd never met before. The session was professionally filmed. The videotape of the demonstration has been enhanced with subtitles explaining many of the finer points of the hypnotic interaction, and is now available as a teaching tool. (See Appendix B for further information.)

Bob presented the problem of having recently made the career switch into doing psychotherapy, only to discover much to his distress that, in his words, he now seems to require too much "external validation" from others. This severely limits his ability to feel good about himself or his new career choice. Specifically, Bob said he requires validation from authority figures that he's doing it "right," and without such validation he feels he is doing it "wrong." In his previous work, he had no such anxieties, and was mystified why now obtaining others' approval would become so important an issue to him.

Let's pause and consider what we know from just these first moments of Bob's problem presentation. We know he wants, perhaps needs, approval from others. Well, who doesn't? Why is it such an important issue *now* when it apparently wasn't one before? He has a new job that is loaded with ambiguity: What's the best therapy? What's the right response? What's the most effective intervention? These and other such questions highlight the many ambiguities associated with doing therapy. *In the face of the ambiguity Bob encounters in his new career, unlike the certainty of his old job duties, he projects failure and negativity.* He demonstrates clearly the process of how people make themselves anxious and unhappy. Bob desperately needs to learn what every experienced clinician eventually (hopefully) learns: Therapy is an inherently ambiguous context, and the goal isn't to do *the* therapy "right." The goal is to do *a* sensible therapy effectively. In fact, there are many "right" ways to do therapy, many diverse ways that can each work in achieving therapeutic goals.

Why "the need for external validation" or approval that Bob defines as excessive? Although I don't know the specific content (who, when, where, why), I do know *someone* significant in his life has withheld approval from Bob. As a general principle, the things we grow up *with* we typically take for granted. The things we grow up *without* typically become our life's mission. Bob wants approval. That's not the problem—the problem is, to whom will he turn to get it?

In the next couple of minutes of the short interview, Bob claims his supervisor is "always" critical of him, even when his clients seem to benefit from his interventions. This is another piece of salient information: Bob's supervisor is perceived by Bob as a withholding authority figure that seems to provide only one-dimensional (only negative) feedback. It's now clear: Bob's response to the ambiguity of therapy is to rely on his supervisor's "expert" feedback, which is only negative. No wonder Bob feels so despairing about his competence, his career choice, and his life.

Note, however, how the themes of this chapter are evident in this excellent real-life example. First, Bob doesn't recognize therapy as inherently ambiguous, so he naively thinks there is a "right" way to do therapy. The "right" way, according to Bob, isn't even based on client improvement. It's based on supervisory feedback which, in turn, is based on how well Bob followed some defined procedure. So, Bob projects failure and negativity into the ambiguity of the context, and then feels emotional distress as a predictable consequence.

Second, Bob doesn't have a reliable discrimination strategy to help him distinguish between feedback that is useful and feedback that is not useful. He doesn't discriminate between whether his need for approval is appropriate and he's paired with a negative supervisor or whether his need for approval is inappropriate and he's paired with a balanced supervisor. Simply put, Bob doesn't know how to tell "whether it's me or whether it's him." Without an ability to rely on an internal mechanism to make these discriminations, Bob will continue to form internal attributions ("It's me"), global attributions ("I'm no good as a therapist"), and perhaps even stable attributions that circumstances will never change ("I'll never be any good as a therapist").

The inability to recognize and tolerate the ambiguity inherent in the job and the inability to distinguish whether the problem is in one's internal need or in one's environment (including other people and organizations) that is too limited to meet that need are constant themes in treating depression. Employees want recognition from bosses, wives want communication from their husbands, husbands want empathy and support from their wives, kids want acknowledgement from their parents, and on and on. There is no need to pathologize these needs or wants. *There is a need to teach people to assess others' abilities to provide what they want.* Otherwise, they may expect or even demand something that will not be forthcoming from someone who simply doesn't have it in order to provide it. The interpersonal model of psychotherapy is based on the hurts that arise in the relationship arena, and this particular issue of wanting what others don't have is a common theme in people's depression.

In Bob's case, I loosely followed the hypnotic strategy structure presented earlier, in his case highlighting therapy as an inherently ambiguous context. In essence, I wanted Bob to know his uncertainty about what's best to do in therapy is justified, and that he could strive to get comfortable with uncertainty. I suggested to him that a client's progress, or lack thereof, is usually the most meaningful feedback of all about the quality of one's work. And, finally, I suggested to him that *before* he asks someone for something, such as approval from a supervisor, he could first assess whether the person was even capable of providing it. Suggesting this led Bob right into an emotional reaction as he related the concept to his troubled relationship with his critical and unappreciative father. A very important and highly personal piece of therapeutic work was accomplished in this session through a combination of direct and indirect methods.

Bob learned to make clearer distinctions, fewer internal and global attributions, and different ways to channel his needs and feelings constructively. Obviously, there is much more to our session than I'm including here, but these are the points most salient to this chapter's topic. The interested reader may well want to watch the entire session to see exactly how each of these ideas and skills were taught.

Following up on our session with Bob several months later (via e-mail), he reported significant improvement both in his general outlook and in his relationships. He felt much less "needy" about approval seeking, and better able to identify what people might offer him before making potentially pointless demands. Bob also reported he was more satisfied in his job now that he was focused on learning how to do good therapy, not "right" therapy.

There are many "right" ways to do therapy. There are many "right" ways to do hypnosis. There are many "right" ways to live life effectively. What this cornerstone clinical chapter has been about is dealing with the despair that comes for all those depressed millions who don't yet know how to "tolerate the ambiguity and just live well."

Focusing on the future 5

In *Hypnosis and the Treatment of Depressions*, I described the pivotal role of (negative) expectancy in the etiology, course, and treatment of depression. I offered the suggestion that the first task in treating a depressed client is to address any sense of hopelessness he or she may have, since hopelessness is directly tied to treatment results in a variety of ways. Hopelessness is a statement of negative expectancy.

Nothing has changed in the years in-between then and now. Hopelessness remains the single greatest factor influencing the spreading scourge of depression, and at the individual level, it remains the first and usually (but not always) biggest obstacle in the path of recovery. Aaron Beck described "negative expectations" as a cornerstone of depression, while Martin Seligman described a "stable attributional style" as depression's foundation (Beck, 1987; Seligman, 1991). Other clinicians and theorists may present such psychological issues as a fear of change, an "analysis paralysis," an existential vacuum, a numbing of the soul which fosters extreme apathy, or any number of other such "deep" framings of the problem. All share a single common denominator: a view of the future that is absent, weak, demotivating, or simply beyond the person's level of skill and/or energy level to try to manage.

Depression remains a terribly under-treated problem. It is estimated that only about one in ten depression sufferers receives adequate help (Hirschfeld et al., 1997). Many people who are depressed don't know they're depressed; they may think they're just not motivated or that perhaps they just drink too much. But, most depression sufferers don't seek help because of the very nature of depression itself. Depression features passivity, a lack of initiative that precludes establishing worthwhile goals and striving to reach them. "Why bother?" is the mantra of depression. It not only sustains the downward spiral into ever-deepening despair, it also makes intervention a difficult process of trying to motivate the (seemingly) unmotivated. A depressed client—*any* client—can defeat a clinician's best intentions and efforts merely by doing *nothing*. We as mental health professionals are not very difficult to beat.

Physicians often complain about the issue of "treatment compliance," the fact that they will prescribe medications the patient doesn't take in the prescribed manner, if he or she takes the medications at all. Psychotherapists similarly complain about the client not doing assigned readings or assigned homework. When clinicians prescribe drugs or activities that can benefit the depressed individual and he or she doesn't adhere to the prescription, it is easy to understand why some clinicians might conclude, "the person must not want to get better—he or she must enjoy or benefit from the depression in some way." It's certainly easier to make an external attribution ("it's the client's fault") than to make an internal one ("maybe I'm missing something"). To blame the depressed client for his or her passivity is to blame the victim, an unreasonable posture to assume. Knowing that the depressed person is feeling hopeless, mired in "why bother? Nothing will ever change," tasks the clinician with finding creative ways to mobilize an expectancy that things can improve.

Even in the drug realm, expectancy plays a significant role in treatment results. Irving Kirsch, Ph.D., of the University of Connecticut, put forth a controversial but not entirely unreasonable position when he claimed that the results of his meta-analysis of antidepressant drug efficacy studies showed that the majority of therapeutic benefit derived was *not* due to the active properties of the drug, but rather to a placebo effect. Kirsch believes patients may have benefited simply by expecting to benefit (Kirsch & Sapirstein, 1999). Kirsch commented, "Why is it that placebos produce such a large change in depressive symptoms, much larger than the changes that they produce in most other conditions? The answer lies with the nature of depression. Hopelessness—the expectancy that an intolerable state of affairs will not get better—is at the core of this disorder . . . For many patients, the administration of a treatment touted to be highly effective can reverse this hopelessness and thereby relieve the depression it causes" (Kirsch, 2000a, p. 12). More studies need to be done, of course, but before clinicians become even less critical about drugs than they already are, they should at least consider the power of expectancy and how else they might use it.

Hopefulness

What is the therapeutic value of hope? The core of hope is a deep and abiding belief that things can change, things can improve. In the absence of hope, people lose motivation to try, and at the extreme, they may even kill themselves. People don't kill themselves when they expect circumstances to improve. They kill themselves when, often in the impulse of the moment, their pain is excruciating and the future seems to offer no chance for relief (Beck, Brown, Berchick, Steward, & Steer, 1990). Hope isn't just a good motivator in therapy. It can save lives.

Every therapy has embedded within it the hope-inspiring suggestion, "Follow these procedures, learn these concepts, and you will improve." For example, training clients to focus on the quality of their thoughts, teaching them to analyze and identify types of thoughts, encouraging them to follow the rituals of writing their thoughts down and restating them in a manner deemed more rational is some of what cognitive therapy is about—and the promise is, "if you do this, you'll improve." Clinicians employing hypnosis do the same thing but in a different way. They tell the client how to sit, when to close their eyes, and the importance of focusing on the clinician's incantations so his or her unconscious mind can make some change that will result in a change of improved feelings and/or behavior.

The power of expectancy in hypnosis has been well researched (Kirsch, 2000b). For a long time, clinicians didn't quite get how much the hypnotic rituals themselves created an expectancy that was the primary therapeutic agent. Even now, those who take what I think of as extreme and untenable positions that the power of hypnosis is either in the technique or is entirely in the client seem to miss the point that *both* matter and only together will fuel the interaction for better or worse. Technique matters, but unless the context supports the technique, the technique will inevitably fall flat. This chapter is about expectancy as a dominant component of the context.

Hurting the people we want to help

I believe mental health professionals have indirectly contributed to the rising rate of depression. We've done this despite our good intentions by unwittingly "enlightening" people, often with damaging misinformation and distorted perspectives.

As an example, in our zeal to protect the underdog, we teach more and more people to see themselves as victims. To define someone as a victim by labeling him or her as such is a terribly incongruous—and ineffective—way to empower someone (Kaminer, 1993). Strength doesn't come from developing the identity of a victim—it comes from developing the resources necessary to transcend that identity. Consider just two therapy examples of teaching victimhood:

- Clinicians teach people with a history of having been abused (sexually, physically, emotionally) to identify themselves as "trauma survivors." On the surface, that sounds empowering. Yet, at the level of injunctive communication, the stuff of which hypnosis is made, the message is "you can define yourself (globally) by your unchangeable personal history." In other words, "you are your history." That is an *anti*-therapeutic message. A therapeutic message would be, "You are MORE than your history." (See how important this message is to Mike, a man with a terrible history of physical and emotional abuse, in the session transcript in Chapter 8).
- Therapists form groups for those who have been given the label, "Adult Child of (fill-in-the-blank)." To label someone, for example, the adult child of an alcoholic, sounds insightful in its ability to explain dysfunctional emotional and behavioral patterns. But, what is

the injunction, if not to say, "you cannot change?" After all, when does the label no longer apply, namely, when is the person no longer the adult child of an alcoholic? (Kaminer, 1993). And how far do we take this concept? When I was in Milwaukee to do a workshop, I saw an ad in the paper from a therapist wanting to form a support group for the "adult children of affluence." The trauma of wealth?

How can we possibly hope to empower people by teaching them to think of themselves as victims? How can we encourage people to take charge of their lives in a proactive, goal-oriented way when we tell them they have a brain disease or neurochemical imbalance that requires drugs? (Valenstein, 1998). We declare them victims of biology when they have no means at their disposal for dismissing or arguing against what seems a scientific/technological view outside their realm of knowledge. So, they succumb to a viewpoint that limits them.

Clinicians routinely tell their clients to "be fully present in the moment," then complain about how impulsive they are. Therapists routinely tell clients to "get in touch with your feelings," and then complain about how irrational they are. Clinicians resignedly tell clients to "do what you want to do," and then complain about how socially irresponsible they are.

Depression is not simply growing in a vacuum. It is rising in the culture that says, "You have freedom and you can do anything you want," but doesn't then teach people how to make decisions both freely *and* responsibly. So, people do what they want to, with little regard for eventual consequences, or for the people they affect negatively through their choices. Viktor Frankl captured the essence of the problem when he said, "The East Coast has the Statue of Liberty. The West Coast should have the Statue of Responsibility" (Frankl, 1971, p. 23). How people make decisions is a critically important factor to consider in the treatment process because the evidence is strong which links depression to bad decisions (Holahan, Moos, & Bonin, 1999).

Plugging holes in awareness: Structuring goal-oriented therapy

In general, therapy strives to help people by developing either their *unde*veloped or *under*developed resources. In this sense, therapy is derived from a process of complementarity, a focus on and even immersion in experiences that counterbalance the symptomatic experiences. In previous writings on hypnosis, I have described a way to use hypnosis diagnostically by identifying the hypnotic phenomena evident in the person's symptoms. For example, when assessing the structural components of depression from a hypnotic perspective, it is easy to see how the preoccupation with the past (the hashing and rehashing of negative history) could be seen as a dysfunctional age regression of sorts. Similarly, the detailed and emotional projection of past and current hurts into the future could easily be viewed as a dysfunctional type of age progression (Yapko, 1989).

By identifying hypnotic phenomena evident in the client's depressive experience, the clinician can more easily determine the kinds of experiences from which the client is likely to benefit. Thus, the hypnotic session has more specific targets to aim at than just relaxation or the absurdity of trite and global session fillers such as, "Every day in every way you are getting better and better."

Beyond hypnosis, this same principle is evident in what we have learned from the therapeutic efficacy literature. To date, the three forms of therapy that are enjoying the strongest empirical support for treating depression effectively are cognitive, behavioral, and interpersonal therapies (Depression Guideline Panel, 1993). It is no coincidence that these approaches have been shown to be effective when they are all goal-oriented and teach specific skills to the client. *None* focus on the past and thereby unwittingly reinforce the depressed client's past orientation. *None* focus on issue content, but rather on the process of *how* someone thinks, behaves or interacts. *None* emphasize insight as the catalyst for therapeutic progress, rather each places an emphasis on *purposeful action*.

Psychoanalytic or psychodynamic therapies have been shown to be the weakest in treating depression (Giles, 1993). That is not a global indictment against such methods, but a recognition that the structure of depression is itself incompatible with the structure of these approaches. As a general principle of brief therapy, *when the structure of a proposed treatment matches the structure of the problem, nothing changes*. To treat a past-oriented, rumination-laden problem like depression with a past-oriented, rumination-laden treatment like psychoanalysis is a poor match. Therapy shouldn't reinforce a client's pre-existing dysfunctional patterns. It should expand his or her range of capabilities.

Hopefulness and a solution orientation

Having a goal orientation in therapy is probably the most compelling way to build therapeutic hopefulness in depressed clients. There are other ways, though. Consider solution-oriented or solution-focused brief therapies and their suggestions for interview questions which are meant to help the client actively look for solutions. The so-called "miracle question" is a popular one, asking the client to consider, "What would happen if you went to sleep tonight and during the night while you were asleep a miracle occurred and when you woke up in the morning your symptoms and problems were gone? What would change or be different for you?" (deShazer, 1985). From the standpoint of this chapter's focus on the future and building expectancy, this is an interesting question. It asks the client to consider carefully the possibility, regardless of how miraculous the catalyst, that things could be different.

Even more powerful is the solution-oriented question, " When doesn't the problem happen?" (deShazer, 1991). By focusing the client on finding the exceptions that can later be amplified through rational discourse and/ or a hypnotic session, the client is pushed to do two very helpful things, both especially salient to treating depression: 1) The client must take his or her typically global perception that "it's *always* bad" and redefine it in more specific terms (i.e., " it's not always bad, but is bad when . . . "); and, 2) The client must take his or her typically stable perception that "it's always bad" and redefine it in more unstable terms (i.e., "it's variable in how bad it is").

The use of solution-focused questioning is hypnotic without the use of formal hypnosis. It carries multiple injunctions which push, cajole, and lead the client to redefine his or her experience as changeable in some way. It facilitates noticing specific situational differences and both internal and external triggers for symptoms worsening or improving. It empowers people to see new possibilities. That is the start of hopefulness, and one doesn't need a formal hypnotic induction to make it possible.

Hypnotically building expectancy

Although a formal hypnotic induction procedure to activate the meaning-fulness of suggestions about developing a positive future orientation isn't necessary, it may be desirable for some of the advantages it offers the therapy: (a) The use of hypnosis models flexibility, imparting the message that "we can relate to each other in a variety of ways"; (b) Hypnosis encour-ages a cooperative relationship, enhancing the therapeutic alliance; (c) Hypnosis highlights the malleability of subjective experience; (d) Hypno-sis empowers people to discover latent resources; (e) Hypnosis can model a goal-orientation; and (f) Hypnosis is multi-dimensional, capable of ampli-fying experience on whatever level is salient to reaching goals. All of these contribute to establishing a positive expectancy for treatment.

In *Hypnosis and the Treatment of Depressions*, I presented a strategy in a contentless step-by-step form for "Hypnotically Building Expectancy" (p. 129). The structure of the process was less specific than the more advanced version offered here. Table 2 describes an enhanced but still generic se-quence for using formal hypnosis to build a client's positive expectancy.

A step-by-step description of the hypnotically building expectancy process

In this section, I will provide a step-by-step description of the generic build-ing expectancy strategy process outlined in Table 2. Clinicians will vary the content, of course, according to specific client characteristics, but the thera-peutic messages embedded within the process are universal in their appli-cability to addressing the hopelessness or stable attributional style seen in depression.

TABLE 2. Hypnotically Building Expectancy

- Orient to hypnosis
- Induction process
- Build a response set regarding the future
- Offer universal metaphors regarding future possibilities
- Distinguish past events from future possibilities
- Feedback the appropriateness and feasibility of personal goals
- Highlight today's *new* actions that lead to tomorrow's improved possibilities
- Identify specific personal resources that can be used in moving toward specific goals
- Introduce distinctions (dissociations) between mood and action
- Highlight action steps as transcending feelings of doubt or hopelessness
- Reinforce the willingness to experiment
- Generalize resources into future opportunities
- Post-hypnotic suggestions for integration and association

- Closure
- Disengagement

The first two parts of the sequence, *orient to hypnosis*, and *induction process*, are described in the previous chapter.

Build a response set regarding the future.   This hypnosis session involves a substantial amount of age progression, namely, an experiential association to the future. Age progression can serve many purposes depending on how it is structured, but generally strives to establish an expectancy (what many might call a "self-fulfilling prophecy") with which the client will then (consciously or unconsciously) align his or her behavior. In conducting hypnosis sessions, the typical intervention pattern is to transition from introducing general ideas to encouraging specific applications of those ideas. Thus, in this session, the clinician introduces truisms (suggestions that are nonspecific and difficult to reject) about the future that begin to engage the client in thinking about the future (but not yet specifically about his or her future). A truism such as, "People often wonder what the future will be like" tends to foster agreement. More truisms, more agreement, and a higher level of responsiveness begins to build.

Offer universal metaphors regarding future possibilities.   In a general, nonthreatening, impersonal way, the clinician begins to establish the point that the future holds many possibilities not yet in existence. By describing how "there will be changes in medicine as researchers find new solutions to currently incurable diseases . . . and there will be changes in the technologies we use each day as more innovations are made that might well change significant aspects of how we live," the client is placed in a position to acknowledge that *what is going on right now is not what will be going on in the future.* This is a vitally important message for the client to absorb in building expectancy.

Distinguish past events from future possibilities.   One of the primary patterns for getting and staying "stuck" is an excessive orientation to the past. Depressed individuals typically focus on the past, recalling and even reliving their hurts, rejections, disappointments, and failures. In so doing, the orientation to the future is minimal, and is generally in the form of extending the past into the future with such self-statements as "I'll never be happy . . . because I never have been" and "I'll never have a good relationship . . . because I've never had one." The past is thus used as the reference point for predicting the future, and the future is viewed negatively through the lens of the past. The goal at this step in the sequence, therefore, is to communicate the therapeutic message that "the past does *not* necessarily predict the future." The associated but indirect injunction is, "Don't use *your* past to predict *your* future." Statements such as, "Nothing in our history would have predicted that in just the last decade people would be communicating instantly with others anywhere in the world on their personal computers . . . or that the five websites that existed when Bill Clinton took office as President would mushroom into more than 50 million websites by the time he left office . . . " are indirect suggestions for acknowledging that profound changes can take place in a relatively short time where the past could not have been used as a predictor.

Feedback the appropriateness and feasibility of personal goals.   Research into therapeutic effectiveness repeatedly highlights the value of the therapeutic relationship transcending any other dimension of therapy, including specific techniques or the modality employed by the clinician (Miller, Hubble, & Duncan, 1997). As stated earlier, if the context doesn't support the technique, the technique will invariably fall short of its target.

In theory, the clinician will already have established some degree of rapport with the client even before beginning the hypnotic intervention, but this phase of the process is meant to deepen it. When the clinician says something like, "You want to feel better about yourself and also have a higher level of satisfaction in your relationship with your spouse . . . and those are certainly reasonable and worthy goals to strive for . . . and I will support you in your efforts to reach those goals . . . ", the client can feel validated for what he or she wants and can feel supported by and connected to the clinician, strengthening the therapeutic alliance. It is a powerful statement to the client when the clinician says, in essence, "I'm on your side, and I want you to achieve what you came here to achieve." It consolidates a goal orientation. The great majority of the time, the clients' goals are appropriate and feasible. They just don't know what to do to bring them about. The clinician's task is to provide and co-create reliable strategies. If the client's goals are *not* appropriate or feasible, then a primary task of therapy would be to establish ones that are. And, a related task is to teach a discrimination strategy to help the client internally better distinguish realistic from unrealistic goals *before* getting too attached to them.

Highlight today's new actions that lead to tomorrow's improved possibilities. There is no more critical message to counter the passivity of depression than, "Take action!" In this stage of the process, the client is oriented to the simple notion that the things he or she does today—or *doesn't* do today—will directly influence what happens next. Suggestions to "become increasingly aware of how the choices you make today will influence what you experience tomorrow," or "You've already come to understand that some things that will happen in your life aren't predictable . . . but some things are . . . after all, you left to drive here with the intention of us having a session together and here we are . . . " are examples of the message that what you do will have direct and indirect consequences. The implication is an indirect suggestion to, "Do something different if you want a different result."

Identify specific personal resources that can be used in moving toward specific goals. Consistent with a philosophical and practical inclination to strive to amplify client strengths over shrinking pathologies, this step offers a specific means for doing so.

When interviewing a client, or simply discussing his or her concerns or issues, the clinician can (and, in my opinion, should) be deliberate in striving to identify client resources. What has the client done successfully, however big or small? What specific resources would he or she have had to have in order to succeed? Can the clinician give those resources a name, a character, a life of their own?

As an example, the client just happens to mention that recently he or she made a move from one city to another for his or her job. That's a relatively uninteresting personal fact—until one considers what it takes to accomplish such a feat. Personal resources are evident in such a transition, including: The ability to let go of the familiar and ability to adapt to the new, an ability to organize the move itself (e.g., arranging for movers, packing personal belongings, prioritizing what to keep, and, therefore, what to discard), exploring a new home, neighborhood and city, finding and then securing the arrangements for a new place to live, meeting new neighbors and colleagues and establishing new friendships, managing the uncertainty of a new life in a new location, adjusting to the demands of a new boss and work environment, and so on. By feeding back to the client, "You did this and you have these resources," the client is simultaneously empowered and taught something about reframing (i.e., cognitive restructuring) his or her experience. The client discovers he or she has resources but has too often overlooked them. (One of the most important strategies in treating depression, "Accessing and Contextualizing Resources," is a more comprehensive one for building on this theme of empowerment. It is described in detail in *Hypnosis and the Treatment of Depressions*.)

Introduce distinctions (dissociations) between mood and action.   One of the most self-limiting ways to choose a course of action, or perhaps more accurately a course of *inaction*, is according to one's mood. When one is depressed, one's mood saps the motivation to do much of *anything*. A fundamental pessimism (hopelessness, stable attributional style, or negative expectancy) makes effort seem wasted when the negative outcome has already been pre-determined. The goal at this stage of the process is to achieve enough degrees of separation between what one *feels* and what one *does* in order to motivate a sensible course of action.

How else do people achieve success in the face of adversity, if not by putting the desired goal ahead of personal feelings of comfort? For example, one puts up with the (temporary) difficulties of school (e.g., taking tests, writing research papers, delivering oral presentations) in order to attain the larger goal of earning a degree. In the midst of test anxiety is a good time to get *out* of touch with one's feelings, not *in* touch. The therapeutic message, therefore, is "you can use other frames of reference for choosing what to do besides your feelings." (A session illustrating this principle is presented in Chapter 7.) In cognitive therapy terms, this message is aimed at the distortion of emotional reasoning. If one's feelings are all one knows how to use as the basis for making decisions, one is severely limited, especially so when the feelings are depressive in quality.

Highlight action steps as transcending feelings of doubt or hopelessness.   Someone wise once said that "Obstacles are what you see when you take your eyes off the goal." Putting the goal ahead of one's feelings implies an underlying belief the goal is achievable. The clinician's task is to convey this message to the client, thus the formal step earlier of feeding back the appropriateness and *feasibility* of the client's goals. But, he or she cannot be expected to have the confidence that he or she will be able to succeed when past attempts have failed and instilled hopelessness. So, the clinician has to extend himself or herself by saying, in essence, "I will provide you with and co-create with you the steps and resources to help you achieve what you want to achieve . . . and the things you will learn to do that are different may well cause you some doubt or even feelings that you just can't . . . but you can use your desire to accomplish your goals to set aside your doubt and stay focused on following the steps . . . doing the things you must do . . . to get the result you want . . . " The clinician is essentially saying, "follow the plan and I'll assure you of things improving." The promise of greater well-being is inherent in psychotherapy of *any* sort, and is the reason why clients submit to even preposterous interventions. They want things to improve, they need direction from the clinician, and they will follow that direction for as long as it seems plausible and benevolently offered. In this context, it is a sensible reminder to the depressed client that, "it doesn't have to feel comfortable in order for it to be a good thing to do."

Reinforce the willingness to experiment.   All along the process, the client has been encouraged, in one way or another, to "do something different." It is an obvious message both in form and intent. Yet, the passivity of depression, the hopelessness that anything he or she could possibly do could result in a step forward is a powerful deterrent to the client experimenting with new ideas or behaviors.

Aaron Beck speaks of "collaborative empiricism," the joint effort of the clinician and client to experiment with the client's self-limiting perceptions (Beck, 1987). The client believes no one would hire him or her, and so doesn't extend even minimal effort to interview for a job. Beck, like any good clinician, would want to put that perception to the test and encourage the client to go on job interviews and let the *employer* decide as to whether to hire him or her. But, these are intermediate steps. The person has to be prepared for the dynamics of job interviews. He or she has to be prepared to dress appropriately, answer questions spontaneously, and somewhat cleverly, and even to deal with the uncertainty of why he or she didn't get hired after a job interview when no feedback is offered. Beyond a good attitude, there are specific skills needed in such contexts.

The main point, of course, is that the client has to be willing to experiment with his or her perceptions, try new behaviors, or do *whatever* must be done that's more likely to succeed. This gets reinforced when the clinician reminds the client, after all that has already been said in the session, that "doing something different increases greatly the chances for a different result . . . and much to your credit, and something to feel really good about . . . is your ever-increasing willingness to do something different . . . and *what* to do differently will be talked about between us and will be made obvious to you . . . so that even you can be surprised at how much more easily you could do something different and helpful to yourself than you might ever have thought. . . . "

Generalize resources into future opportunities.   The same life lessons or specific skills the clinician wants to teach the client to improve his or her immediate situation are lessons and skills that will undoubtedly apply to other life situations both now and in the future. The more concrete the client, though, the less likely he or she will be to generalize the learnings to other contexts. For example, we may talk in session about "having greater empathy for your spouse," but that will not automatically translate into your having more empathy for others. "Others" were never discussed, and so fall outside the established "therapeutic frame." If the clinician wants the client to learn greater empathy with his or her spouse, but also wants the person to apply that new skill in other relationships, he or she will have to be deliberate in suggesting that to the client. It is up to the clinician, especially in using hypnosis because of the phenomenon of trance-state specificity, to make a point of helping the client extend new skills into a variety of contexts, not just the most immediately symptomatic one. (Trance-state specificity refers to the formation of the suggested response during hypnosis which does *not* automatically carry over into the rest of the person's life after the hypnosis unless a mechanism like post-hypnotic suggestion is used to extend the hypnotically based response.)

This issue is the basis for what many hypnotically experienced clinicians call the "ripple effect" with hypnosis: An idea or skill introduced during hypnosis is self-applied by the client in contexts the clinician didn't even address. In fact, Mike, the client in Chapter 8's case transcript, demonstrates this phenomenon beautifully in regards to sleep improvement, an issue I did not address in the session. The point is that, in most cases, clients need additional directions applying new skills in different and even seemingly disparate contexts. The clinician can simply suggest something general like, "in the future, you'll have many more chances in a variety of situations to try these new behaviors and experiment with them." In this way, the process provides a concrete means for not just solving a problem, but starting to teach problem-solving.

Post-hypnotic suggestions for integration and association.   The chief function of the post-hypnotic suggestion is to associate new learnings or associations to contexts beyond the hypnotic interaction. In the previous step, the notion of generalizing resources to other contexts was introduced. The more general the post-hypnotic suggestion, the less likely it is to establish a meaningful association between a specific resource and a specific context. Thus, in this stage, it is best if the clinician offers specific suggestions for specific applications of specific resources. Continuing on with the example of developing increased empathy in one's marriage, a clinician might suggest something like, "And as you continue to become more aware of the effect you have on your spouse . . . more sensitive to and caring about his or her reactions to the things you say and do . . . you can notice that when you're talking with your son and daughter . . . together or individually . . . you can also recognize the strength of your influence with them . . . and so choose your words more carefully and more protectively of them . . . and when you notice your spouse and children feeling close to you . . . through the things they say and do . . . it can feel so good to you . . . that you took the time to learn . . . how to be more closely connected in a loving and respectful way. . . . "

Post-hypnotic suggestions provide the bridge between what is accomplished during the hypnosis session and the rest of the person's life. Thus, if the therapy is to succeed beyond the immediacy of the clinician's office, the post-hypnotic suggestion is a vital step in the intervention.

Closure and *disengagement* are described in the previous chapter.

A sample transcript of a "building expectancy" session

The following is a transcript of the building expectancy hypnosis session called "The Power of Vision," which is included in my *Focusing on Feeling Good* audiotape series for treating depressive symptoms with hypnosis. (See Appendix B.) It is a general session for building positive expectancy and incorporates much of the structure described in this chapter. It is offered here simply as a sample of how such a session might be structured in a generic, non-specific form.

Find yourself a comfortable place to sit, and then sit in a position that is very comfortable for you . . . Arms and legs resting on the chair . . . or on the floor . . . or on the bed . . . or wherever you happen to be. But the important thing is to make sure that your body has good support, because you'll discover that as your body gets really relaxed, it tends to get really heavy. So, you probably don't want to have your arms or your legs crossed. Once you have settled into a comfortable position that you can sit in for a while . . . Then I'd like you to allow your eyes to close . . . so that you can start to build an internal focus . . . a focus within yourself . . . so that you can find within yourself . . . those parts of yourself . . . that most need to experience comfort . . . relaxation . . . the experience of being soothed . . . with the words that I say . . . the new and helpful ideas and realizations that I bring to you . . . because in that way, you can fully expect . . . to absorb new possibilities . . . and use them skillfully . . . in your own behalf. Out of all the things that there are to focus on at this moment . . . you can turn your attention to . . . the feelings of sitting comfortably . . . noticing how each breath that you take in . . . allows you to grow more comfortable . . . more relaxed within yourself . . . and you now have these many minutes . . . of absolute freedom . . . the freedom to not have to think . . . to not have to analyze . . . to not have to spin your thoughts around in so many different directions. It means that little by little . . . your thoughts can begin to get more focused . . . your mind can get more comfortable . . . just as your body can get more comfortable . . . and little by little, the experience develops . . . more completely and more fully . . . of being deeply relaxed . . . wonderfully comfortable. Now there are many different things that I can talk about . . . but the very first thing that I want to talk about . . . is the mind . . . your mind . . . after all, that's what we're dealing with . . . your thoughts . . . your feelings . . . your way of looking at things . . . and my guess is that you already know how enormously complex the mind is . . . there isn't anyone who understands all of it. The fact that your mind is so complicated . . . is precisely why . . . you can have mixed feelings about things . . . why you can have . . . conflicting motivations about things . . . how you can consciously feel hopeful . . . and at the same time . . . concerned . . . but you know there are different levels of awareness . . . and some of the most powerful experiences that you are capable of having . . . take place at levels much deeper than just conscious awareness . . . much deeper. Whether you call that deeper part of yourself . . . the unconscious mind . . . or the subconscious mind . . . or your deep self . . . doesn't really matter . . . it's just very important for you to know . . . that there is a deeper part of you that learns . . . and absorbs . . . new understandings . . . and it's that deeper part of yourself . . . that you can come to know and understand . . . by listening to this tape and each of the tapes of this tape series . . . because the whole reason that I created this tape series . . . is because I know . . . and you know . . . that you want things . . . to be better in your life. I know you want to feel better . . . and feeling better can happen . . . when you begin to do *things . . . differently. So, you're learning . . . about your mind . . . you're learning about the relationship . . . between the things that you think now . . . and feel now . . . and do now . . . and what happens later . . . the eventual results of the choices that you make. What would you like to experience differently? Go ahead and take a few moments to have a wonderful image of how life would be when it's more satisfying . . . create a vision that's detailed and vivid about what your life could look like . . . and how it could* feel good *and satisfying to you. Now I don't know if you could create that kind of wonderful vision right now . . . this moment . . . or whether that kind of powerful personal vision can evolve for you over the next few days or weeks . . . but you know and I know that there's nothing more powerful than a person with a vision . . . what is vision? It's a possibility . . . a possibility that is so motivating and compelling . . . that you* start doing positive things now *. . . that make your vision possible . . . eventually. There are, I'm sure, important things in your life . . . that you have accomplished . . . that if you have a high school diploma or a college degree . . . you didn't get it by . . . sending in two dollars and a Cheerios box top. You got it by consistently going to class . . . consistently taking and passing tests . . . consistently . . . writing papers and turning them in . . . and were there times that you didn't want to go to class? Of course . . . there were times that you didn't want to go to class . . . but you went anyway . . . and what you discovered is that . . . your feelings of a lack in interest in going . . . comes and goes . . . but the diploma stays . . . the college degree stays. It's a very valuable realization . . . that the goal of eventually graduating high school or college . . . kept you going . . . even when you really didn't feel like it . . . that's the power of vision . . . the ability to see beyond the moment's discomfort. We can take that new principle . . . and we can apply it in such a way . . . that whatever it is that has been hurting you in the past . . . you can now develop a new vision of learning new skills . . . changing the things that you say and do . . . slowly and gradually . . . doing more things for tomorrow's successes than today's comfort. You know, it's a very common metaphor . . . to talk about the unconscious mind . . . .as fertile soil . . . and that through hypnosis you can plant seeds . . . that will grow. And even though that isn't even my most favorite metaphor . . . it's a useful one. Now, fewer and fewer people live on farms these days. Most people live in cities . . . and there is something lost by living in a city . . . because in the city the emphasis is on "right now." It's very different when you grow up on a farm . . . when everyday . . . your lifestyle requires you . . . to think in much more long-term . . . ways . . . a farmer . . . spends time tilling the soil . . . preparing it for planting . . . preparing the soil . . . adding nutrients . . . planting seeds that . . . the farmer knows aren't going to yield anything for . . . weeks or months . . . and he has patience . . . and he knows that making the vision . . . of a good crop yield . . . become a* *reality . . . will take time . . . but you learn to do things actively* now *to create the possibility for a good crop yield . . . if you're going to be a happy, successful farmer. I'd like* you *to learn to think in terms of planting seeds . . . preparing yourself . . . for the changes about to come . . . in your life. There are so many powerful and great things . . . that can happen in your life . . . and when you realize that . . . at a very deep level . . . as I hope that you're starting to . . . then you can nurture your feelings of . . . optimism . . . that things can change . . . things can improve. You* can *learn things that you didn't know before . . . you can practice at developing new skills . . . that you didn't have before. And so . . . I can safely predict . . . that there are important experiences . . . that you're going to have in your life . . . that will be wonderfully valuable . . . and they will really teach you something . . . they are experiences that haven't happened yet . . . and there will be places that you will go . . . that you haven't been yet . . . places that will be powerful . . . places that will be happy . . . places where you'll feel good. And I can safely predict . . . that you will meet people that will influence you in important and wonderful ways . . . that you haven't met yet . . . people that will care about you . . . people that will become friends . . . people that will become teachers . . . people that you haven't even met yet . . . that will contribute . . . to the higher quality of your life. Now whoever it was . . . that said there are no guarantees in life . . . there are only opportunities . . . had the right idea . . . opportunity speaks to the future . . . and the future hasn't happened yet. And everyday . . . many times a day . . . it's as if you come to a fork in the road . . . and when you come to that fork in the road . . . if you go in the same direction . . . you can visit and re-visit the same old places in your tired past . . . or, you can take the other direction and move enthusiastically into the future . . . in a way that is powerful and motivating . . . and when you feel that wonderful feeling of hopefulness and optimism . . . that's the feeling that can join . . . with your deeper understanding . . . that you can* make choices now *. . . that will bring you more of the things that you want for yourself in the future . . . and then that rich, vivid, detailed image . . . your vision of your future . . . can be what pulls you forward in your life . . . having that image . . . is wonderful . . . and learning to be detailed . . . about generating the step by step sequences . . . the actions that you can take every single day . . . that, too, requires a vision. And so as more and more of you . . . begins to turn your attention to . . . future possibilities . . . you can expect . . . to find yourself . . . starting to* do things differently *. . . and I think you'll be happily surprised to discover . . . that you* are *starting to do things differently . . . more in line with your evolving vision . . . and it is the power of the future . . . .to draw you in . . . in ways that feel great . . . that can guide your daily choices . . . choosing carefully what to say and do . . . for the results you want tomorrow, the next tomorrow, and all of your tomorrows. And so nurture these seeds of optimism that you're planting today . . . let them grow . . . let them grow. Now take whatever time you want to or need to . . . to absorb these important ideas and possibilities . . . and to integrate at a deep level . . . the strength of these messages . . . about possibility . . . and future . . . and growth . . . and change. When you've had enough time to enjoy this experience of comfort . . . then that's when you can bring this experience to a comfortable close. So, when you're ready to bring yourself out of hypnosis . . . you can start to re-orient yourself at a rate that is gradual and* *comfortable . . . slowly alerting yourself. And when you're ready . . . you can re-orient yourself completely . . . fully alert yourself . . . and allow your eyes to open . . . bringing back with you the best feelings . . . of feeling relaxed and comfortable . . . and wonderfully optimistic . . . as you remind yourself . . . in the nicest of ways . . . that the future hasn't happened yet . . . but it's going to be great!*

Putting it all together

The necessity for building positive expectancy in the face of hopelessness cannot be overstated. Hypnotic suggestions are not magical or somehow different than what clinicians strive to accomplish through other suggestive means, and so the overlap with other methods for building positive client expectations is to be acknowledged and utilized. There is something special though, about the use of formal hypnosis. It brings subtle responses to a fuller development, it makes things left unsaid assume a power that rivals and sometimes even surpasses that which has been said.

But, hypnosis doesn't "just happen." Sessions are purposeful and structured to achieve particular outcomes. Deliberately striving to co-create a vision with the depressed client (or *any* client, for that matter) of what is possible, when vision has so much power to motivate and transform, is a most worthy use of valuable session time.

Clearly, you can/can't have it all 6

Cognitive approaches to understanding and treating depression take a number of different forms, but all share an emphasis on examining the interrelationships between contingencies, cognitions, and behavior. Contingency is the relationship that objectively exists between an action a person takes and the consequence of that action. Cognition is how a person perceives, explains, and even predicts in subsequent contexts the nature of the contingency. Behavior is the course of observable action an individual takes based on his or her cognitions and the nature of the contingency (Peterson et al., 1993).

This chapter focuses on the issue of contingency from two vantage points: 1) *Controllability*, when an individual's actions can reliably produce specific and predictable outcomes; and, 2) *Uncontrollability*, when the relationship between an individual's actions and the outcomes is random. Individual's perceptions of controllability feature greatly in major depression as a major force in its onset, course, and recovery (Seligman, 1993).

It does not seem a coincidence that the rates of depression are rising in every age group at a time in social evolution when our culture—including the influence of many mental health professionals—spreads a popular philosophy of controllability. People are routinely taught by the "experts" that with the "right attitude" or the "proper technique," they can control virtually anything in their lives, from their children's interests to their own physical health. Clinicians cannot avoid dealing with client perceptions of controllability as a cornerstone of treatment, since it is fundamental to the client's world view. How a clinician addresses this issue has direct consequences for the quality of the client's recovery from depression and the likelihood of relapses.

The "learned helplessness" model of depression originated and developed over the last three decades by Martin Seligman and others has had a profound impact on our current understandings of depression. "Learned helplessness" is a cognitive model, describing the cognitions and behaviors of depression that arise from perceptions of uncontrollability. Simplistically, an individual is exposed to aversive and uncontrollable stimuli who may then form the erroneous overgeneralization that when he or she is being hurt, effort at self-help is futile. The emotional and physical consequences may well be anger, despair, depression, and a lowered immune capacity (Buchanan, Rubenstein, & Seligman, 1999).

The supply of "aversive and uncontrollable stimuli" in modern life that can lead many people to suffer depression is plentiful. Families, which once provided safe haven, no longer do so for many: Marriages that endure throughout life are increasingly uncommon, resulting in painful divorces and associated financial and social burdens. Families breaking up means children getting squeezed through custody battles, visitation fights, estranged parents and inconsistent visiting opportunities, separate parent households with differing and often confusing expectations and rules, and the imposition of adapting to a parent's new dating patterns or the uninvited presence of a new stepparent and stepsiblings. Despite the popular, guilt-alleviating myth that divorce doesn't hurt children, there is strong evidence to the contrary (Hetherington, Bridges, & Insabella, 1998).

Beyond marital and family inconsistencies and even traumas, there are other social factors contributing to a widespread sense of helplessness in people. Jobs are no longer secure, because the economic and business climates have changed radically. Young entrepreneurs can make tens of millions designing and selling internet companies that don't even necessarily show an actual profit. People get laid off from jobs for seemingly arbitrary reasons and at times of year that never happened before. Technophobes feel helpless in their ignorance of how computers and the internet work or why they'd ever want to go web surfing. Information hounds feel oppressed by the extraordinary amount of information that already exists merely for the asking plus the additional burden of the volume of data ever-increasing. "Can't catch up" is the mantra of life these days for people pressured under the weight of all the responsibilities they have assumed just to stay afloat. "How am I supposed to control my life when I can't even control my hair?" is more than just an amusing bumper sticker. It's the common sentiment of people feeling overwhelmed by life and powerless to change it. The result is that more Americans now report feeling they are on the verge of a "nervous breakdown" than ever before (Swindle, Heller, Pescosolido, & Kikuzawa, 2000).

It's no wonder, then, that a sense of helplessness grips so many. A cultural milieu such as we currently have would be predicted by the learned helplessness model to lead to higher rates of depression, and indeed, that is precisely what is happening. We don't really need more research to tell us what has already been established: An escalating sense of helplessness is a large contributor to the rise in depression. We need more research to tell us what we can actually *do* about it.

Where's the control?

We need to get clinicians clear about the fact that medications can not and will not be an adequate reply to the problem. They don't clarify what's controllable. Nor will more people espousing the popular philosophy, "You can control it if you want to." The flip side of an illusion of helplessness is the illusory belief that one has control over all one's circumstances. To someone who is floundering, feeling like part or all of life is out of control, just before or perhaps even while in a state of helplessness, the individual may well seek out someone who is perceived as expert or powerful enough to restore control to him or her. In fact, isn't this the most common scenario for someone seeking treatment? The person feels "stuck" or "trapped" or "hopeless" or "victimized" or any of a thousand other adjectives to describe feeling the despair of being unable to solve a pressing problem. The person comes to therapy hoping, but not necessarily believing, that somehow the clinician will be able to say or do something to help alleviate distress. Just how vulnerable is someone in distress to the guidance of another person who is deemed a "benevolent expert?" As we have learned from the social psychological studies of power, obedience to authority, and conformity, the vulnerability can be great (Aronson, 1999).

So, what happens when the benevolent expert voices the belief or philosophy that "you can control your disease," whether it's depression or cancer? How attractive is it to someone who wants to believe he or she can make the problem go away with a mere adjustment of attitude? The capacity to suffer an "illusion of control" is widely encouraged as a psychotherapeutic and even a life philosophy.

Associating hypnosis to control

The "illusion of control" may be an especially appealing illusion to practitioners of clinical hypnosis. In the clinical literature and in the clinical presentations sponsored by professional hypnosis societies around the world, the extremes of human experience and the seeming magic of hypnosis are displayed and taught as if they are common experiences in which all people can share. So, the man who can develop an anesthesia in a matter of seconds is used as a demonstration subject with no clarification that this person's talent makes him a statistical anomaly. Or, the woman who volunteers for a demonstration who can develop a deep dissociation with hallucinations and a reversible amnesia is a wonderful object of curiosity, but can *anyone* do that if just properly motivated or skillfully approached with the "right" technique?

Clinicians who are attracted to hypnosis are typically impressed by the greater degree of personal control a client develops through hypnotic interventions. Certainly that has been a basis for my own attraction to hypnosis, for it is deeply impressive to discover hidden abilities in clients that they do not know how to get to consciously that somehow surface in meaningful ways during the dissociative process of hypnosis. I do not need further convincing of the reality of the mind-body relationship, or of the value of suggestion in significantly altering peoples' perceptions of themselves, their bodies, their relationships, time, or almost any other aspect of life.

But, the larger issue, one that is amplified even further in the realm of hypnosis, is what limits, if any, there are to the degrees of control an individual has over his or her experience. Is there a danger in leading people to believe, for example, that if they have cancer, they can use guided imagery to cure themselves? How many people can actually do this and what are we to make of the person who can't—that he or she didn't try hard enough, or perhaps wasn't properly motivated, or maybe even had an unconscious wish to die?

Complicating treatment with misperceptions

The relationship of an "illusion of control" to depression is a strong one. Consider another common example: An unemployed man is financially stressed, frustrated from going on numerous job interviews with reasonably high hopes that are dashed when someone else gets the job. Increasingly, he feels hopeless about ever getting a job, and eventually becomes depressed when no amount of his effort seems to make any difference in his getting a new job. He announces to his therapist that he has a new job interview scheduled later in the week, and the clinician tells him to do self-hypnosis and get himself "pumped up" so he can go into the interview confident and well-prepared and act as if he's the only logical choice for the position.

The clinician's intentions are good ones, of course, but he or she has now set the client up for the depression worsening if he doesn't get the job. How? By leading the client to believe it was up to him to "make it happen." The client was led to focus only on the things he could and should do to be ready for the job interview. His focus was narrowed to only consider the things he could do to get the job, an indirect message that getting the job is in his control. So, if he doesn't get the job, who *must* he blame, if not himself? The result is, his depression worsens because of the clinician's intervention, well-intended though it was.

Instead, the clinician should have helped the client carefully evaluate the issue of controllability, insightfully acknowledging there are some factors in his control (e.g., scheduling the job interview, updating his resume, researching the company and how he might fit in, gathering information from anyone he knows who might already work there, rehearsing answers to obvious questions, showing up on time, etc.) and there are some factors outside of his control (e.g., who else is applying for the job, the interviewer's mood, biases and expectations, what he is asked to say or do in the interview, etc.). To instill a belief in the client that what happens in one's body, or in one's interactions, are all determined only by one's attitude is so one-dimensional as to be damaging when the oversimplification is discovered through more complex real life experiences.

Earlier in this book I spoke about the respectfulness inherent in assuming a position of creating possibilities with the client. Controllability represents another facet of ambiguity, and certainty is difficult. Therefore,

I will not say, "hypnosis will heal you," but I am willing to say, "I'll be curious to see how these principles or methods might be helpful to you." The therapeutic interaction is an opportunity to discover where the limits of control are and where, if *anywhere*, they might be expanded.

With depressed clients in particular, there is an extra precaution. As soon as a well-meaning clinician says some variation of, "Others have been able to do this," the depressed client can get even more depressed because of a perception of personal helplessness, such as, "Others may be able to do it, but *I* can't" (Abramson et al., 1985). The wary clinician, observant as to the quality (i.e., degree and pervasiveness) of the client's helplessness, must take it into account when formulating an intervention. Teaching a philosophy of "you can control your depression" to someone who feels helpless to do so can actually foster more helplessness and depression, not less. That is one reason why the expectancy issue, discussed at length in the previous chapter, is so important.

Discriminating controllability

An insightful clinician would have to examine his or her beliefs about the issue of controllability. Specifically, how do *you* determine what is and is not controllable in a given situation? How do *you* determine when a client is limited in some way and those limits should be accepted and respected versus when those limits should be rejected by the client who should instead strive to transcend them? When can the unique attributes or talents of one individual be viewed as "humanly possible" for others to achieve, or when should such skills be viewed as unique to that person and not generalizable to others? These are the very same questions a client would need to be able to answer for him or herself in order to ward off the depressing effects of an illusion of either helplessness or control.

The potential for making errors in forming such subjective judgments should be obvious. Communicating such subjective judgments as an authority to a suggestible client is a potentially hazardous process. Clearly, the clinician needs to have a good discrimination strategy, once again, only this time for the purpose of discriminating what is from what is not controllable in a given context.

External versus internal aversive, uncontrollable stimuli

The sociological perspective of depression, well developed in the interpersonal model, considers the role of victimization in the onset of depression. Social inequities that groups or individuals may suffer, such as racial or gender discrimination, can lead to depression by instilling a sense of hopelessness and helplessness (Jack, 1999). If one expends effort to find a job, for example, and continually gets turned down because of an uncontrol-lable factor (e.g., age, race, or gender), one can easily adopt a perception of uncontrollability, namely, no amount of effort will be likely to succeed, squashing any motivation to even try. The "giving up" behavior of many depressed individuals is a direct result of effort resulting in failure.

In the learned helplessness research, the empirical evidence is sub-stantial for the relationship between perceptions of uncontrollability and depression. The research has largely focused on aversive, uncontrollable stimuli in the *external* environment—abusive parents, unfair professors, re-jecting peers, and the like. But must the aversive and uncontrollable stimu-lus be external? What happens when the aversive, uncontrollable stimulus is *in your head*?

In fact, it's the internal factors that most often torment people. People have far greater capacity to walk away from a bad marriage, bad job, bad *whatever*, than they do the ability to escape themselves. People are rou-tinely victimized by their own poor decision-making (the subject of the next chapter), impulsivity, ignorance, perfectionism, and unrealistic expec-tations. The thoughts and feelings a person has hold such enormous power for shaping the quality of one's life experience. To encourage a client to spend more and more time focusing on and amplifying his or her subjec-tive world is potentially hazardous with the depressed client in particular, since the disorder of depression is itself a disorder of subjectivity. For the client who is ignorant of his or her own feelings, values, needs, wishes, and fantasies, focusing on and relating well to one's subjective world can be therapeutic. However, when the client is living in a subjective reality that makes little use of "reality checks," the potential for depression arising and continuing is at its peak.

Perfectionism

Consider perfectionism as an example. Perfectionism is highly correlated with depression in several ways. It reflects the cognitive error of dichoto-mous (all-or-none) thinking by essentially stating, "It's not perfect so it's bad." It reflects a lack of ability to compartmentalize, a primary mecha-nism for developing acceptance and compassion, namely, "You don't have to be perfect for me to love you." Perfectionism provides the basis for re-peated deep disappointment with self and others when behaving imper-fectly, harming one's relationship with self and others. It adds to the high level of anxiety, when making mistakes is a terrifying prospect. It also in-creases the overall level of emotionalism one experiences when so much rides on the hope for a particular (perfect) outcome (Basco, 1999).

In practical terms, perfectionism precludes a genuine acceptance of one's self or others. The client who meets someone, feels a deep romantic attraction toward him or her, gets heavily emotionally and sexually involved quickly with this new "perfect" person and then pulls away when his or her flaws are discovered, is a common client presentation most clinicians have seen many times. Such a person cannot compartmentalize well enough to allow flaws to peacefully co-exist with strengths. Instead, flaws contaminate all else that is right with the person. If you love someone, and have the ability to compartmentalize, you know his or her flaws and can love that person anyway. But for the person who is global and perfectionistic, no amount of analyzing this person's childhood, especially his or her relationship with the opposite-sex parent, will teach the vital skill of compartmentalization needed to make an intimate relationship succeed. This is one of the mistakes of therapy when clinicians treat from a particular theoretical model. Instead of examining what specific skills a client would need to succeed, in this case compartmentalization, they examine how someone came to not know what they should know, as if having insight into the deficit's origins will somehow magically impart the salient skill.

The perfectionistic client doesn't just play out the perfectionism in dating relationships. That person will be just as likely to establish the same kind of relationship with the clinician. In the first session, the client thinks the clinician is brilliant, insightful, profound, and witty. By the sixth session, the client thinks the therapist is a moron. Assessing perfectionism at the start of therapy has predictive value for the client's view of the therapist and the therapy (Blatt, Zuroff, Bondi, Sanislow, & Pikonis, 1998).

Perfectionism also affects the client's view of himself or herself as a therapy client. When the well-meaning clinician tells the client, "You can likely recover in six sessions," what must the client conclude if he or she *doesn't* succeed in six sessions? If he or she has an external attributional style, the conclusion will likely be "the therapist was lousy." If the client has an internal attributional style, more likely in a depressed client, he or she will likely conclude, "I'm a failure." Thus, the clinician's well-intended sharing of information about average lengths of treatment can become an instrument of self-flagellation for the depressed, perfectionistic client. Similarly, managed care companies should be pushed to recognize they can make depressed and perfectionistic clients worse by setting arbitrary cut-off dates that establish a standard that can only make some clients worse by not living up to it.

The larger point of this section is that perfectionism, like other self-limiting perceptual patterns, is an internally generated aversive, uncontrollable stimulus. The constant barrage of self-criticism that accompanies a focus on one's imperfections can be difficult to ignore or manage, and is a primary factor in one's mood state. How you talk to yourself in your thoughts and what you specifically say creates an internal atmosphere. When the self-talk is critical, mean-spirited, even vicious in the things you might say to yourself that you would *never* say to another human being, distress is inevitable.

Self-criticism

One cannot escape self-talk, nor can one escape self-evaluation. If one has a conscience, a sense of social responsibility, a desire to do well in the things one does, all of which are enormously positive, one will engage in self-evaluation, strive for competence, and thus be self-critical. Being self-critical is *not* the problem. Attending to and non-critically believing whatever self-criticism one makes is the problem. Depressed individuals have negative self-talk going on routinely ("I'm no good, life is terrible, I'll never be okay . . . ") and it is not unlike an inescapable negative hypnotic induction. In fact, *all* people have such negative self-talk, at least some of the time, but the people who generally feel good don't sit and listen to it and passively accept it. They *actively* argue against it, they *actively* manipulate it in some way. Here is yet another way the passivity of depression sustains the disorder. The clinician has to teach such clients how to actively manage such hurtful self-talk rather than being its passive victim. To do that, a clinician must provide assistance in helping develop a discrimination strategy: How does one know what to listen to as useful feedback, from both one's self and others, and what to reject as simply malicious? (In "The Case of Mike" in Chapter 8, hypnosis was used for this very purpose.)

Expectations and victimization

Just as perfectionism and negative self-talk are internal sources of potentially depressing victimization, one's expectations can also be victimizing. The previous chapter's focus on negative expectancy and hopelessness highlighted this relationship between expectancy and depression. In this section, however, we can consider the role of expectations in the onset and course of depression in other contexts.

Expectations directly relate to the issue of control, hence their inclusion in this chapter. To the extent that we expect someone to behave in a particular way, we will exert pressure on them—attempting to control them—to fit with our expectations. For example, if I expect you to be open with me, I might well exert pressure on you to "C'mon, tell me what's bugging you!" when you seem unusually quiet and pensive.

Depression, marriage, and expectations

Our expectations of others directly affect our level of satisfaction in our relationships with them. The leading predictor of marital satisfaction, for example, is how well your partner lives up to your expectations: If your partner does the things you expect him or her to do, you're much more likely to see the relationship as a good one (Heim & Snyder, 1991). But, the converse is also true: When your partner doesn't do the things you think he or she "should" do, the relationship is seen as unfulfilling or even distressing and depressing.

In fact, there is a very strong direct relationship between marital satisfaction and depression. In the Epidemiologic Catchment Area (ECA) study, a large and heavily referenced epidemiologic survey of American mental health issues, marital distress was both correlated with as well as a reliable predictor of depression. In fact, where marital distress was reported, there was a 25-fold increase in the rate of depression (Weissman, 1987). In similar research, a 10-fold increase in the rate of depression existed when a marriage was distressed, a lesser figure but large nonetheless (O'Leary, Christian, & Mendell, 1993).

Clearly, marital distress is a strong factor in depression. The astute clinician *must* ask a married depressed client about the quality of his or her marriage. Even if the marriage itself isn't the basis for depression, the clinician must know that depression adversely affects others in the family (children *and* spouses, but especially spouses), and therefore evaluate any negative impact of the depression on the marriage and treat it as a risk factor for worsening the depression and generating relapses. (For a detailed consideration of the effects of depression on marriages and families, see my book, *Hand-Me-Down Blues: How to Stop Depression From Spreading in Families*.)

Depressed individuals are generally known to have disturbed relationships with others. This includes more interpersonal conflict, lower relationship satisfaction, less social support, less social interaction, and greater pessimism about the future of their relationships (Joiner, Coyne, & Blalock, 1999). Other people are often at the base of an individual's depression. They are hurt—and often depressed—by others' rejection, abandonment, betrayal, humiliation, withdrawal, manipulation, and other means of interpersonal harm. Almost everyone knows the mood consequences of relationships—the euphoria of a new love when things are going great, and the deep despair when things are falling apart. Other people feature in depression directly or indirectly, again pointing to the absurdity of adopting the singular position that "it's all in your neurochemistry." When people do not have the social skills to manage relationships effectively, they can easily be victimized by others and they can be victimized by their own ignorance or unrealistic expectations, or both. Depression can be the result. To make the point even more emphatic, behavioral marital therapy not only succeeds in alleviating depression when the depression is maritally related, as it is in *at least half the cases*, it does so at a rate that matches medications and with a higher rate of producing marital satisfaction, something no medication can do (Beach, Whisman, & O'Leary, 1994).

The relationship between expectations, marital satisfaction, and depression is vital to consider in treatment planning. There is a cartoon I show in my clinical trainings of a woman turning away from her husband with a look of obvious disappointment on her face as she says, "If you really loved me, you'd win the lottery." Clearly, her expectation is terribly unrealistic, but apparently she doesn't realize it. Consequently, she is unhappy with her partner. Consider all the people who get into marriages with similarly unrealistic expectations that their partner is unable to live up to (or perhaps, in some cases, down to). They want, and expect, this emotionally unaware person to talk about feelings. They want and expect this workaholic to care less about work. They want and expect this sexual opportunist to maintain fidelity. They want and expect this asocial person to be social. In every one of these cases, what the person wants and expects is *not* unreasonable—but he or she fails to insightfully consider who he or she asks for it. The expectation in such examples is not unrealistic and victimizing—only the person chosen to fulfill it. Can the person change his or her expectations? Can the partner learn to change and eventually live up to the expectations? In the face of ambiguity, the clinician must again offer direction that will help the client intelligently address such significant, life-determining questions. Again, a discrimination strategy must be learned: How do you know if your expectations are realistic? How do you know if your partner (friend, boss, child, colleague, parent . . .) can do what you expect or hope he or she can do?

One of the most powerful means for empowering the depressed client is to teach him or her to identify and evaluate the quality of his or her expectations in *any* and *all* aspects of his or her life. If the person never evaluates and distinguishes what a realistic expectation is, he or she can forever go on getting hurt by his or her own unrealistic expectations. For the person with an external attributional style, and a global one, too, the probability of saying, "Life is so unfair" is great when the world doesn't perform as expected. The clinician has to teach the skill of using feedback from people and situations in order to determine whether expectations are realistic. When your partner is emotionally unaware, for example, you can't ask for or expect sharing emotional support or insight together. Adjusting one's expectations to be realistic is proactive, empowering, and holds the preventive potential to save a lot of grief later (Kramer, 1997).

Expectations, helplessness, control, and anger

The relationship between expectations and anger seems obvious: When someone or something doesn't fulfill your expectations, frustrating your wishes, anger is the consequence. Consider the woman in the cartoon described earlier who says, "If you really loved me, you'd win the lottery." The fact that she has an unrealistic expectation has obviously escaped her own notice. Let's take it a step further, though. She clearly makes the external attribution that it's *his* fault he hasn't won the lottery. Somehow, in her view, if he were properly motivated he would be able to win the lottery. She sees it as in his control, to her personal dissatisfaction and to the detriment of the relationship. One can too easily imagine her taking her anger to a clinician who advises her to "pound on the chair with this bat to get your anger out," instead of teaching her to recognize when her anger-generating expectations are unrealistic.

How much of the anger that people feel arises from their unrealistic expectations and their attempts to control the uncontrollable? By not recognizing that one's expectations are unrealistic and by attempting to manipulate circumstances to fulfill those expectations, failure is a predictable result. For the melancholy depressive who makes internal attributions but without clarity, the global conclusion is, "I'm no good and it makes me angry." For the aggressive depressive who makes external attributions, the conclusion is, "He/she/it is no good and it makes me angry." Internalizing anger is stressful and typically involves the type of ongoing self-criticism discussed earlier; it reinforces victimization and, in turn, depression. Externalizing anger involves blaming others, taking no personal responsibility for one's inappropriate expectations, and trying to control other's behavior in order to obtain compliance with their expectations. Anger can be used as a controlling behavior towards others when it is used inappropriately and at levels of intensity that are out of proportion (excessive) to the circumstances.

What did that chair ever do to you?

For years many therapists have been saying, "Get your anger out." They've been telling people to beat on chairs, pound on walls, scream and yell, and hit pillows. Such interventions focus on and thereby amplify a feeling—anger—and they do it outside of "real life" contexts. There are very few, if any, real life interpersonal contexts in which the best response for resolving a conflict is to suspend the interaction and go pound a wall. Conceptually such interventions don't make sense—and, as it turns out, clinically they don't either. Hundreds of studies have led to the same conclusion: Focusing people on their anger makes them *angry—not* better. (For an excellent review of the salient literature, see *Anger: The Misunderstood Emotion* by Carol Tavris.) Realistically, how can someone "get your anger out" as if it is a static property, when, in fact, the person is still generating even more anger through the combination of unrealistic expectations and inappropriate attributions?

Can beating on a chair provide a positive result? Perhaps. Helping someone verbalize or express anger that has been "bottled up" may be helpful in being able to acknowledge and "own" it. But, at best, such an intervention is a stepping stone on the path to developing a more realistic view of anger and its management. The angry person has to learn specific skills such as: (a) How to discriminate what is and is not realistic in terms of one's expectations; (b) How to develop impulse control to allow sufficient time to critically examine one's expectations; (c) How to recognize anger in degrees—namely, catching it and responding to it when something is merely irritating rather than when it's enraging; (d) How and when to express anger appropriately, without the use of intimidation or by physically or verbally abusing someone; (e) How to tolerate others making decisions that are personally disappointing but are within their right to make (e.g., your child's decision to go to an out-of-town college); and, (f) How to compartmentalize so that the anger can be handled appropriately, resolved, and let go so there isn't a persistent grudge infecting subsequent interactions.

Clinicians unclear about controllability and uncontrollability can too easily offer direction to clients that perpetuate their anger and controlling behaviors towards others. When teaching clients what is uncontrollable, "other people" should be at the top of the list. You may control them temporarily through a variety of manipulative tactics, but the seeds of rebellion are planted in this way and the relationship's eventual failure is assured. In the long run, most people will usually do as they wish.

Primary and secondary control

One of the useful distinctions about controllability, especially in relation to hypnotic interventions, is the distinction between primary and secondary control. Primary control is defined as an individual's ability to proactively adapt the environment to his or her expectations or wishes. Most of what this chapter's discussion of control has focused on are the mood consequences for adopting the belief that the external environment can be adapted to one's wishes independent of what may actually be possible.

Secondary control is defined as the individual's ability to proactively adapt himself or herself to the environment. The person has somehow quickly assessed the environment as unyielding to any personal efforts to control it, and has tasked himself or herself to "deal with it." While primary control is a person's typical first and most preferred response in the face of perceived uncontrollability, secondary control allows for a successful management of the situation when primary control is not possible (Rothbaum, Weisz, & Synder, 1982).

Many forms of psychotherapy emphasize secondary control strategies. "Reality therapy," in whatever form it takes, essentially tells the client, "Stop reacting to the world in terms of the way you wish it would be and start reacting to it in terms of the way it really is." In other words, the message is, "You can't change the reality of your (age, employer's unfair policies, culture's emphasis on material success over spiritual development . . .), but you *can* change your reaction to it." Whether we call it cognitive restructuring, strategic reframing, or whatever, the goal of such fundamental interventions is to increase the range of secondary control strategies when primary ones are deemed inappropriate.

Hypnosis and the art of secondary control

The skilled application of clinical hypnosis is especially evident in enhancing secondary control. It could be reasonably said that enhancing secondary control is what hypnosis does best. Clinicians use hypnosis to help people manage pain, for example, in which the reality of the pain requires an effective adaptation. Clinicians use hypnosis to help people manage anxiety in situations where the perceived threats in the world won't change but their responses to them can.

Depression requires a careful consideration of both primary and secondary control. The often distorted perceptions of controllability (perhaps evidencing an illusion of control) and uncontrollability (perhaps evidencing an illusion of helplessness) found in depressed individuals is based on an inability to reliably discriminate controllable from uncontrollable. Wanting to "empower clients" is a constant aspect of doing psychotherapy, but it cannot be a global empowerment. The more global the individual is, the more he or she generates one-dimensional responses of trying to control *nothing* or, conversely, trying to control *everything*. Either type of rigid pattern will inevitably lead to multiple failures, of course, and even depression if the (mis)attributions support its onset.

The goal, therefore, is to teach the client to proactively strive to identify what is controllable *in a given context* and *do that*, and identify what is *not* controllable and do a "risk assessment" before deciding what to do next. Something may be out of one's control, and yet a person knowingly decides to gamble. Gambling knowingly and intelligently is not necessarily a bad choice. As a simple example, buying a lottery ticket is not a foolish thing to do *if* you can afford the dollar and *if* you don't suffer the illusion that because you picked your mother's birthdate and daughter's age that you are definitely going to win and *if* you can take it in stride (i.e., won't get deeply disappointed or even depressed) when you lose. There are people, though, who don't grasp what "odds" (risk assessment) means. So, even when they buy a lottery ticket that is 20 million-to-one against them, they still think they'll win and then suffer when they don't! *Getting 100% emotionally attached to something over which one has no control is a reliable risk factor for depression.*

Assessing controllability

At advanced trainings on treating depression, I will ask attendees, all well-educated and experienced professionals, to assess the degree of controllability an individual has in a variety of vignettes I present to them. For example, I might ask, "what degree of control does a woman have in curing herself of her breast cancer using self-hypnosis?" Some in the group will say "no control" and others will say "total control." Can professionals get any further apart in their perceptions of controllability than those replies? One wonders what these clinicians with such extreme perceptions are telling their clients in private, and whether it is helpful to tell them that.

As a cognitive intervention strategy, I regularly use the exercise I described in detail in *Breaking the Patterns of Depression*, called "Assessing Controllability." I want the client to *list every factor* that will influence the outcome he or she is striving to create (e.g., whether she gets the job she's applying for, or whether she'll say yes when he asks her to go out with him, or . . .). Then, I want the person to evaluate the *degree* of controllability of each factor, rating it from zero (no control at all over it) to one hundred (total control over it). Then I ask for an overall rating of controllability. I may use additional strategic exercises, such as assigning the person to actively attempt to control the uncontrollable (e.g., "Do something to make it rain in the next 5 minutes in that corner of my office") as an experiential means for pushing the client to give thought to and make assessments of what is and is not controllable in everyday contexts.

Clients have to develop the skill of knowing when to take action because at least some control is available, and when to walk away because no amount of effort will make a difference. The more the client has accumulated an extensive history of experiences of misjudging controllability, the more experiential and multidimensional the process of teaching discriminations should be.

A distinguishing feature that separates controllability from uncontrollability is the *objective* degree of control or degree of influence one's actions have over the outcome. In the following hypnosis session transcript targeting the issue of controllability, that point is emphasized both directly and indirectly. Consider the structure of the session, especially its key emphasis on making discriminations with information, not feelings. (This transcript is taken from my audiotape program for depression, *Focusing on Feeling Good.* See Appendix B for further information.)

Hypnosis session transcript: Is it in your control?

And so to get yourself started now in this hypnosis session . . . I'd like you to arrange yourself in a position that is comfortable . . . and I'd like to encourage you to use your knowledge of your self now . . . to recognize . . . how you can gradually guide yourself into a wonderful state of comfort . . . of mind and body . . . and if you haven't closed them already . . . go ahead and close your eyes . . . so that you can effectively close out all of the external distractions. Of course, the external world is naturally going to go on as usual all around you . . . but in terms of your inner experience . . . you have the ability to control . . . the direction of your thoughts . . . the quality of your thoughts . . . and so you can *create . . . a wonderfully comfortable state of mind and body . . . where you give yourself . . . plenty of room . . . plenty of distance . . . from all the everyday . . . demands and responsibilities. And that's why . . . in a way . . . right now it doesn't even matter what goes on out there . . . but what does matter a lot . . . is what goes on inside you. When you learn . . . what you discover that helps you feel better and stronger . . . I think what is most enjoyable about experiencing hypnosis . . . this deep state of relaxation and comfort . . . that is growing ever deeper . . . moment by moment . . . is that it reminds you in a very powerful way . . . to the very core of who you are. That day-in and day-out . . . you get to choose . . . you get to choose . . . where your thinking goes . . . you get to choose what new skills . . . you want to learn . . . you get to choose . . . what you want to do with your time off . . . what you want to think about . . . when you have free time . . . you get to choose . . . whether to express your feelings . . . and if so, you get to choose how and when to express them . . . and to whom. And what does it mean to* be in control? *It means recognizing and using . . . your ability to choose . . . the* power to choose *. . . and when you use your power and your wisdom to choose wisely . . . the quality of your life . . . continues to grow . . . the depth of who you are . . . continues to evolve . . . I think sometimes . . . what I find troublesome . . . is when people don't realize that they have the power to choose . . . perhaps you've had earlier experiences in your life . . . where you felt trapped in negative circumstances . . . and maybe you still feel trapped in negative circumstances. And I really don't know whether someone else would agree that you're trapped . . . but it's interesting to consider . . . that when you deliberately challenge yourself . . . to actively take the steps to step outside . . . the boundaries of what you believe . . . you can dare to ask yourself a question, "What if? . . . What if? . . . What if I'm open to exploring and discovering new possibilities and doing something different?" You might actually discover a sense of excitement . . . the kind of excitement that builds when you take intelligent risks in your own behalf . . . And if you look at other people's lives that you admire . . . you can appreciate there were no guarantees of success given them . . . just because someone enrolls in a college program . . . doesn't guarantee that he or she will definitely graduate . . . but enrolling . . .* creates the possibility *of taking a course and passing it . . . and taking another course and passing it . . . and another . . . and another . . . and eventually graduating . . . and it is in your control whether you go to class . . . and it is in your control whether you study . . . and it is in your control whether you write term papers thoughtfully and turn them in on time . . . and that's so much of what getting a college degree is . . . it's showing up for class and doing the work . . . and enduring exams and lectures . . . and if you keep showing up long enough . . . and you do your work well . . . you graduate. And in a way, that's what the rest of life is about . . .* creating possibilities *. . . striving to make them realities . . . and so it's time for you to carefully consider . . . What has previously seemed out of your control? What have you managed to convince yourself you can't do anything about? . . . and now start to ask yourself . . . "What if? . . . What if?" . . . And of course . . . at those times you just don't see any alternatives . . . you always have the option . . . of talking to someone else . . . and getting another viewpoint . . . so many times it happens in life that . . . what seems like a trap to one person . . . is a welcome opportunity to another. So often, my clients come in . . . and they feel stuck . . . and helpless . . . and they feel bad . . . and they truly want to feel better . . . but I can see things . . . that they can't . . . everyone has . . . what might be called blind-spots . . . in their field of vision, I have them, too . . . and when I get stuck, it's nice . . . that I have people around me . . . that I can ask . . . for another opinion . . . or another viewpoint . . . or that I can ask questions . . . and learn from other people . . . who have learned to handle it well . . . who can describe to me what it takes to handle it well . . . and give me a target to aim for in planning my own behavior . . . and strategies. You didn't learn to be the way you are all by yourself . . . you don't have to solve problems all by yourself . . . and one of the things that* is *in your control . . . is choosing . . . to find an ally . . . a knowledgeable or caring person . . . that can support you in your efforts . . . and* *day-in and day-out . . . you face all kinds of situations . . . and all kinds of circumstances . . . and you can take these ideas . . . and make them so natural . . . within you . . . so automatic within you . . . that you almost instantly recognize when to step into . . . and absorb yourself . . . in a situation and make something good happen . . .* because *you can influence it . . . to one degree or another . . . you may not have total control over it . . . but you* can *influence what happens . . . you can create an opportunity . . . you* can *create a possibility . . . and, in other situations . . . you can almost instantly recognize . . . here is something that you have little or no control over . . . and you can for the record, state your opinion . . . or do what you need to do to feel good about yourself . . . but at the same time . . . you can emotionally . . . pull yourself back enough . . . that you're still comfortable . . . with what happens. You can always remember . . . to never fully invest yourself in something you only have partial influence upon . . . The power to choose . . . is a very important one. You have the freedom to choose . . . you know that you are responsible . . . for the choices that you make . . . and* only *the choices that you make . . . and it's a gift . . . a wonderful gift . . . to have that freedom to choose . . . which people you will allow into your life . . . because they make you feel good when you're around them . . . what you'll choose to do with your time . . . because it stimulates you and pleases you . . . where you'll choose to go . . . when you'll choose to do something . . . because it's time for you to do what helps you . . . I think you can feel the freedom now . . . .you're* not *stuck . . . you're free to choose . . . and* you're *in control . . . and you can take the time and gather the facts in order to choose wisely . . . and so when you hear these phrases running through your mind . . . over and over . . . the freedom to choose . . . the power to choose . . . it can really feel good . . .* really *feel good . . . and so with those good feelings . . . flowing through you . . . you can feel the power . . . and what it means to be in control . . . in control of your body . . . as you breathe comfortably . . . and feel the deep relaxation in your body . . . the freedom of your mind to think, and problem-solve, and anticipate . . . the freedom of your spirit . . . to know that your life is yours . . . and the choice of how you use your life . . . is yours . . . and these are all the things that are* definitely in *your control. And so whenever you start to feel things aren't going your way . . . you'll remember . . . the power to choose . . . the freedom . . . to do something different . . . in order to feel better . . . and to reaffirm . . . you can move through life more easily and skillfully. And so take whatever time you'd like to . . . to stay with these ideas and consider them deeply . . . and absorb them deeply . . . into your very being. And then, when you've had enough time to process and learn from this session . . . then you can bring this session to a close . . . a comfortable close . . . feeling good about yourself and feeling as though you've finally settled something important. And when you're ready . . . to end for now . . . then you can start the process of slowly reorienting yourself . . . at a rate that's comfortable and gradual . . . take your time in doing so . . . and then when you're fully prepared to . . . you can alert yourself, re-orient yourself fully . . . and open your eyes.*

Creating possibilities

When some people feel beaten down, or when they feel like they have been hurt or are continuing to be hurt by other people, or by life situations, or by problems that seem too huge to deal with, they may retreat into a sense of personal helplessness, feeling they are victims of situational and emotional forces too great to overcome. I don't know if I have ever encountered anyone who was depressed who didn't make errors, often serious and depressing errors, about the issue of control. Most of the time, the ability to control circumstances is not an all-or-none phenomenon. One can usually put forth some well-focused effort to *create some positive possibilities*. As I have previously said, one can strive to create possibilities, but there aren't many guarantees in life. What success is about is when some of those strategic possibilities start to become realities. But, people often need to be reminded that not every attempt one makes will succeed. After all, no one succeeds at *everything*.

Since the goal is to create possibilities in life through making good choices, whether on a professional level about what type of hypnotic suggestion to use with a particular client, or whether on a personal level to marry that person, the importance of good decision-making abilities cannot be overstated. These are the focus of the next chapter.

Coping styles and 7
the right to choose
. . . wisely

If you were to go to your case file drawer right now and pull out the files on those clients you have treated or are currently treating for depression, what percentage of those individuals would you estimate either were or are suffering from self-generated problems? I'd venture an educated guess that most of those depressed clients suffer depression by being trapped in negative circumstances, real or imagined, of their own creation. There is no legitimate basis for believing people actually *want* pain or suffering, rather it is often a direct or indirect consequence of the bad choices they make.

In this chapter, I will explore the relationship between coping styles (decision-making and problem-solving styles) and depression, and the positive value of hypnosis in helping transform these styles. Consistent with all the ideas and techniques presented in this book, my focus is on the *process* of choosing, not the content of a specific choice. In other words, the focus will be on *how* someone makes decisions or chooses a course of action (including *in*action, since choosing not to choose is also a choice), rather than what the specific choice is.

Depression and undermining the self

Depressed people typically maintain ways of thinking, feeling, and behaving that may both generate and maintain depression. *Self-destructive choices* to harm one's body (with drugs, alcohol, cigarettes, poor nutrition, physical inactivity, etc.) may sometimes provide some measure of immediate comfort in the short run, but eventually are likely to cause problems that will further compound one's depression. *Self-generated negative perceptions* that bend neutral and even positive feedback in negative directions in order to sustain a poor self-image is an active process of expending effort to maintain the status quo when the status quo is hurtful. *Inappropriate social behavior* (poor social skills) invites rejection, disappointment, even humiliation, especially powerful in causing and maintaining depression, particularly in light of the strong evidence for the emotional and physical health benefits derived from having positive relationships with others (Giesler & Swann, 1999).

There are different levels of analysis possible for considering the many ways depressed individuals will undermine themselves. The first line of consideration in evaluating the quality of the problems an individual experiences is this: Are the person's problems self-generated, or are they imposed through external means? An example of each can clarify the point: People who happily smoke cigarettes and rebelliously blow their smoke in the faces of concerned people (e.g., friends, relatives) who question their habit may well end up depressed eventually when confronted with serious illness (e.g., lung cancer) derived from their smoking. This is an example of a self-generated problem. Someone who must manage an elderly parent suffering Alzheimer's faces difficult and often painful choices that can be oppressive and even depressing. But, this is not something derived from making poor personal choices. Rather, this is a hurtful circumstance that is imposed on the person, and he or she must find an effective means to cope with such circumstances without succumbing to depression.

In either instance, depression can result from having to deal with negative circumstances (e.g., lung cancer or an ailing parent). At that level of analysis, the goal is the same—help the person cope with the negative circumstances. But, at a level of analysis of the control issue, the distinction between primary and secondary control, discussed in the previous chapter, becomes important to the intervention. Is the client to learn to make choices to change his or her circumstances (assuming primary control)? Or, is the client to learn to make choices to adapt to his or her circumstances (assuming secondary control)? Both the clinician and client need to be clear on this point in order to choose an intervention strategy wisely. The purpose of this chapter is to encourage developing and using strategies for choosing intelligently.

Coping with life

No one escapes the pains of life. Our bodies age and are vulnerable to illness and injury, people we love die, jobs and budgets get cut, marriages disintegrate, and on and on. Why isn't *everyone* depressed? How do some people manage to stay out of depression when facing problems even as serious as life-and-death ones? (See "The Case of Vicki," a session with a 42-year-old woman with terminal cancer, for an inspiring example of facing death *without* depression. Further information about this case is available in Appendix B.) The general (global) answer is, they cope. More specifically, they process information and make decisions in ways that help insulate them from a deep, enduring or pervasive distress.

Can depressed individuals be taught the kinds of coping styles and decision-making strategies that will help insulate them, too? Yes. Each of the therapies that currently have the greatest amount of empirical support (cognitive, behavioral, and interpersonal) for effectively treating major depression do exactly that as a fundamental part of the treatment process. As individuals are empowered to not only manage their current difficulties, but the additional difficulties they will inevitably face as life goes on, an episode of depression can lift and future episodes can be curtailed.

What are the coping styles that increase or decrease one's vulnerability to depression? There are many different coping styles one could describe, but I will focus on three in particular: The avoidant, ruminative, and active styles. Each has profound implications for every phase of the therapy process, from whether the individual even seeks therapy, to whether the person participates in the therapy and applies what he or she learns to personal advantage (Holahan et al., 1999).

Avoidant coping styles

Many clinicians use the phrase, "in denial," to describe an individual who is seemingly unable or unwilling to deal with the severity of his or her problems. Rather than describing someone as being "in denial," I prefer to describe the process by which some people so greatly underestimate the seriousness of a problem that it leads them to ignore it or respond to it in an understated, ineffective way. Why someone might be motivated to distort a serious reality in a milder direction is easy to understand if one thinks in terms of psychological defenses against anxiety-provoking, personally threatening stimuli. Less analytical but equally true, for *whatever* reason, the person simply doesn't recognize a threat when he or she sees one. It may seem to provide some small temporary comfort to the person to turn a blind eye to percolating problems, but to do so poses additional hazards: Most problems don't just go away if one ignores them. On the contrary, they tend to get worse.

Furthermore, it is inherently disempowering to essentially state, "The problem is more powerful than I am in my ability to address it." The result is one becomes victimized not just by the problem itself, but by one's reaction to it. Without deliberate strategies for problem-solving, including strategies for managing problems that *can't* be solved, an individual can easily feel overwhelmed and then retreat to the illusory safety of avoidance.

Let's put this idea into context by adding some realistic situational details: Mary has a 12-year-old daughter named Alice. Mary is depressed, and though she manages to function and do the things she has to do, she struggles to keep her life going. Alice is playing in her room with her toys, scattered all over in a genuine mess. Mary comes to the door and says, "Alice, please clean up your room," and disappears. A half hour later, Mary comes back to the room and Alice has done nothing to comply with her demand. Mary repeats herself, only a little louder, and disappears again. When she returns a half hour later to check on Alice's progress, she discovers Alice still playing and doing nothing to clean her room. Mary yells,

"Clean your room!" and then disappears again. When she comes back a half hour later, Alice has still done nothing to clean her room. Mary throws her hands up in the air in resignation, says out loud, "I can't deal with this," and walks away defeated. She feels totally victimized by a 12-year-old, avoids confrontation, and becomes further depressed.

And what of Alice? Alice has already learned that if she ignores mom long enough, eventually mom will go away. Alice has already learned the avoidant behavior that will be a risk factor for her own depression at some later point in life—maybe next year, maybe in twenty years (Joiner et al., 1999). This transgenerational phenomenon is some of what I termed "hand-me-down blues": The depression and depressive risk factors which are transmitted in families through means other than (and in addition to) genetics. Mary's avoidant style has been demonstrated countless times in such routine family interactions, and by age 12, Alice already shares it. Add to the mix additional distortions, such as Mary interpreting Alice's passive refusal to clean her room as evidence of covert hostility that must be brought to the surface by "aggression training therapy," and one can appreciate how messy diagnosis and treatment can really get.

Evaluating avoidance

Is avoidance *always* a bad strategy? No. Sometimes if one ignores problems they *do* go away. So, again we see the need for an effective *discrimination strategy*. How does one know when to avoid and when to step in and take charge? This can't be done "intuitively." The only way to answer the question realistically is with refined foresight, namely, being *accurate* in one's predictions as to whether conditions will better or worsen by ignoring them. Those who are simply aviodant are *not* accurate, typically either missing or misunderstanding the available evidence which indicates things will worsen. The ability to predict likely outcomes with accuracy is a crucial life skill, but cannot be taught by clinicians who defer their responsibility to teach such skills by touting the "be present in the moment" philosophy. Nor can they be taught by clinicians who impart the philosophy that the future is unpredictable. Some of it is, and some of it isn't.

If people are to be genuinely empowered in therapy, clinicians will have to do more than manage a symptom with a pill or a simple relaxation strategy. People will need to be taught ways of thinking ahead, solving problems, preventing problems, and seeing life as manageable when equipped with the right tools.

Ruminative coping styles

Rumination is the cognitive process of spinning around the same thoughts over and over again. Rumination is generally an agitating process and is directly responsible for much of the anxiety associated with depression. In turn, it helps generate the insomnia that represents the most common of the vegetative symptoms of depression, as discussed in the first chapter. Thus, simply teaching self-hypnotic relaxation skills is *not* an adequate reply to an ongoing ruminative process. One can perform a lengthy and wonderfully relaxing hypnotic induction that shows the client through direct experience that he or she can reduce agitation and anxiety which may help build positive expectancy for treatment. But, as soon as the client opens his or her eyes again, and the ruminations begin again, whatever relaxation was generated during the hypnosis session instantly dissipates. The client may become disillusioned that anything can really help for more than just moments.

Ruminative coping styles are directly linked to depression. Where this relationship has been studied to the greatest extent is in the area of gender differences in depression. We have known for a long time that women are more depressed than men by a ratio of almost 2:1 (Kornstein, 1997). There are those who claim that men and women are equally depressed but men express depression differently through anger or drug abuse (Real, 1997). It's an important claim to consider, but is somewhat problematic. How are we to reliably recognize depression if it is merely inferred from other problems, like drug abuse, and not because of the overt symptoms of depression itself? Why pick depression as the inferred base for one's problems and not a personality disorder or some other disorder equally plausible but not directly observable?

The greater ratio of women to men suffering depression has been reaffirmed numerous times (Culbertson, 1997). In fact, as long ago as the mid-1980s, the American Psychological Association set up a task force to study women's higher rate of depression, and in 1990 released a powerful monograph called *Women and Depression* which went a long way in explaining the reasons for the gender differences (McGrath, Keita, Strickland, & Russo). Subsequent research by a number of prominent social scientists and clinicians has specifically focused on women's greater tendency toward rumination as a coping style as a significant contributing factor to their higher rate of depression (Nolen-Hoeksema, Grayson, & Larson, 1999).

A ruminative coping style means engaging in a greater degree of intellectual analysis of a problem rather than any specific behavioral action taken toward its resolution. Thus, the kind of stereotypical interaction results that comedians have poked fun at whenever joking about the perils of marriage: She comes home from a bad day at work and tells her husband she needs to talk. He sits and listens to her describe the stressors of her day, and then he proceeds to tell her what she can do to remedy the situation. She gets angry at him for telling her what to do when all she wanted was to tell him how she felt. Puzzled, he says that since she feels bad, she should do something to change things. She blows up, storms out of the room, declaring him "impossible," while he tries to figure out what he did wrong.

Such a scenario reflects a key difference in coping between ruminative and active styles. It will also affect the therapy context: When she goes to a therapist, since she doesn't feel she can talk to her husband, she will likely seek out a clinician who will listen empathetically and *won't* tell her what to do. She might *feel* better working with such a clinician. But, she will *do* better if she works with someone who will push her (gently, respectfully, therapeutically) to take sensible action (if there is some to take) in a timely way (Ellis, 1994). Clinicians who merely offer support may well end up supporting the client through a depressive episode that eventually lifts, as most are likely to do, and inadvertently set the person up for later relapses by never directly addressing the issue of coping style.

It is no coincidence that all the therapies with the strongest empirical support encourage taking sensible *action* in one's life. Likewise, it is no coincidence that those therapies that encourage rumination, particularly psychoanalysis (coupled with a past orientation, another damaging focus for depressed clients), have proven themselves to be the weakest approaches for depression. The common term "analysis paralysis" is a good descriptor of what can go awry with a ruminative style.

Evaluating rumination

Is rumination *always* a bad coping style? Of course not. The ability to spin things around in your mind, consider them from various angles, and analyze them for possible solutions can be extremely beneficial at times. But, when is it creative problem-solving and meaningful consideration, and when is it utterly useless obsessing? At what point might one *accurately* recognize that *no* amount of further analysis will yield anything useful and then "let it go"? It requires an effective discrimination strategy to know when to "stay with it and stay focused on it," and when to "let it go and move on."

Socrates said, "The unexamined life isn't worth living." The depression research makes it abundantly clear that neither is the *over*examined life (Just & Alloy, 1997).

Active coping styles

The ability to recognize something needs to be done, knowing what to do and when to do it, and then doing it, are the sophisticated abilities of someone with an active coping style. Avoidance and rumination may even be initial reactions in such a person, but quickly pass as the will to take action and achieve an effective resolution takes over.

An active coping style is inherently empowering. It implies that the individual recognizes his or her ability to make something useful happen and acts on that recognition. How does the person recognize this? A primary mistake made by passive (ruminative, avoidant) individuals is in thinking that they have to have the confidence to act *before* taking action. This is a sequencing problem amenable to hypnotic intervention. In most contexts, the action one takes *must* precede a sense of self-confidence. Consider your own clinical training as an example: If you waited until you felt confident that you were a good clinician *before* seeing your first client, you would likely still be waiting to see your first client. Instead, one gathers the academic training, the intellectual infrastructure into which clinical experience will be integrated. The infrastructure will be modified as clinical experience dictates, in an ongoing process of lifelong learning and adaptation in one's career as a clinician.

The importance of an action-orientation in overcoming depression cannot be overemphasized. Hypnosis to encourage action can be a vital part of therapeutic interaction because its very use models an action orientation. Hypnosis has been described, perhaps most articulately by Paul Watzlawick (1978), as the language of injunction. There is at the very least an implied message, and perhaps a direct one as well depending on the way the clinician structures his or her hypnotic suggestions, to "Do something" even while, paradoxically, telling the client to "Relax and do nothing." The paradoxical aspects of hypnotic communication have been especially well described by Jay Haley and are evident in such statements as, "I can only hypnotize you to the extent that you let me hypnotize you" (Haley, 1973). If the client gives the clinician control of him or her, a persistent myth regarding hypnosis, then who is really in control?

Hypnosis is an especially well-suited intervention style for depression because of its active nature. People sometimes mistake the client who is in hypnosis, sitting there quietly and seemingly doing nothing, as evidence of passivity. In fact, in one psychotherapy conference, I was paired with one of the primary developers of solution-oriented psychotherapy, for a spontaneous conversation about the similarities and differences in our approaches (deShazer & Yapko, 1998). I admire and routinely use aspects of this man's work, but couldn't relate to his meaning when he commented that he stopped doing hypnosis because it made him "work too hard." He perceived he was working harder than the client at promoting change, and didn't like it.

His viewpoint was noted by some (apparently) suggestible people in the audience, one of whom later attended my clinical demonstration ("The Case of Bob," described in Chapter 4) and saw me structure and deliver a hypnotic intervention where I spoke more than the client. She commented to me at the end of the demonstration that it appeared to her that I "worked too hard." But, that is a terribly superficial appraisal of the hypnotic interaction. In fact, the client in hypnosis is also working hard, but in a different way. The client is likely to (and certainly encouraged to) engage in an active search for relevance, namely, "how does this suggestion or metaphor apply to me?" Also, the client is actively building new associations, new understandings in the course of the hypnosis session. After all, it isn't the mere fact of being hypnotized that is therapeutic, rather it is the new associations (whether cognitive, emotional, temporal, or *whatever*) that are formed *during* the hypnosis. Furthermore, the client is directly or indirectly encouraged to actively engage in effective problem-solving, since the clinician is doing hypnosis for a reason: There's a therapeutic goal in mind, which presupposes its viability and the need for action steps to be taken in order to achieve it.

Men are generally socialized to be more action-oriented than women, a basis for the gender differences in the rate of depression. For example, a man gets fired from his job and his reaction is to go out and get drunk. A woman gets fired from her job and goes home and analyzes it: "What did I do wrong? Should I have been more politically astute? Should I have worked longer hours? Should I have socialized more? Should . . . ?" The next day, he's out looking for work, but she's barricaded in her bedroom, ruminating about the deeper meaning of losing her job. Her ruminations may yield some ideas about what to do differently in the future, but they aren't going to get her a new job. Action will.

The man getting drunk as a response to his getting fired is hardly what one would call an effective response, action-oriented though it seems. It is avoidant on one level (emotions) and is action-oriented on another (doing something other than ruminating). The goal is *not* taking action just for the sake of taking action, though. The goal is to take sensible, purposeful action in the direction of solving a problem. The related goal is to learn effective problem-solving.

Evaluating action

Is action *always* a good coping style? Of course not. By now you might be getting ahead of me, anticipating correctly the need for an effective *discrimination strategy*: How does one know when to step in and take charge, and when to passively let circumstances slide by? The foundation to the answer lies in all that has been discussed thus far about ambiguity, hopelessness, and helplessness. In any given context, an individual would have to have the skills mentioned at the outset of this section: Recognizing there is a problem, evaluating one's role in either creating it or being responsible for addressing it, delineating specific steps of possible resolutions, assessing the degree of controllability, and anticipating realistically the likely outcomes of implementing possible solutions. As you will see later in this chapter, hypnosis can be a most useful tool for helping develop these skills.

Hypnosis and decision-making

The focus on ambiguity as a risk factor for depression in Chapter 4 highlights the issue of how one's style of decision-making affect one's quality of life. In the face of uncertainty, potentially life transforming decisions have to be made.

"Decision-making" is a global construct. Rare is the individual, if such a person exists at all, who makes all of his or her decisions in the same manner or style. Realistically, people will likely make business decisions differently than the way they make personal decisions, and they will probably make book buying decisions differently than home buying decisions.

In this section, we will consider the process of decision-making as it relates to depression. Consider as an example the choice of a marriage partner. Marriage can be wonderful, but even under the best of circumstances, a good marriage requires ongoing effort. It is effortful to make compromises, communicate openly and regularly, often about sensitive or difficult issues, and take on additional responsibilities for the benefit of the relationship. When you have two high functioning partners, sensitive to the implications of the commitment they made, the work of the relationship is considerably easier.

But what happens when one partner, or *both* partners, are unable to participate fully in the relationship, such as when severely depressed? Or, what happens when the relationship is a painful place to be, victimizing one or both partners?

Decision-making, marriage, and depression

Given how much wisdom and integrity it takes to make a marriage work well, how is it, then, that so many people end up unhappily married? Why do they choose someone to partner with who, assessed with some objectivity, can not provide any of the things a healthy and stable relationship would require? The choice of a marriage partner has profound implications not only for survival of the marriage itself, but for the likelihood of depression in one or both of its members (Hammen, 1999). As described earlier, someone is at least ten times more likely to either already be or to become depressed when the marriage is distressed (Beach, Sandeen, & O'Leary, 1990).

Worse yet is when children are produced by a couple who came together for all the wrong reasons, lacking both insight and foresight. A depressed mother or father makes a poor parent, increasing the risk of depression in his or her children by a factor of three over the children of non-depressed parents (Weissman, Warner, Wickramaratne, Moreau, & Olfston, 1997).

Clinicians can take to heart and put into practice the reality that *depression is contagious*—not in the viral or bacterial sense, but in the social sense. Marriage partners affect each other powerfully, and parents profoundly influence their children. Knowing this lends an urgency to focusing not just on what decisions have already been made and dealing with their aftermath, but what decisions are being made unintentionally each day in each interaction and what decisions have yet to be made.

A clinician's decision-making style deeply influences his or her style of intervention with clients. Why are some clinicians so cerebral, deciding emotions are unimportant? Why are some so "touchy-feely" that their unexamined feeling is that emotions are the most important part of a person on which to focus? Why are some clinicians so global that they speak only in "psychobabble" terms that convey little meaning (e.g., ego-strengthening, self-esteem, countertransference), while others are so detail oriented they miss the bigger picture of what the client is trying to tell them?

Frames of reference

Smart people can make poor choices. Intelligence has little to do with having an effective strategy for making good decisions. What constitutes an "effective strategy for making good decisions?" It's using the best possible frame of reference—the one most consistent with—making the client's goal(s) attainable.

Consider the mental health profession's current preoccupation with "therapeutic efficacy" and "empirical validity." If someone asks, "What is the best therapy for depression?", my answer would be, "Best for what?" It's not a sarcastic or evasive answer—I just want to know what frame of reference the person asking the question will be using for evaluating the information I provide. If he or she wants to know what's "best" for least demand on the client as a participant in treatment, I'll answer "medication." If he or she wants to know what's "best" according to what's cheapest for a 3-month treatment time-frame, I'd say "medication." If the person wants to know what's "best" for teaching rational thinking, I'd say "cognitive therapy" in one form or another. If the person wants to know what's "best" for developing an ongoing relationship with a caring therapist who can be an empathetic "touchstone," I'd say "long term supportive psychotherapy." When efficacy studies describe the "best" treatments, they tend to describe them in terms of their length of treatment, degree of symptom remission, and relapse rates. Clearly, there are different frames of reference for deciding what the "best" therapy for depression might be.

If someone hasn't evaluated or decided upon a meaningful frame of reference for making a decision, the person can feel "stuck" and unable to move forward. This is the case with Consuelo, a psychologist from Italy I conducted a hypnosis session with that is presented for analysis later in this chapter. As you will see, the importance of developing the right "yardstick" to measure the approach most likely to succeed is a vital step toward making effective decisions—the kinds of decisions that don't blow up in your face later as depressing failures.

Hypnosis and exploring options

Hypnosis can be used to help clients feeling "stuck" to actively make both emotionally and intellectually intelligent decisions. Hypnosis can also be used to impart the powerful teaching that each decision must be made on the interplay of the unique characteristics operating at a given moment between personal characteristics, situational demands, and future consequences. (A decision made that seems alright now can be disastrous later, and prevention should always be a focal point of clinical consideration.)

Table 3. Hypnosis and Exploring Options

- Induction process
- Build a response set regarding "choice"
- Describe possible frames of reference
- Present alternative frames of reference salient to the problem context
- Establish a goal orientation
- Identify personally plausible options
- Age progression to explore each option's consequences
- Identify specific action steps
- Associate action to problem context and reinforce
- Post-hypnotic suggestions for integration
- Closure and disengagement

Table 3 above describes a generic hypnotic process called "Hypnosis and Exploring Options." This strategy, adaptable to the individual needs of a particular client, contains a series of steps intended first to mobilize an insightful exploration of possibilities available to one in some situation of concern that may have been overlooked, and then a foresightful consideration of how any of these possibilities might be helpful in the long run. The process amplifies the important message that decision-making has to be an active process involving the abilities to move in and out of alternative frames of reference while evaluating the merits of each.

A step-by-step description of Hypnosis and Exploring Options

Induction process.   Either a structured or conversational approach to se-curing then focusing the client's attention.

Build a response set regarding "choice."   As previously described, the hyp-nosis session should build a momentum in the direction of the therapeutic goals for the session, moving from general suggestions about choices to specific suggestions for making specific choices. So, a series of general sug-gestions (e.g., "You can choose the moment at which you let your body get even more comfortable . . . you can choose to notice which of your thoughts are the most soothing . . . you have the ability to choose a physical posture that makes it easy for you to listen . . . ") can be offered to begin amplifying the notion of choice without making any demand to choose something related to the session's issues.

Describe possible frames of reference.   A primary way people get "stuck" is by having only one frame of reference for making a decision. Earlier I used the example involving the question, "What is the best therapy?" For HMOs, the answer is rigidly and unfortunately, "whatever is cheapest." Cost is the frame of reference for HMOs answering the question. For re-searchers, the answer may be, "whatever has the greatest empirical sup-port." For clinicians, the answer may be, "whatever lets me do the therapy

I like to do." For clients, the answer may be, "whatever makes me better."

In this stage, then, the goal is to introduce the notion that there are multiple frames of reference for making a decision—almost *any* decision. One does this by describing this point to the client in some common context, such as deciding which car to buy: "Someone asked me what I think the best car is to buy . . . and I had to ask, best for what? . . . For looks? . . . For resale? . . . For comfort? . . . For reliability? . . . For status? . . . There are many different frames of reference for deciding which car to buy . . . or for making even more important personal decisions . . . "

As the client begins to think about different factors to consider in order to make a decision, it starts to become clearer to him or her that there are limitations to only using one's feelings or one's comfort level for making a decision. The client can begin to discriminate between what's *easiest* (i.e., most comfortable, most familiar) and what's *best* in terms of the goal(s) he or she hopes to achieve.

Present alternative frames of reference salient to the problem context. At this stage, the clinician can start to move closer to the clinical issue at hand, or the decision to be made, addressing it more directly now that therapeutic momentum and a therapeutic alliance have been established. The clinician can offer such suggestions as, "I can see how one person, who cares most about keeping things the same even though they're not very good, would tell you to do this . . . and I can understand how someone who's a hotheaded, impulsive type would tell you that you should do this . . . and how someone who was more concerned about other's safety more than his or her own would advise you to do this . . . "

The clinician can offer viewpoints that parallel the different "voices" of the client's own internal dialogue, an internally focused strategy. Or, the clinician can encourage the client to use others outside himself or herself in order, an externally focused strategy, to present a range of viewpoints. I did this with Consuelo, the client in the session transcript presented later in this chapter.

Establish a goal orientation. The client is encouraged to consider which of the viewpoints will be most effective to adopt if his or her goal is to be reached. Again, the goal is to reinforce that the choice to be made *must* be based on what it takes to reach the goal and *not* on what is easiest or least threatening. In Consuelo's case, where she wants to re-establish control over her professional commitments, it would not be comfortable for her at the start of our session to have to say no to people asking for her help, but would be necessary if she were to have more time to do the writing she wanted to do. So, a suggestion such as, "Out of the many different ways there are to choose what you will do . . . you can choose the path to follow that will take you where you most want to go . . . even if it is a path you have never taken before . . . "

Identify personally plausible options.   Presenting different choices that the clinician happens to think of, or that occur to others, doesn't necessarily make them instantly desirable or acceptable to the client. At this stage of the process, the goal is to make the choices seem more personal, therefore more demanding of a better and more meaningful response. As the clinician gently but firmly brings more pressure to bear on the client to make a choice, a good choice, an effective choice, the client now has the opportunity to more seriously consider "doing something different." Whether it's adopting a suggested choice or self-generating a new one, the client gets more focused on what he or she can actively implement. Suggestions such as, "Out of all the different possibilities . . . you can choose one in particular that seems sensible to you . . . even if somewhat unfamiliar . . . and you can consider it carefully from a variety of angles . . . to increase your confidence . . . that it really is sensible . . . and decide to follow it through with action . . . or you might choose to let it go . . . and choose another possibility instead . . . that seems even more effective . . . "

Age progression to explore each option's consequences.   Given the negative expectations typical of depression, it is often the case that the depressed individual has difficulty imagining a future without depression, or *any* future at all beyond a mere extrapolation of what is or what has been. The goal of this step, therefore, is to teach foresight, a predictive ability sufficiently accurate to warrant saying, "If I do this, then this is the likely result." Such skill is *vital* to recovery from depression as well as to preventing relapses. It's important for the client to know that while not all things are predictable, many things are. This can help motivate the client by helping him or her see that following a sensible plan really can generate positive results. So, the clinician encourages the client at this stage in the process to explore consequences perhaps by suggesting something such as, "follow a decision to see where it takes you . . . and you can imagine *in detail* that it's been months since you chose a new path and began to follow it . . . notice how it feels to have decided . . . and what it has led you in these months to do differently . . . and what you like better in yourself now . . . and what it has allowed you to do that before you felt unable to do. . . ."

As the client gets more absorbed in the age progression and the details of the changes the clinician draws to his or her attention, he or she has more of an experiential basis for accepting or rejecting the various alternatives. The client is encouraged to "think ahead" when deciding, an especially important and reliable path out of ambivalence.

Identify specific action steps.   This step provides a reinforcement to the client that "there is *at least* one good option to pursue, and these are the clear steps to follow in order to pursue it intelligently."

Associate action to context and reinforce.   Knowing what to do is one thing, actually doing it another. Meant to further counter the passivity and help-lessness of depression, this step involves establishing a link (association) between a specific action step and a specific context. The clinician suggests something such as, "When you find yourself dissatisfied with what happens in that troublesome situation you described to me . . . you can stop and you can think about the different ways available to you to decide what to do . . . and you can decide what you'd most like to see happen . . . and you can use your growing ability to step out of the moment in order to see where each choice will take you . . . and then you can decisively do what you know will eventually be helpful . . . taking one step at a time . . . on the path you've chosen . . . until sooner than you might have expected . . . you are where you want to be . . . "

Post-hypnotic suggestions.   Giving suggestions for helping make the steps of "exploring options" more automatic (i.e., integrated) is a worthwhile goal. One of the primary advantages of employing hypnosis in treatment is in its ability to make changes sometimes seem less effortful for clients. Post-hypnotic suggestions such as, "You may be pleasantly surprised at how automatic it becomes to you . . . to make decisions according to what's best in the long run . . . and not what's easiest in the short run . . . and you can feel good about how quickly you seem to reach well-considered conclusions . . . and implement purposeful action that benefits you . . . and helps you feel so much better about yourself and your life . . . "

Closure and disengagement.   A suggestion to bring the experience to a comfortable close, followed by a suggestion to reorient.

Exploring options in context: The case of Consuelo—a session transcript with commentary

In December, 1996, I conducted a clinical demonstration at the Brief Therapy Congress in San Francisco organized by The Milton H. Erickson Foundation. Attended by more than two thousand delegates from all over the world, it was a dynamic setting for exploring brief therapy options.

I entered the scheduled demonstration hour with the idea that I would simply spontaneously ask for a volunteer from the audience to work with who was feeling "stuck" in some way. As I entered the auditorium, though, Consuelo approached me and asked if I would work with her in the demonstration. Consuelo and I had previously met through mutual friends, but had no relationship beyond polite greetings. I accepted her offer to be my partner in the demonstration, and so we began. (This session was professionally videotaped and enhanced with explanatory subtitles for teaching purposes. See Appendix B for more information.)

Transcript

Commentary

M: Hi, Consuelo

C: Hi.

M: Can you provide a little bit of background about yourself?

C: Yes. First of all, I am Italian, and I live and work in Milano. I have various kinds of jobs. I teach in the university, I train managers about communication and I am a psychotherapist, too, using hypnosis. I am here because I would like to spend less time working and more time in writing. I'd like to write, and I think you are the most important person now to help me in this; I am stuck in writing and I would like to express myself in writing essays or even a book.

Consuelo provides very little background about herself beyond the most rudimentary self-description. *Consuelo is from another culture, she is experienced with hypnosis, and she is quick to reveal her goal-orientation.* She has a specific problem to work on, and a clear motivation for resolving it.

M: Really? (Showing interest in her goal.)

Nonverbal reinforcement of her worthy goal.

C: Yes. This is my . . . the reason why I am here.

M: Okay, and specifically what you would like to do in this session then is what?

Clarifying her specific goal(s) for the session in light of her larger goal of writing.

C: Not to be stuck and to have more options. To understand better what I'd like to do in my professional life.

Consuelo has picked up and started to use my language—the terms "stuck" and "options" I used in my introduction. She seems responsive to and willing to use my framework, believing as she said earlier she thinks I can help her. She is obviously familiar with "utilization."

M: Okay. Now, as you have been considering this kind of change in

Identify the pattern (structure) of how (*not* why) she *isn't* writing, your professional focus to include writing, what are the kinds of things that you have become aware of as obstacles or things that seem to be holding you back?

namely, how she gets "diverted" from her goal.

C: Yes, the obstacles are the time that I spend in working. I don't say "no" when some work is coming; I say "yes, thanks." So, I don't have time to write.

Consuelo clearly identifies her excessive workload as the problem. She further identifies her inability to set limits effectively as the path to becoming overburdened.

M: How do you decide which things you are going to choose to do?

Identifying her strategy for determining priorities at a given moment (her frame of reference for choosing her commitments).

C: (Long pause). I don't know . . . Maybe it depends on if the thing that is being offered to me is challenging, is new, is something that gives me the opportunity to learn something new. You know, to teach this new thing.

Her obvious confusion indicates her "experiential deficit." Ultimately, she concludes she takes on commitments if they represent an opportunity to learn or grow in some way. She does *not* indicate that she takes its time demand into account vis á vis her time availability.

M: Okay, so if I'm understanding you correctly, you are saying that in the short-run, then, what you'll choose to do is based on what is going to be interesting to you at that point in time?

Double-checking that the essence of her strategy is choosing according to what's interesting, *not* according to what she has time for in terms of her greater priorities.

C: Yes.

She validates my characterization of her decision-making strategy.

M: But, by making that choice, sometimes it interferes with your ability to do other things that may take longer.

My first allusion to the ineffective nature of her decision-making strategy.

C: Yes. Yes, yes. Short-term, yes, you are right.

She strongly validates that the deficit of her strategy has been identified.

M: Let me divert my attention from you for one second and point something out to the group. Part of what I'm interested in, of course, in exploring options, is how people go about making decisions, not *what* the specific decisions are so much, but *how* they go about making decisions. You see, in many ways it is the equivalent of when people ask a question like, "What is the best car to buy?" Best for what? For speed? For looks? For endurance? For comfort? For resale? And part of where people get stuck in the frame that they're in, the perceptual frame that they're now experiencing as being too rigid, is when they're using a set of criteria to make decisions that aren't really helpful with what they are trying to accomplish.

Since Consuelo had previously picked up and utilized ideas I presented to the audience despite their lack of being personal, I chose to use that same mechanism here. I introduce the key notion how *decisions can be made according to different frames of reference* through the car metaphor. She has already acknowledged that her strategy isn't working well, and I am now striving to build her responsiveness to adapting a new, more effective frame of reference for choosing what she will and won't take on.

M: Now, you'll notice in my asking Consuelo the question, "How do you decide what you're going to do?", it took her a moment, but then she was able to say that it is based on what she finds challenging at the moment. And so (turning my attention back to Consuelo), part of what I'd like to do in this hypnosis session, then, is provide some other possible ways of making those same kinds of decisions about what you're going to do and what you're not going to do.

Defining the session's purpose, and reinforcing Consuelo's goal.

C: Uh-huh.

Consuelo agrees to the session's goal as I've defined it, affirming our therapeutic alliance.

M: Now, you mentioned, of course, that you have been trained in hypnosis, you use hypnosis—this is something that you are already familiar with in terms of your own experience.

Orienting Consuelo to the topic and experience of hypnosis as the lead-in to the formal induction.

C: Yes.	She acknowledges she is hypnotically capable.
M: Okay, that being the case then, what I'd to do is begin . . .	Initiating the formal hypnotic induction.

Focus: Six Primary Goals For My Hypnosis Session With Consuelo

1. Create a safe and comfortable atmosphere to address her issues both directly and indirectly, respecting her ability to make use of new ideas in her own way.
2. Diminish any sense of personal inadequacy or self-criticism Consuelo experiences by reframing the problem as one of an ineffective strategy; the message is, "it isn't you, it's the way you go about it."
3. Identify Consuelo's key experiential deficit relative to her goal, namely prioritizing according to the criteria of what's new, interesting or challenging, without considering what her time actually permits. (Redefining priorities.)
4. Help Consuelo expand her "strategy for choosing" to include the factors of time and the eventual consequences, and not just according to what's interesting or challenging *now*.
5. Provide a concrete means (attitude and technique) for Consuelo to set limits and say "no" to work invitations/opportunities in order to create and protect time to write.
6. Reinforce the worthiness of her goals and enhance both her ability and motivation to accomplish them.

M: (Resuming session): . . . So, orient yourself in whatever way you want to or need to . . . use your experience now in your own behalf to help yourself . . . start to develop the kind of internal focus . . . that I know you have experienced . . . at other times that you've done hypnosis . . . And being able to use your background . . . of having worked with hypnosis . . . having experienced hypnosis . . . I think you already know . . . what the experience is like for you . . . how you feel . . . as you start to experience yourself . . . getting more internally absorbed . . . And, of course, you also know . . .	Induction with the naturalistic approach of "accessing previous hypnotic experiences."

Enhancing her internal focus. |

that as the outside world goes about its business . . . that you can still be aware . . . of this very comfortable distance . . . a *very* comfortable distance . . . between what's out there and what is inside . . . And out of all the different possible focal points . . . all the different things that you could notice . . . I really don't know . . . what you'll *choose* to notice . . . whether you'll focus on something external . . . that passes through your awareness . . . or whether you'll focus on something internal . . . perhaps a thought . . . or a particular feeling . . . certainly you get to *choose* . . . Whether it's a particular physical sensation . . . all I know is . . . that there is a number of possibilities . . . each valuable . . . in its own way . . . and when you take the time . . . the way that you are now . . . to start to notice . . . the different aspects of your own experience . . . it can make it really easy for you . . . surprisingly easy . . . to explore that . . . very strong relationship . . . between the choices that you make in this moment . . . and the eventual possibilities that unfold . . . And certainly you know . . . how much planning goes into . . . organizing a trip to come to a meeting such as this . . . and you've come a very long way . . . and it really wasn't a last minute decision . . . in the literal sense . . . I know that there are some people . . . who find it astounding . . . even puzzling . . . why someone would travel so far . . . I've had people ask me . . . why I go to other countries . . . when America has so much . . . And as someone who travels . . . as you obviously

Building a response set re: options (choosing focal points).

Reinforcing the ability to choose from a variety of positive possibilities.

Establishing the link between choices made now and the eventual consequences.

Introducing a metaphor re: planning for specific desired outcomes.

De-emphasizing a singular frame of reference (each culture offers possibilities).

do . . . you already know . . . that the way that things are done . . . in Milano . . . aren't quite the same as they are in San Francisco . . . And you can recognize . . . at a very deep level . . . that wherever you go . . . you have the beliefs . . . the experiences . . . the values . . . the perspectives . . . of someone from Italy . . . Just as I know that wherever I go . . . I have an American frame of reference . . . (Consuelo takes a deep breath) To be able to step outside that frame of reference . . . That's right . . . and to experience . . . different ways of looking at . . . food . . . relationships . . . manners of dress . . . and each country that you travel to . . . creates different options . . . and ways of living . . . You already know that, Consuelo. But one of the things that . . . you start to discover . . . is that the choices . . . each carry a result . . . there are things that you want to be able to say . . . things that you want to be able to do . . . Now, I can describe an experience to you . . . and at first, you might even wonder . . . why I'm talking about this . . . right here . . . and right now. But I wouldn't be surprised if . . . at a much deeper level . . . you understood something . . . that later you might talk about . . . or might write about . . . Now I don't know what it's like in the hypnosis trainings you do . . . But one of the questions I get asked all the time is . . . "Where do you get the metaphors from?" . . . And the way I answer that . . . even in the things that I've *written* . . . is that when you're living life . . . the messages are everywhere. So, even earlier today . . . I was standing in line . . . waiting to get lunch . . .

Acknowledging/utilizing current frames of reference.

Indirect deepening suggestion.

Identifying a specific frame of reference as starting point for making personal choices.

Even basic aspects of life involve making choices.

Culture as a frame of reference.

Reinforcing the association between choices and consequences.

Feeding back her desire to express herself; enhancing positive motivation.

Framing the forthcoming metaphor.

Indirect suggestion for using this current experience as a basis for writing later.

Reinforcing common frame of reference, enhancing rapport.
Reinforcing the value of written ideas.

Introducing a metaphor re: the need to set limits.

really nothing particularly special about that experience . . . until you start to notice . . . and I started to notice . . . that someone stepped into the line . . . a few people ahead of me . . . turned and said to the person that they just cut in front of . . . with a great deal of charm . . . "I'm sorry, but I'm really in a hurry. Do you mind?" . . . And didn't even wait for an answer. Now those are the little spontaneous experiments . . . because the woman that he cut in front of . . . who was considerably more charming than he was, said, "Then you can just hurry . . . to the back of the line." . . . Now, when that interaction happened . . . I really didn't know that I'd be telling you about it . . . just a few hours later. And now that I've told you about it . . . you have an opportunity . . . to perhaps . . . consider . . . that there is a deeper meaning than just a lunch line story . . . You might choose to consider it . . . as an interesting observation about people . . . Or, you might choose . . . to think about it . . . differently . . . And then at a whole other level . . . you can wonder . . . "What does that have to do with writing?" . . . But, now there's a whole other thing . . . that I'd like to describe to you . . . Now, I don't know if this whole episode . . . made its way onto the Italian television . . . or into the Italian newspapers . . . but a very interesting thing happened about six months ago . . . in the life of Hillary Clinton, the President's wife . . . because she was working with someone who invited her to . . . close her eyes . . . and to think about a particular problem she was having . . . and she was invited

Something that may seem mundane on one level can have value on another—an indirect suggestion to be less self-censoring.

Message: Socially redeeming characteristics do not obviate the need for good personal boundaries.

Message: Others will impose their needs, if you let them.
Message: You can still be nice even when you're setting limits and saying "no" to someone, male or female.
Message: A personal boundary isn't negotiable.

Encouraging the search for personal relevance.

Presenting alternate frames of reference (options) regarding the story's significance.

Associating the metaphor's message to the stated goal.
Transition to a new therapeutic metaphor.
Alluding to the recognition that what seems important at one time and place may not be in another time and place.
An indirect suggestion for adapting to changing circumstances.
The story's principal character is a powerful woman.
Establishing the common link of both seeking hypnotic experience,

to think about . . . how someone very famous . . . and how someone very inspirational . . . might talk to her about that very problem . . . And she chose several different . . . very important people . . . from American history and world history . . . She chose Gandhi . . . she chose Eleanor Roosevelt . . . she chose Jesus . . . Now, I don't know who *you* would choose, Consuelo . . . Who you think of as having a very different viewpoint . . . that could tell you something . . . that would really make a difference . . . Who you would choose . . . and what that person would tell you . . . It's an interesting experience . . . based on a very real belief . . . that people know more . . . than they sometimes realize . . . But it would certainly be an interesting thing . . . to ask a writer . . . how she makes time to write . . . Or how anybody does *anything* . . . But even now as you're sitting here . . . you might have noticed . . . as I have . . . shifts that have taken place in your breathing . . . and the muscle tone of your face . . . And so, in just a moment, Consuelo . . . I'm going to ask you . . . to describe for me out loud . . . what you are aware of at this moment . . . And you'll find that you can describe to me quite easily . . . quite effortlessly . . . and that even as you describe your experience . . . it can deepen your involvement . . . And so if you would now . . . describe for me . . . what you're aware of . . .

encouraging an identification.
Indirect suggestion to identify respected voices of alternative viewpoints (options).

Indirect suggestion to choose multiple alternative viewpoints.

Indirect suggestion to identify specific, personally meaningful others to represent alternative frames of reference.
Encouraging her to generate specific helpful feedback to herself from another perspective.

Truism facilitating acceptance of alternatives.

Direct suggestion to interview others to acquire a variety of strategies for accomplishing her goal.
Generalizing the point about effective strategies beyond just writing.

Reinforcing hypnotic responsiveness.
Anticipation signal regarding speaking in order to provide verbal feedback regarding her experience.

Facilitating verbalization.

Verbalization as a deepening method.

(Consuelo opens her eyes and smiles.)

External reorientation.

C: When you tell me about my travel, I went immediately in the place where I was born. It's a very nice small town in Sardinia. And then I've seen all my houses—in Sardinia, then in Milano. I was comparing the Italian culture and my family, my friends, and the American culture, and I heard my mother telling me, "You want too much, slow down." And, then when you were telling me about the writers, the first one was you and then I said, "No, I want a woman," and I didn't find a woman, it was Christa Wolf but I don't write these kinds of things, and then I have chosen (Italo) Calvino, especially because he was very fond of American culture, and because of his last book about lightness in American literature, it's a chapter about lightness. And, this was what [was going on] . . .

Projection from her own subjective frame of reference.

She accepted the invitation to consider cultural differences as alternative frames of reference.

She chose her mother as the significant person providing a helpful message reinforcing the need to set limits.
Associated the message to writing/writers, and went from me to others with relevant helpful characteristics.

M: Okay, alright. Go back inside now (closes her eyes) . . . that's right . . . and start to reabsorb yourself . . . immerse yourself again . . . and notice how quickly . . . and easily . . . you can begin to recapture . . . a very deep sense of awareness . . . and what you've just described so beautifully . . . is your direct experience . . . of knowing . . . *really* knowing . . . that culture represents a choice . . . of being able to choose what   you most appreciate and value . . . in your culture . . . in my culture . . . *any* culture . . . and what you start to realize . . . when you think about it . . . is that, in a way, each human being . . . is a culture . . . all her own, all his own . . . your own language . . . your own customs . . . your own way of doing things . . . and you get to

Her description is accepted and she is given suggestions to re-enter hypnosis.
Encouraging a more rapid development of hypnosis.

Reinforcing her ability to communicate as a core component of her self.

Reinforcing her allusion to cultural differences as a basic frame of reference.
Reinforcing her flexibility in seeing some value in each perspective.

Transition from a general point to a more personal meaning.
Ratification of her point of view in general while encouraging her to

choose . . . which aspects of your culture . . . you want to continue to honor and make good use of . . . and which aspects of the way thing have been . . . you're ready to let evolve and change and grow . . . but there's one other thing . . . that I think would be really *deeply* helpful . . . that in the same way someone might ask . . . which is the best car to buy? . . . and you've heard my answer . . . Best for what? . . . Then *you* might ask . . . What's the best use of my time? . . . And I think you can safely predict . . . how I'd answer . . .

. . . And so you can make some choices   according to . . . what feels best . . . and some choices according to . . . what's the safest . . . and least threatening . . . and some choices based on . . . what the goal is . . . and some choices . . . according to what will get the most approval . . . and so out of all the different ways there are to choose . . . I wonder if you're now much more aware of which path of choice will help you get things written . . . Now I don't know that I would say this *all* the time, Consuelo . . . but every once in a while . . . it's not a bad idea to listen to Mom . . . (Consuelo laughs) . . . Now, out of all things that I've talked about . . . from lunch lines to houses in Sardinia . . . I wonder which things you'll bring back . . . that can stay with you now . . . and be with you the next time . . . and each next time . . . you're at that point . . . of choosing to do something that is challenging now . . . or choosing to do something that you'll be able to . . . hold in your hands later . . . Take whatever time

think critically about which aspects to maintain and which to change.

Allowing, rather than forcing, change to occur.

"Marking" the word "deeply" as a deepening technique.

Reiterating an already accepted example of the validated time utilization, and encouraging a new association between effective time usage and accomplishing her goal.

Reviewing possible frames of reference for time utilization strategies. Highlighting different ways to structure one's time, drawing attention to the option most likely to make writing possible.

Indirect suggestion to choose the option consistent with accomplishing her objective.

Modeling selectivity.
Reinforcing Mother's message stated earlier to not do too much, a key to accepting the need to set and maintain limits.
Reviewing and reinforcing key ideas from the session through indirect associations.

Post-hypnotic suggestions for integration of key ideas.
Contextualizing the resource of choosing options according to desired objectives rather than imme-

you want to or need to, Consuelo . . . to process your thoughts . . . and to bring this experience to a comfortable close . . . And when you feel like you're ready to and want to . . . you can start the process of reorienting yourself, bringing yourself back . . . Take your time, and when you're ready you can fully reorient yourself . . . and allow your eyes to open . . .

diate factors.
Alluding to a tangible, written product.

Suggestions for closure.

Permissive disengagement.

(Consuelo opens her eyes slowly and stretches.)

M: Hi.

C: Hi. (Smiles and nods.) Well, in the . . . May I say something?

M: Please.

C: In the last four years, I bought two houses, one for me and one for my son. Now I don't need any more to work so hard. So, I can spend my time different ways. Instead of . . . yes, I think that, now I have accomplished this very important task for me and for my son, now I'm free.

Self-reinforces the realization that with changing circumstances she has new options.

M: You know, people will keep presenting things to you to do that are very interesting and challenging.

Testing her resolve to choose according to a new goal-oriented strategy.

C: What did you say?

M: I said, people will keep presenting things to you that are very interesting and challenging.

C: Yes, I think so. Well, (laughs). I . . . um . . . Maybe I can say no.

The conflict between being immediately accessible to others and setting limits to make attaining the goal possible is evident.

M: (Feigns a look of surprise.)

C: Maybe, I don't know . . . yes, it depends on . . . if . . . yes, I can say no. "No thanks!" Okay.

Consuelo resolves the conflict with the acceptance of the need to set limits in her own behalf. The session goal is accomplished.

M: Any other comments that you'd like to offer about the experience?

C: No, it was very moving for me, especially the first part. The second part was very exciting, and I was . . . yes.

M: Nice.

C: I think that something's changed. Thank you.

M: Thanks, Consuelo.

(The tape continues with questions from the audience.)

Follow-up

This session illustrates well the process of "Hypnosis and Exploring Options." While it loosely follows the generic structure outlined in Table 3, it is clearly adapted to Consuelo's unique attributes. It seemed especially important to integrate both cross-cultural and gender factors into the process.

Approximately two months after the session, I contacted Consuelo (via e-mail) in order to obtain some follow-up information. Here is her reply, minimally edited:

> Dear Michael,
>   . . . I am in transition phase. I am finishing some tasks already taken and in the meantime I am organizing my job in a different way. For instance, I am accostomed to do every thing by myself, and I have discovered that I am loosing a lot of time in menial thing that can be done by other person like, a secretariat. So I am looking for a helper who can do all the job I can delegate.
>   I am making list of thing that are necessary and thing that can be postponed so I organize the "queue." As far as saying no to new job it is still hard for me. My son has moved in January, but his home is not finished yet and I'd like to restore my apartment too.

But the best new is that next week I will send to an editor a book I have been writing in the last three years. During Christmas I made a lot of corrections expeccially cutting difficult parts or writing in a lighter style. I hope that the editor will like it and will publish it.

I am also showing your tape, or if I can say "our" tape, as a teaching instrument as I can show not only your technique but also the reaction of the patient.

I thank you so much for helping me in becoming more clear about what I really want and how to overcome my difficulties ...

Consuelo

Several weeks after receiving the above, I spontaneously received another follow-up correspondence from Consuelo:

Dear Michael,

I am very happy and I like to share with you my happyness. My book will be published by Franco Angeli (a well known Italian editor).

The title is "The art of leading training groups: Schopenhauer's porcupine."

This for you is a real demonstration that you have done a very good job. So thank you again.

As soon it will be published I will send you a copy.

Consuelo

Feeling stuck and having resources

Consuelo was a delight to work with. She is bright, resourceful, and motivated. But, what about depressed clients? Especially those that *aren't* bright, resourceful, and motivated?

The content of Consuelo's problem can too easily mislead one. In fact, she models what is most typical of depressives: Feeling "stuck" and unable to achieve what she wants. She's smart enough to know, though, that instead of "beating up on herself," she can go in search of solutions. This is the heart of a preventive approach with true depressives: We must teach them that instead of sinking into despair when they feel stuck and don't know what to do, *they can take action* and find out what to do. To her credit, Consuelo did that. And, she modeled well that when people *experientially* discover better choices, they typically use them.

In *Hypnosis and the Treatment of Depressions*, I described a strategy called "Accessing and Contextualizing Resources," a means for hypnotically finding and using the "best" parts of a person for therapeutic gain. I'd suggest revisiting that strategy as a response to any concern about depressed clients. Suffice it to say here, depressed clients shouldn't be blamed for their depression. If one looks for pathology in *anyone*, one will find it. And, if one looks for resources, one will find them. This book is about focusing on the positive, and hypnotically empowering people to find and use their abilities.

The case of Mike: 8
breaking patterns
of depression
(An unedited session transcript
with commentary and analysis)

Introduction

In early 1998, I was invited by Jeffrey Zeig and Suzi Tucker of Zeig, Tucker
& Theisen, Inc., Publishers, to participate in a new educational videotape
program they were planning to develop. The video series was to be called
Brief Therapy: Inside Out, and would feature a dozen well-known psychotherapists with varying approaches and philosophies regarding the practice of brief therapy. The purpose of the series was to have each practitioner both describe and demonstrate his or her methods to interested viewers.
The series participants are each highly skilled clinicians and teachers, and
it was an honor for me to be included among them.

The arrangement was to be as follows: I would fly to Chicago in December (1998) and proceed to Governors State University. There I would
conduct four therapy sessions with bona fide patients who had either sought
therapy at the school's counseling center or responded to locally placed
advertisements for recruiting purposes. For my sessions, depressed individuals in particular were solicited. Those who wanted to participate would
receive a therapy session at no charge in exchange for granting the rights
to Zeig, Tucker & Theisen, Inc., Publishers, to professionally film and later
distribute the teaching tape to professional audiences. I would meet the
clients at the film studio at the university, conduct the sessions, and then
choose which of the four sessions I thought best represented my work for
inclusion in the series.

As it turned out, only three of the four volunteer clients showed up for
their sessions. (One of the unfortunate side-effects of depression is how
many people are too depressed to get help, even when it's almost right in
front of them.) Each of the three sessions I conducted was instructive in

one way or another, but the session I chose for inclusion in the video series and in this book is particularly informative.

The hosts of the video series are Jon Carlson, Ph.D., and Diane Kjos, Ph.D. Each did an excellent job of drawing out key points about my theoretical understandings of treatment as well as the practical aspects of my interventions. (The videotape is called "Breaking Patterns of Depression: Hypnosis and Building Resources." For further information, see Appendix B.)

Background of the session with Mike

As a volunteer for a therapy session with me for this educational series, Mike agreed to particiapte in what was clearly defined as a one-time-only meeting. Mike and I had never met or spoken prior to our session. When I arrived at the studio for the filming of our session, I was introduced to Mike, and was informed that he was currently in counseling with a student intern at the university. In the few moments immediately prior to beginning our session, I was also told he had seen several previous therapists as well. No specific information about them or his therapy experiences with them was provided, nor was there enough time to obtain any such information before the cameras began to roll.

As I discovered afterwards, Mike did not have any information about me before the start of the session, either. He had no idea what to expect from our interaction, since he didn't know what kind of background I had or what approaches to therapy I was likely to employ. This session is, therefore, particularlarly illustrative of how clinical hypnosis can be effectively introduced into a therapeutic interaction in a first session, even with a totally inexperienced client.

Mike arrived on time, was seated, "wired" for sound, and we began our session.

The verbatim (unedited) transcript

The interview

Commentary and analysis

MDY: Hi. What is your name? And what would you like help with?

Mike: Um, Mike, and, um, I've been carrying like alot of emotional baggage for a long time. And, um, you know, it just seems to affect me, you know like daily. You know, I can't

Mike's opening statement reflects his past orientation, typical of depressives.

He makes it clear he is constantly

seem to, like, break free of things, you know, and uh, it just seems like I, you know, have constant reminders of things that have happened in the past.

focused on the past and that he strives to find a way to keep his past from controlling him.

MDY: So, when you say "emotional baggage," what do you mean exactly?

Asking for a definition of terms.

Mike: In what way you mean? Or, where did it come from? Or . . . ?

MDY: All of the above.

I'm interested in assessing the quality of his attributions about his past and his symptoms.

Mike: Okay.

MDY: Reader's Digest version.

I want less content and more structure in his reply.

Mike: (laughs) Well, alot of it, you know, is from, like, the last 34 years, you know, in my life. It just seems like one bad thing after another, you know. Alot of it stems, I think, from my father, you know.

Mike's reply reflects a global attribution, as well as dichotomous thinking. His statement suggests he believes his *entire* life has been bad, filled with only negative experiences. **A target for intervention**, since no one's life is unilaterally good or bad. He also attributes his problem to his father, an external attribution reflecting his sense of victimization.

Growing up was just, it seems like, full of twists and turns. A lot of hittin', kickin', slappin', throwing down stairs, hit with bats, belts, boots, um, you know, I've verbally been called every name you can think of, um, you know, past is filled with running away, foster homes . . . whew, that's just like the tip of it.

Mike reveals a history of extreme physical, emotional, and verbal abuse. His reply has minimal affect associated with it, attesting to his having told the story many times and suggesting the need to go into the details is much less important than offering him coping tools, such as compartmentalization.

MDY: So, with that kind of pretty nasty background, how does it affect the choices that you're making today?

I want to know specifically how his inability to compartmentalize the past is currently affecting him.

Mike: It seems a lot of times that I second-guess myself all the time. You know, I'm not really sure exactly which way to move without constantly replaying things in my head. Or, you know, it just seems like I'm kind of stuck in a gutter, you know, and can't get out. And so . . .

Mike states explicitly that when he faces ambiguity (uncertainty) he uses the *past* as the reference point rather than a goal-orientation, **a target for intervention**. The past is generally not a good guide for trying to move forward in life, thus his sense of being "stuck."

MDY: Stuck in terms of your ability to do what?

What is Mike's goal, what would he be better able to do, if he weren't feeling stuck?

Mike: Function alot of times. It seems like it weighs me down and uh, you know, I'm married and I have two children and it seems to affect them also, you know, um, where there's an emotional distance a lot of times.

He simply wants to function, not a very ambitious goal, but a clear statment as to how much the depression has him in its grip.
He also reveals he has a family, and has the insight to realize he is affecting them adversely because of his depression. This is **a target for intervention**, since the children of a depressed parent are three times more likely to become depressed themselves. His depression and resulting withdrawal from his family represent strong risk factors for his family that must be addressed in any meaningful intervention. Even though his family is not present, a systemic perspective allows them to be taken into account in my intervention with Mike as an individual.

MDY: How does . . . How do those kinds of past experiences become a basis for emotional distance in your own family?

By asking "how" rather than "why," I can uncover the sequence of behavior I'm trying to interrupt or modify.

Mike: Because, it seems, whether I talk to people or things, you know, there's a lot of times there could be facial expressions that people make, or smells, or just *anything*, and it seems like pictures click when that happens and somebody may say

Mike describes with great accuracy the many ways he is triggered into having flashbacks that effectively disconnect him from others in the present. He describes an extreme internal orientation, **a target for intervention**, typical of both trauma something, whatever, and then for a long time after I get home I may just be in another world, you know, just thinking.

and depression. In effect a "negative self-hypnosis," this is the moment I decided to formally utilize his hypnotic ability with the goal of redirecting it positively.

MDY: Stewing about it, thinking about it?

Assessing his degree of rumination.

Mike: A little of both, you know. And then always, you know, thinking, "Well, maybe I should have done this better or different."

Mike's pattern of continually replaying the past is highlighted again.

MDY: Alright, so when you say those kinds of things to yourself, then what happens?

Defining the sequence I may need to interrupt with an intervention.

Mike: I seem to get caught up in it, you know.

Again describing his ability to engage in (negative) self-absorption. My personal perspective is that this reflects more of his hypnotic ability in its natural (though symptomatic) form than any formal suggestibility test would be likely to do.

MDY: Do you always have that kind of running commentary going on through your mind? That kind of evaluation about yourself? That kind of assessment about how you're doing . . .

I want to assess how pervasive his self-doubt and ruminations are, since they are a likely **target of intervention**.

Mike: Always.

He describes them as everpresent.

MDY: . . . and what you said and what you did? And do you always pay attention to it?

My question introduces the possibility one might not pay attention to ruminations.

Mike: Alot of times. I shouldn't say one hundred percent of the time but, yeah, a lot of times I do.

He modifies his response from "always" to "alot of times," potentially a significant redefinition.

MDY: How do you know whether it's worth listening to?

Assessing whether he has an internal discrimination strategy or only a "one-size fits all" response of passively listening to whatever he happens to generate.

Mike: (head drops, long pause) I don't.

His "experiential deficit" is identified—an inability to discriminate what is from what is not worth focusing on.

MDY: Have you ever had the experience of discovering that some of the things that run through your mind aren't particularly helpful to you and you don't really need to focus on them?

Looking for exceptions to his rigid pattern to build upon, a simple solution-oriented strategy.

Mike: Yeah, there's been times that, you know, I think that, you know, that what somebody said or something just doesn't amount to a whole lot.

Mike claims there are times he can keep from getting caught up in the negativity.

MDY: And then do you let it go?

Assessing whether his response is effective.

Mike: Yeah, sometimes I do, but it just seems like words can hurt worse than punches, you know.

He indicates it's not a reliable strategy. He then restates in a different way the pain of having been abused.

MDY: Okay, but if I criticize you, how do you know whether to pay attention to it, how do you know whether to listen to it, how do you know whethether to take it seriously or whether to dismiss it?

He has previously stated when the source of criticism or doubt is *internal* (himself), he is essentially defenseless. I now ask whether that is equally true if the source is *external* (me).

Mike: I seem to take a lot of things seriously. It could just be joking, whatever, but I do take it serious.

He essentially restates he takes in deeply and responds strongly to anything perceived as negative or critical, even if in a joke.

MDY: Okay. But the question I'm really asking is how do you know whether you should take it seriously? You're telling me that you do take it seriously, but I'm asking a question of how you know whether you should?

Through my question, I reintroduce the notions to him that his pattern of sensitivity and negativity has been a product of passively accepting the negative and that he can start to think in terms of actively fighting against it.

Mike: (head drops, long pause) I don't.

MDY: Okay. It seems to me that that would be a really valuable thing for you to be able to have is some internal mechanism that helps you decide whether it's worth paying attention to. And one of the things . . . I don't know if you've ever talked to other people about the inner voices that they have inside their own heads where they replay bad things that have happened and the self-criticisms that they generate and all the junk that goes on up there, but if you were to do what I do, which is when I have hundreds of people in a room and I ask them, "Who among you has good self-esteem?" Hands go up—not many—but some hands go up and I ask them, "Do you have an inner critic? Do you have a voice inside your head that criticizes you and says rotten things to you and puts you down and says mean and horrible things to you?"

And every single one says yes. Then I ask them, "If you have a voice that says rotten things to you, how can you have good self-esteem?" And the interesting reply—it's always a little bit different—but the common bottom line is they don't listen to it! When I ask them, "How do you not listen to it?" that's when I start learning all kinds of different strategies. One person will say, "Well, I picture it as being on a volume control knob and I just turn the volume down. Somebody else says "I picture it as a barking dog tied to a tree, and I just keep walking." Somebody else says, "Uh, you know, I have another voice on my shoulder that says good things

Reaffirms his experiential deficit, **a target for intervention.**

I introduce a specific *goal* to Mike that involves him in developing a specific skill he clearly does not have that would eventually be beneficial to him—the use of *metaphor* to introduce to him the concept that just because someone has self-critical ruminations or hurtful internal dialogue (or imagery) doesn't mean he or she has to focus on it, amplify it, or believe it. I describe some mental activity as "junk," a *reframing* of the notion that all thought is somehow valuable or meaningful, thus requiring a discrimination strategy. Furthermore, by describing people by the hundreds as having a similar presence of what I frame as an "inner critic," it has the effect of *depathologizing* his pattern, a key step in *motivating* the person to want to develop a skill instead of coping with a "disease."

Deframing Mike's belief that the problem is his past and *reframing* that it's his passively listening to his inner critic.

Modeling actively searching for effective strategies to cope with symptoms.
Using other peoples' strategies as metaphors to encourage him to adopt one or develop his own.

to me." But the interesting thing is that every single person has that inner critic, that critical voice. It's just a question of whether they listen to it or not. Now, to me, that was a very, very powerful learning from being around and asking those kinds of questions of literally thousands of people. But you'll notice in the question that I asked you, "Do you have some mechanism whereby you don't have to listen to it?" where you decide, "It's not offering me anything valuable here. All it's doing is keeping me stuck in the gutter," as you said.

Normalizing the inner critic.

Reiterating the need to actively argue against the inner critic in order to feel good.

Without that kind of a mechanism, you're always going to be stuck listening to it. And when is it ever going to say anything to you other than negative stuff?

Restating the need to develop a mechanism, a skill, for negating or ignoring the inner critic. Repetition of a new concept and technique is essential—it is unrealistic to think you can introduce a new idea just once and the person will instantly "get it."

Mike: Right.

MDY: It's not as if it's ever going to say to you, "Gee Mike, you're great!," "Gee, Mike, you're wonderful. Aren't you the best? Aren't you lucky to be who you are?" You know, that's not what people who feel good about themselves do. So, in a way, I'm kind of giving you a target to aim for, that having the ability to develop a mechanism for not listening to it when it's taking you someplace that you really don't want to go, because when are you ever going to escape all the triggers? When are you going to escape the sounds, the smells, the images? You can be watching a television show, you can be watching a movie, you can, I mean, the triggers are always going to be out there. We're not going to be able to change the external world. But, what goes

Emphasizing the potential value of the suggested skill in dealing with negativity, and again normalizing the inner critic's negative focus.

Using humor to get across the point that people with good self-esteem aren't saying ridiculously self-flattering things to themselves, they're simply using the skill I'm suggesting he learn to ignore or negate the negative. By giving him a target, something he has not previously had, and implying there is a way to reach it, Mike becomes very focused on the hope things can change. *Building expectancy* is a powerful means for motivating participation and the willingness to experiment in the client. Part of building expectancy is establishing realistic expectations, in this case that the reminders (triggers) will still be "out there," but he can expect his reactions to them to be different.

on inside your mind is eminently negotiable.

Mike: Okay.

Mike accepts that idea easily.

MDY: So, now, have you ever evaluated the value of the things that you tell yourself? Has it ever been an option for you, in other words, not to pay attention to it?

Encouraging Mike to review how the absence of the skill has led to his "feeling stuck in a gutter."

Mike: I try to, but a lot of times it, you know, I seem to remember and it kind of always comes back, you know?

Reaffirming he hasn't been able to do what I'm suggesting to his own detriment.

MDY: It will, but now the question is how you respond to it when you have the memories or when you have the images. When you have a memory come up of something bad that's happened to you, you can either focus on it, or not. I'd like to hear about the times that you do either. Tell me about the times that you do focus on it and what happens, and tell me about the times that you don't focus on it and tell me what happens.

Establishing the expectation that there is no miracle here—the triggers will persist, but he can develop a new way of keeping them from being destructive to him by changing his focus. I ask him to draw upon his own experience, if relevant, to determine the effects of how and where he focuses.

Mike: The times I focus on bad things, I just . . . I guess my escape from it, you know is, I just feel it build up, you know, and, uh, a lot of times at work or something I just have to get out of there real quick, you know, and I just seem to cry for a long time, you know, and um, that's probably how I just try to vent it out, you know.

Mike describes well what we know to be true—when you focus on something, you amplify it, for better or worse . . . in this case, worse. The crying spells he has are a common depressive symptom. His "venting" strategy clearly does not work—a general limitation of the "get your feelings out" perspective that inevitably fails when the person is still regenerating more (anger, depression) than can be vented.

The good times . . . when, you know, people say things, you know, I guess there's a lot of times you just try to

Mike uses some of his own experience to affirm that when he actively argues against the negativity, he prove them wrong, you know, and uh, I know that alot of times when people say things that I guess it just . . . it seems to just . . . you know, like a magnet or something, you know, it sticks on you and it's hard to get away from it but a lot of times I just try to tell myself like, "No, Mike, you know that's—that's not true, you know, and so it's hard, you know, I mean it's, it's not easy to just say, "Aw, forget it, you know, it's not right, you know, so . . . "

does better. But, he isn't able to do that consistently, and generally succumbs to it.

MDY: No, it isn't easy. But, it's a skill worth developing, because you will have how many things thrown at you for the rest of your life? And the idea is to get good at being able to dodge 'em, and weave around 'em, and *not* take 'em in, *not* be the magnet for these things sticking on you. And there are a lot of different ways of accomplishing that. Have you done any kind of focusing work, hypnotic work, relaxation work, imagery work, ever?

Validating his perception that it isn't easy to dismiss the criticism or hurt, but reaffirming the value in becoming more skilled at doing so and thereby motivating him to want to develop the relevant skills.

Introducing the idea that there are structured ways to develop the relevant skills, one of which is hypnosis. I use many names to introduce the possibility of working hypnotically to diffuse any possible negative reaction to the word "hypnosis."

Mike: No.

Mike has no previous experience with hypnosis, thus requiring a little extra time to orient him to the process.

MDY: Now, that would be a very interesting way for you to get absorbed in a different style of thought about these kinds of things. And if you're actually open to doing that kind of a section—session, I'd love to do that with you.

Defining hypnosis for him as a process of absorption similar to what he's already doing, but with a different focus.
Asking for his permission to do the hypnosis session.

Mike: Okay.

Mike grants permission.

MDY: Feel okay about doing that?

Double-checking his agreement to be sure.

Mike: Yeah.

Mike reaffirms his permission.

MDY: Okay. What I'm going to do is just talk about some different ideas, different possibilities, there really isn't anything that you have to do, but what I hope will happen is that as you're listening to me and you start to get more absorbed in the things that I'm talking about, that it'll start to open up some different possibilities for you, different ways of responding, because as I said, it's not the world that's going to change. It's going to be your internal experience, how you respond to these things. So, if you feel okay about doing that, then I'd say just sit back in the chair, get yourself comfortable and, uh, let me introduce the idea of focusing to you. Alright?

Orienting him to what I will do and what he can expect from the experience.

Framing the goal as evolving possibilities for new responses to old triggers.

Orienting him to and engaging him in beginning the process of hypnosis.

Pause in the transcript to define my goals for my session with Mike

1. Establish rapport and a *therapeutic alliance*.
2. *Deframe* his viewpoint ("It's my past") and *reframe* the salient issue ("It's the need for an ability to ignore some negative feedback").
3. Encourage the development of a *discrimination strategy* ("What's worth listening to?").
4. At times of uncertainty, help Mike shift his focus to *future possibilities* rather than past abuse to guide his choices.
5. *Re-associate Mike to his family*, relating to them positively and with an absorption in the recognition that they are a realistic source of optimism and pride.
6. Introduce hypnosis and other focusing methods to Mike in a safe, non-threatening way, and encourage his further development of such skills as a means of *symptom management* and *personal empowerment*.
7. *Reinforce critical thinking* by addressing his global and dichotomous thinking as well as his pattern of personalization.

The hypnosis session (cont'd)

MDY: If, um, you're comfortable the way that you're sitting that's fine. What I'd suggest that you do is let your eyes close, take in a few deep breaths, and just orient yourself for a couple of minutes to the notion of absorbing yourself in a different way of thinking about your own experience. Now, you probably haven't thought about it this way before, but when you get absorbed in the past, the negative feelings of things that have gone on, you can get so aborbed in it that you really don't see other ways of thinking . . . other ways of feeling . . . but one of the things that's potentially valuable . . . about taking a few minutes to sit quietly the way you are now . . . is that it gives you the freedom to explore . . . other parts of yourself . . . you know that you're much, much more than your past, Mike . . . and that phrase of being much more than your past is going to surface at different times . . . in different places . . . but when I encourage you . . . to start thinking a little differently about yourself and your experience . . . and to go exploring within yourself . . . there are strengths that you have . . . that you used to cope . . . that you've used to build a different life for yourself . . . being married, having your own family . . . things that you have clearly left behind . . . now in this kind of an experience . . . where I invite you to step outside your usual experience of yourself . . . there are several things . . . that can be especially important . . . and it's for you to know that your internal experience is changeable . . . and of course

Beginning the hypnotic induction— a typical conversational approach to induction.

Providing a general framework for the purpose of the process to enhance motivation to participate. Feeding back how he has used this process of absorption to stay stuck, but suggesting he can now use it to move forward. This is termed "utilization."

Suggesting that through this process he can discover relevant learnings, insights.

Refuting his global self-definition of essentially being his past and encouraging a more liberating—and accurate—view that he is *more* than just his history to use as a guide.

Seeking to *amplify his strengths*— philosophically and pragmatically a different approach than striving to "shrink" pathology. Encouraging differentiation (thus compartmentalization) from his family of origin. Solutions typically lie outside the boundaries of usual awareness.

Encouraging an unstable attributional style through the recognition that his experience is change-you'll notice that first in superficial ways . . . breathing slowing down . . . muscles getting more relaxed . . . mind wandering less and less . . . and little by little as the momentum builds . . . and you start to discover yourself . . . places and things that feel good to you . . . situations even memories that you've forgotten about that were quite nice . . . the good people that you've met along the way . . . people that went out of their way to do something nice for you . . . small things that you'd forgotten about . . . and little by little . . . the reality of what I mean when I say that you're more than your past . . . can start to drift into your awareness . . . you have goals . . . ways that you want the future to be different than the past . . . ways that you want to be able to connect with your wife, your kids . . . ways that you want to evolve friendships with people . . . and all the while knowing that it's the things that you say to yourself . . . through your thoughts . . . that make all the difference . . . in how you feel . . . now certainly you know that your mind is capable of generating lots of different things . . . audio clips and video clips . . . from different life experiences . . . but it's so interesting when you're in a more comfortable state of mind to realize . . . that those are things that can just drift past and never really stick to you . . . things that can just float by . . . that you never latch onto or give time to . . . and when I said everyone has the voices . . . what's interesting is how they can grow quiet . . . how they can become easy to ignore . . . how other aspects of your experience can take over . . .

able, not fixed.
Suggesting hypnotic responses as evidence of malleability of experience.

Refuting his global perception that his whole life has been bad by reminding him of positive experiences he's had but neglected to keep in his awareness.

Further encouraging Mike to no longer define himself by his past.

Encouraging a future orientation.
Positive associational suggestions to his wife and children.
Positive associational suggestions to having a social life and support network.

Extending the positive interactions to include those with himself.

Acknowledging his mind is capable of generating flashback images and memories, but suggesting that he can now look at them as intellectual curiosities at most, but are generally uninteresting enough to give much time or thought to.

Suggesting diminished intrusiveness of the past and a refocus on other things more enjoyable.

There are already things you've done, Mike, that you wouldn't have predicted from your past . . . and it's easy to appreciate that . . . on impersonal levels as well as personal ones . . . A hundred years ago nobody would have predicted space shuttles and space stations . . . things change . . . A hundred years ago nobody would have predicted paved roads everywhere in this country . . . or flying around the world in a matter of hours . . . and, of course, what I'm really saying is for you to use your past to predict the future . . . becomes more and more difficult . . . as you begin to fill your future with more things that remind you . . . that you're more than that . . . and it's literally as if a wall is built . . . between what you're experiencing now . . . and what you'll experience tomorrow . . . and what you experienced before . . . and whether you use the actual image of a wall to separate the past from present or the present from future or you use some other divider . . . all I know is . . . the things that have gone before . . . have increasingly less and less influence . . . on the choices that you make today . . . tomorrow . . . all of your tomorrows . . . I want you to notice . . . your breathing has slowed, Mike . . . muscle tone is more relaxed . . . to get absorbed in a comfortable way . . . to know you can go inside yourself and find good experiences . . . simple pleasures . . . the look . . . on your child's face . . . when you do something funny and unexpected . . . the simple things that remind you . . . of the extraordinary range of feelings you're capable of . . . perceptions you're ca-

Introducing the notion that the past is not an accurate predictor of the future, reinforcing the worthiness of a future orientation rather than a past one.
Metaphors describing contexts in which past did not predict future.

Suggesting as his orientation becomes more future focused, it will be much easier to detach from the past in positive ways.
The concrete imagery of a wall to use as a vehicle for encouraging the ability to compartmentalize his experience of the past from the present and future.

Encouraging Mike to rely less on the past to guide him and more on what he wants to have happen in his life.

"Trance ratifications . . ." (i.e., feedback to Mike he is succeeding in his participation as a means to reinforce responsiveness).
Expanding Mike's ability to get internally absorbed to include positive things since previously his internal absorption has been unilaterally negative . . . Indirectly suggesting he can use humor with his children as a means for demonstrating his enjoyment of them, crucial to their well-being. Reaffirming he is capable

pable of . . . understandings that you're capable of . . . and to slowly but steadily build a wall around what was . . . in order to create an endless array of possibilities . . . for what can be . . . and in the same way that I say . . . you're more than your past . . . I also want to remind you . . . the future hasn't happened yet . . . now you've noticed some shifts . . . even in the way your body feels . . . and perhaps even in your thoughts and perceptions as well . . . I really won't know until you're describing those understandings to me . . . in a little while . . . .but here's an experience that you allowed . . . because you trusted yourself in this very new situation with me,who you've never met before . . . you trusted yourself to deal with whatever I might say or do . . . you trusted yourself to deal with the spontaneity . . . the unexpected . . . .and that's an important thing, Mike . . . because there doesn't have to be trust out in the world . . . or predictability out in the world . . . or even safety out in the world . . . there only has to be your internal awareness . . . that you can deal with it . . . as someone wise once said . . . that the best way to predict the future is to create it . . . and with every interaction that you have with your own family . . . the one that you've created . . . you have an opportunity . . . to do things better . . . you have an opportunity to discover . . . what's right about you . . . and so, at this point . . . take a moment just to review different things that I've said . . . your reactions . . . the things that you can take with you from this experience . . . that you can really use . . . and if you find yourself remember-

of generating more than just negative feelings, particularly when he has "walled off" the past's ability to intrude.

Refocusing him on the hopefulness of his future in light of the fact that he can make new choices that will yield different consequences.
Associating a suggested change in his perceptions to the visible changes already established in his body.

Introducing the notion that there need not be predictability in the world or security in the world (indirectly commenting on the triggers for his traumatic memories); by re-associating him to the idea that he is resourceful and strong he can evolve the ability to deal with things spontaneously and evolve self-trust, a core component of self-esteem.

Empowering Mike to be proactive in creating a good life for himself.
Re-associating him to his family and the sense of responsibility he should feel to make his wife and children safe from his depression by engaging positively with them and presenting them—and himself—with what's good, strong, and healthy about him.
Moving towards the hypnosis session's closure, and so encouraging Mike to do whatever additional processing of salient learnings he might wish to do.

ing . . . that there are a lot of different ways of responding . . . to voices from the past . . . from turning down the volume button . . . to picturing a barking dog tied to a tree and just walking right past it . . . or the ever popular therapist response, "Thanks for sharing!" . . . or any options you generate . . . .that make it abundantly clear . . . you don't have to listen . . . Take whatever time you want to, Mike, to process your thoughts . . . feelings . . . reactions . . . Take a moment to consolidate . . . absorb the deeper implications . . . and then when you feel like you're ready to and want to . . . you can start the process of reorienting yourself . . . reconnecting with this environment and me . . . letting your eyes open whenever you're ready . . . take your time . . .

Post-hypnotic suggestion for integrating and applying the notion of responding differently to the traumatic memories and inner critic.

Permissive suggestions for closure.

Permissive suggestions for disengagement.

Post-hypnosis session discussion

Commentary

(Pause as Mike reorients and repositions himself)

Hi. How are you doing?

Reconnecting.

Mike: Good.

MDY: You want to tell me about it?

Asking for feedback, critical to identify and correct any possible misinterpretations and to reinforce correct ones.

Mike: I saw a lot of things. That I'm capable of feelings . . . That I've used talents that I thought I didn't have, but I have.

Clear statements he is able to start redefining himself now.

MDY: Were you thinking of specific examples? Or, just a general awareness?

If he had specifics, I'd have wanted to reinforce them.

Mike: Just general. Yeah.

Just a global sense Mike has.

MDY: And how did that feel?

Tying his emotional state to the quality of his perceptions.

Mike: It felt good.

The general sense of well-being typically experienced during and after hypnosis.

MDY: It did?

Mike: Yeah.

MDY: Good.

Mike: It felt real good.

MDY: Good.

Acknowledging and reinforcing Mike's good feelings.

Mike: Um, almost like I could imagine, like, a wilted flower. But I could imagine, just, even though things have got me down, that I am capable of standing up. Um, the other thing that I realized was that I'm limiting myself . . . to everything. Whether it's work or, you know, um . . . I also noticed I processed real quick just different things that people have said over the past . . . but they *aren't* true. Um, I also, you know, like, saw my children, you know, and I realized I have a terrific influence over them. Whether it's positive or negative, I have that influence over 'em.

Mike's imagery of a fragile but resilient flower is an appropriate self-reference.
Mike feels empowered to fight back.

Mike insightfully realizes it isn't circumstances holding him back—it's himself.
Mike is showing his ability to "consider the source" rather than just believing what he hears.
Mike re-associated to his children and took in the notion that he is responsible for their well-being.

MDY: It's great that you realize that.

Reinforcing that very serious insight.

Mike: And, the thing that . . . the distance-wise, I kind of really focused on that for a minute. And I'm living in the past, I'm not living in the present. And so I'm not accepting things for what they are. I've already got 'em doomed before they start. I, uh . . .

Mike considers the effects he is having on his family and realizes he is hurting them through his preoccupation with the past.

Mike realizes he gets so wrapped up in his idea of how things should have been that he misses how they really can be.

MDY: A very important realization.

Reinforcing more optimistic appraisals.

Mike: And I understood about the walls, you know, uh, it's almost like doors and windows. I'm allowing, whether it's emotions but I pictured water coming through windows and doors.

Mike adapted and used the image of a wall as a vehicle for compartmentalizing. And, he takes responsibility for allowing it rather than seeing himself as a victim of it.

MDY: Mmm. That's a great image.

Reinforcing the appropriateness of his imagery.

Mike: And so, I'm the one that has to close these windows and doors. And . . . the other thing I saw was like, I pictured like when you're cold you get a blanket. It was real interesting . . . And I also realized I can be whoever I want to be or do whatever I want to do, you know.

Mike accepts he must be proactive in helping himself.

MDY: There will always be people who tell you you can't. What are you going to do?

Testing his vulnerability to others' negative feedback to see if there's a difference from before.

Mike: Well, what I realized or, had thought about was when I was talking about different abilities or things, I'm capable of making things happen on my own. And I've used that throughout my life, but never took the time to think about it.

Mike reaffirms his internal attribution that he is able to assert control over his life experiences.
A value of hypnosis is its creating a context for self-exploration and self-development.

MDY: Great. But my point about people are gonna tell you that you can't do what you want? I'm hoping your response will be some variation of, "Thanks for sharing!" (Mike laughs). Your own individual response that way, but to not take it in, because exactly of what you were saying about you're the one who makes it happen. So, you get to choose. YOU get to choose.

His response was tangential to my point about his reactivity in the past to others' negativity, so I repeat the question as to his current state of vulnerability to others and answer for him what I hope he will have internalized as a strategy.

Reinforcing an internal locus of control.

Mike: Right.

MDY: The fact that people throw stuff? So what?

Diminishing the impact of critical others.

Mike: But I have a choice to listen or not to listen. And so, I should . . . I need to take in the positive things and really process what people say in the sense, like, I can draw off things, you know, encouragement. But the funny thing is, and this is what I can't get over, it's like, I never took, not even five minutes to just . . . (exhales slowly and deliberately) relax. I kind of walk around stressed. I walk around . . . but for just, I don't know whether it was a minute, two minutes, three minutes, whatever it was, but I actually felt (again exhales slowly and deliberately) . . .

Mike states his perception that he now has a choice as to whether to listen, an obvious gain made from the session. He realizes also he can use the positive feedback to enhance himself.

Mike has been so absorbed in ruminations and his struggles just to cope that he has never had the experience of "stepping off the treadmill" long enough to see what else was possible. A primary benefit of hypnosis.

Evidence of time distortion and a nice nonverbal description of the positive feelings engendered through the process.

MDY: Could even see it in your body, as well as in your face.

Reinforcing the effects were dramatic and obvious.

Mike: (laughs) Yeah.

Mike enjoys that affirmation.

MDY: See, to me, that's an important thing for you to be able to spend time with yourself in a way where you like what's in there. Where you can go inside and say, "There's good stuff in there!"

I emphasize to Mike that his internal experience isn't all bad as he had believed—that he has good experiences he can focus on that will thereby enhance his quality of life.

Mike: Yeah.

Mike accepts that idea.

MDY: You know, I can run and play and do whatever I want inside my head and it doesn't really matter what's going on externally at those times.

Suggesting it is possible to dissociate from external factors (implying the flashback triggers), and maintain a sense of comfort despite them.

Mike: Right.

Mike accepts that notion.

MDY: That's what's rejuvenating, that's what's replenishing, that's what highlights for you exactly what I meant at the end when I talked about the range of things that you're capable of. And when you've got this much range to just stay right in one narrow band is certainly unnecessarily limiting.

Reinforcing the notion that you can be responsible for making yourself feel good by focusing on the things that are enjoyable, inspiring, and motivating.
Focusing on the negative is unnecessarily constrictive.

Mike: Yeah.

Mike accepts that notion.

MDY: And you seemed to get that.

Reinforcing his acceptance.

Mike: What come (sic) to mind is, I remember seeing on TV one time where somebody took a piece of paper and put a little dot, and said, "What do you see?" And you focused in on that little dot.

Mike offers an appropriate metaphor highlighting the same point, clearly indicating he grasps the message about subjective perception.

MDY: Yeah. Yeah. So you're saying it is all about perception, and it seems like you got that . . .

Reinforcing his understanding the point.

Mike: Yeah.

MDY: . . . Which is great. Is that the kind of experience . . . uh, given that it was your first time with it and you did this well, um, something that you'd be interested in pursuing?

Indirectly suggesting he continue with developing his hypnotic ability since he so clearly benefited from applying it.

Mike: Oh, yes.

Mike indicates his willingness.

MDY: I think it would be a good skill, a really good skill, for you to develop, and there are ways of doing that from uh, um, perhaps the counselor that you're working with can pick up and do these kinds of things with you. But, certainly there are, there's a world full of tapes, relaxation tapes, visualization tapes, guided imagery tapes. Those are great things. More importantly developing

Offering Mike ways to continue to develop his hypnotic skills.

the ability on your own. To be able to just sit down wherever you are, whether it's at work, or whatever, or even when you come home stressed, which is going to happen, and you don't want to take it out on your family, so you go spend ten minutes calming yourself down, where you can come back in and you feel great about being with them. And it shows. And it shows. And those are the things where you highlight to yourself over and over again, "I'm good! You know, I can do these things."

Reinforcing an internal locus of control.

Casually reminding him again to proactively insulate his family from his moods.

The emphasis is on *demonstrating* the pleasure in being with his family.

Encouraging positive re-self-definition.

Mike: Yeah.

MDY: You know, reinforce for yourself . . .

Mike: Right.

MDY: . . . that you're way past whatever was before. It's important.

Reinforcing Mike dissociating from his traumatic past.

Mike: Yeah. (Spontaneously starts to laugh).

Mike manifests obvious pleasure in his experience.

MDY: That's good?

Mike: I feel real good.

Spontaneously self-discloses his pleasure.

MDY: Well, that's good!

Mike: I do!

MDY: That's good.

Mike: I'm, I'm, I need to step outside of what I'm in.

Mike realizes he is not a victim of circumstances.

MDY: Always. Always. I mean, to me one of the things that I hope will be a lasting thing from this session is,

I reinforce he has more control than he realizes, and that applies to what he thinks or tells himself as well.

that anything that floats through your brain isn't worth air time until you decide it's worth air time. I mean, your brain is capable of generating all kinds of junk. My brain is capable . . . I mean, the percentage of thoughts that I have that are actually worth paying attention to . . . I'd hate to put a number on it, but, put it this way, there's a lot of things that go floating through my mind that just aren't worth paying attention to . . .

Mike: Right.

MDY: . . . and that's true for any human being. Not every thought is golden, not every insight is meaningful and not every perception is worth following up on. And for you, who hasn't previously had a discrimination strategy, an ability to decide, "Is this worth focusing on, or isn't it?", where it's just been automatic for you to take it in and respond to it, I imagine it's been very, very stressful trying to keep up with all that—sort it and live with it.

Mike: It is.

MDY: And, um, what I'm hoping you now have as a choice is filtering out a whole bunch of stuff, spending time with yourself in a way that's comfortable, and just getting a charge out of the little things—the smiles, the touches, the sunsets, the . . . all the little things that make life good.

Mike: Yeah. And, it is good! You know, it is good, because . . .

Reinforcing the normalcy of having negative thoughts using myself as an example (since the therapeutic alliance is clearly a strong one.)

Acknowledging empathetically how much distress he had been in and implying those are now feelings of the past.

Summarizing the goals of the session.

Reinforcing the shift of focus to some of the pleasurable things in life.

Mike now redefines life as a positive experience.

MDY: Overall.

A reminder to consider all factors, but not to be all or none in his thinking.

Mike: Yeah, it is.

Mike accepts my feedback.

MDY: Overall. I mean, there's always crummy things that happen in life, but there's good things that happen, too.

I reinforce life is not all good or all bad, but model a reasonable conclusion that despite bad things happening, life can still be good.

Mike: Yeah.

Mike accepts that framing.

MDY: And it sounds, actually, like you've got some good things going.

Praising Mike for having done some things in life quite well.

Mike: I do.

Mike acknowledges that's true.

MDY: Yeah, it sounds it.

Mike: I do.

MDY: Enjoy it.

A final suggestion to notice more of what's right.

Mike: I will!

Mike accepts that suggestion.

MDY: Very nice to meet you, Mike.

A formal close to the session as we part amiably.

Mike: You, too.

MDY: Thanks.

(Session ends.)

Follow up to the session with Mike

Following our session, Mike and I had a few minutes to talk further about his experience. I encouraged Mike to continue working on some of the specific goals established in our session. I was especially emphatic about the value of being more goal-oriented, more well connected to his wife and children, and more aware of his own personal resources. I suggested he could focus more on these issues in his ongoing counseling.

Just a few weeks after the session, I contacted Mike via e-mail for some early feedback. His report was a very enthusiastic and positive one. He indicated he was feeling much better about himself and his life in general.

I didn't want to probe too much, choosing instead to simply reinforce his positive comments. So, I accepted his general description.

Five-month follow-up

Five months after our session, I again contacted Mike for some more specific follow-up information on his progress. Here is his verbatim, but lightly edited, reply:

> . . . *Things have gotten better. I'm not going to say overnight, but I am on the upswing. I have been able to sleep now straight through the night for five months now (Hooray!). Things are getting better with my wife. I listen to what she has to say and act on it (not that I never listened to her before but my head was not on straight). My marriage has improved (not that it was bad but I was occupied with other things and not giving her the attention she needed). I was constantly living in the past and there were blocks in our relationship and also with my children. It has not been easy by any means but it takes daily commitment . . .*
>
> *. . . Every day I am thankful to just get up. I refuse to be defeated by the past. Instead I look forward to conquer the future. I really feel as though I have been given a new lease on life. I do not want to waste it. Thanks again for everything.*
>
> *Mike*

A couple of months after that communication, Mike contacted me via e-mail with a request for specific advice. He said that he had continued to see his therapist intermittently following our session, but that each time he did so she wanted to focus on elaborating the details of his childhood abuse. When Mike told her he wanted to "move-on" from continuing to revisit and describe the abuse he suffered, she told him she thought that he was "avoidant." She declared his lack of full cooperation in her efforts to further explore the episodes of abuse was evidence of "denial."

Mike felt the problem was not his own denial, rather his therapist's rigid adherence to some treatment formula that he didn't find at all helpful. Mike asked me if it was reasonable of him to want to work with someone else instead, someone who might be more able to offer him helpful life skills as I had done. He said that no one else he had ever seen for therapy ever focused him on what's right about him or tried to teach him practical skills for managing his life and symptoms. Now that he had a glimpse of his ability to feel good, he wanted more opportunities to do so. I encouraged him to talk to his therapist again directly about his wish to move forward in his therapy with a focus on skill-building. Then, if his therapist seemed unable or unwilling to provide him with specific practical tools, he might decide to change therapists. I reminded him it's not his job to catch his therapist up to where he is.

Twenty-month follow-up

In August (2000), Mike spontaneously sent an e-mail to me describing his progress. Here is his message to me in lightly edited form:

> Hello, Mike,
>   Just wanted to drop you a note and tell you all that has happened to me. I have been faithful to the tapes (note: Mike refers to the audiotape program Focusing on Feeling Good I sent him as a thank-you gift following our session for his volunteering to work with me) . . . I really feel great. I've been sleeping the whole night through . . . I feel a lot of self-confidence, I feel myself getting stronger every day, relationships are getting better . . . but most of all I don't carry around all that hate and bitterness. I am glad to get up in the morning (except for going to work). I feel 100% better.
>   Thanks,
>   Mike

Final comments

I find it interesting that Mike was ready to "move on" in his life even though his therapist apparently was not. The tendency for clinicians to follow a protocol that mandates "focus on the past" or "focus on the pathology" is often at odds with the more sensible goal of "focus on the client" and "focus on amplifying strengths." Mike was highly focused on and responsive to me, clear evidence of his sincere desire to get some practical tools to help him cope with his abusive past and related depression. He didn't want or ask for a shoulder to cry on. In my experience working with depressed clients, that is highly typical. Despite those theorists who promote the misguided notions of "no pain, no gain" and instruct us to "look for the secondary gains," both the clinical efficacy research as well as my own clinical experience make it clear that depressed individuals are most likely to improve when they learn specific strategies for coping with and even transcending their symptom patterns. Blaming depressed people for their hopelessness and passivity by suggesting they are motivated to be that way is grossly unfair.

Mike hadn't spent any time looking for or defining his personal resources, nor had he been encouraged to do so in his previous therapy experiences. He hadn't considered how he might do a better job of "considering the source" when attacked or criticized. He hadn't fully realized the potential negative impact on his family of his withdrawal from them. He hadn't fully considered that the past didn't have to define him. These were all valuable contributions derived from this session. The "ripple effect" of improved sleep, something I should have but didn't ask about, is evident in his follow-up communication. The inclusion of the formal hypnosis session appears to have been invaluable to Mike in many different ways.

The reader will notice that as I introduced hypnosis to Mike, I didn't provide a lecture on hypnosis, I didn't ask him to sign a release or legal consent form, and I didn't lecture him about myths and misconceptions about hypnosis. I don't like the idea of a consent form for hypnosis any more than a consent form for a specific cognitive-behavioral therapy homework assignment or a recommended social skills reading. Hypnosis is part of therapy, and when the clinician and client agree to the goals and methods of treatment, the goal of informed consent is accomplished. The therapeutic alliance, key to the success of *every* form of therapy, is served by utilizing the client's capacity for absorption and directing it towards health. There is no magic in hypnosis, just a sensible use of communications that influences the client's experience respectfully.

There are many other things I would like to have had the chance to do with Mike. My compassion runs deep for people like Mike: People who are sensitive, caring, wanting to do what's right in life for themselves and their families, and who are suffering because they just don't know how *not* to.

Mike has my respect and gratitude.

Hypnosis and 9
suggestions
for prevention

One of the things most limiting the mental health profession's ability to curtail the rising rate of depression is its emphasis on what Martin Seligman once appropriately termed "mop-up" (Yapko, 1988). By "mop-up" he referred to the profession's self-imposed reactive position of striving to help people who are already depressed to somehow get over their depression. By the time someone comes in for the help of a health professional, he or she has already suffered whatever abuses, hurts, losses, and disappointments are a part of his or her unchangeable personal history. The clinician's prescribed role is to help the person find a way to live with whatever has happened as asymptomatically and as skillfully as possible.

Helping someone learn to manage his or her depression is only possible, of course, when the person even bothers to seek the help of a mental health professional, which we know occurs in only a minority of cases. Most people suffering depression never get the help they need (Gabbard, 1998). Clearly, maintaining a focus on "mop-up" and trying to do effective therapy one case at a time is becoming much too much like trying to empty the ocean with a (leaky) bucket. Depression sufferers will always need clinicians capable of providing effective therapy, of course, but clinicians can also do additional things to help on other levels.

We have learned a great deal about depression in the last couple of decades. It is at once a complex disorder, and paradoxically, a simple one. On the side of complexity, it affects every aspect of a person's life and has many contributing component factors all interwoven in often puzzling ways. And, on the side of simplicity, it most typically arises when people are devalued and poorly prepared to meet the demands of life. We can do much, much more with what we've learned than just react. We can expand our views of ourselves to see the opportunities for prevention.

Is it genuinely possible to move from a "mop-up" response to a preventive approach with depression? Is it possible both at individual and interpersonal (social) levels? The answer is yes to both questions.

The weakness in strength

People so often focus on their perceived shortcomings, or what they consider their weaknesses, as the vulnerable entry points for depression in
their lives. They are right to do so. But, their weaknesses are not the only
appropriate concern. It may require a slight shift in one's perspective to
also recognize that *one's strengths also represent one's potential vulnerabilities*. If one has health, one is vulnerable to disease. If one has a strong
marriage, one is vulnerable to the loss of the spouse. If one has a wonderful
job, one is vulnerable to losing it. (Consider as an example the demotivating
effects of managed care on once-happy independent clinicians whose vulnerability was in losing their professional freedom.) Thus, no one is immune to the problem of depression. The more one builds a solid life, the
more one has, the more one potentially has to lose if and when lightning
strikes.

As potentially depressing as this may sound, in fact there is a hopeful
message of prevention within the point. We as mental health professionals
can do much more to help people understand that depression isn't only
about hurtful life circumstances any more than it is only about brain chemistry. We can help people understand that life is filled with constant challenges to all of us to keep growing, keep transcending, and keep thinking
at least a step or two ahead of predictable problems. We can encourage
people to live up to higher standards and take the initiative to build better
lives.

Reconsidering the message we send

But, these aren't the usual messages the mental health profession spreads.
So, the drug companies usurp our ability to teach people what it means to
think about their lives and to behave with integrity by pushing them to
simply meet life's challenges chemically. The very medical model that holds
the rock-bottom lowest potential for preventing depression (after all, drugs
can *only* be prescribed after the depression appears) gets the greatest exposure until it's a noncritically accepted belief at a cultural level that depression is entirely about neurochemistry gone awry. It's more than that.

Biology matters, of course, and drugs are often a valuable treatment
tool for many individual depression sufferers. But, medicalizing depression promotes a misleading perspective with too much power to transmit a
wrong message. If the National Institute of Mental Health, the drug companies, and psychiatrists don't get away from pushing that one-dimensional
"neurochemical deficiency" sound byte, we will *all* pay the rising price in
human suffering. The strength of the medical model is its weakness when
it misleads people into thinking of depression as a disease to cure one pill
at a time.

Psychological approaches have a different set of vulnerabilities: downplaying biology despite the fact that there is lots of evidence that genes and biochemistry do, in fact, play pivotal roles in the onset and course of depression; overemphasizing everyone's right to be a victim of something or another; divisive internal bickering over whose therapy is better; and clinicians getting their benevolent missions hijacked by researchers who often seem to miss the vital differences between controlled clinical studies and real life *uncontrolled* clients. After all, clinicians can't reasonably be expected to function well in providing a high demand service while being bombarded with often unreasonable demands to follow arbitrary protocols while having to explain or defend themselves every step of the way. Research data are helpful in making informed decisions, but there is still no substitute for good clinical judgment. I hope this book serves to enhance clinical judgment.

Prevention at the individual client level

Throughout the therapy process, clinicians can strive to not only help the client manage depression, but prevent future episodes as well. (This is important to do, but is also "mop-up." Ideas regarding helping people *before* they become therapy clients will be discussed shortly.) The skills listed in Table 4 have all been highlighted throughout this book as vital skills for an individual to master if depression is to be managed and prevented.

Each of the skills listed in the table holds significant potential to reinforce the key learning that *one has to forever be responsible for monitoring and actively directing what goes on in one's head and heart.* Instead of reinforcing well-intended messages ("You have an inner sage with great wisdom") that can misdirect people into developing an unwarranted noncritical self-trust, we can reinforce that although we are all capable of great things, we are also capable of terrible things. What we choose, passively or actively, will determine how we experience ourselves and how we will affect others.

TABLE 4. Skills to Manage and Prevent Depression

- Recognize and tolerate ambiguity
- Distinguish facts from inferences
- Learn impulse control and cause–effect thinking
- Generate multiple viewpoints
- Accept and utilize one's uniqueness
- Manage and prevent stress
- Build and maintain good relationships
- Be action oriented
- Focus on solutions, problem-solving
- Distinguish between contexts and strive to adapt accordingly
- Develop foresight

Hypnosis: Focus on prevention

It is possible at any time in the course of therapy to introduce the client to concepts of prevention simply by pointing out how each new skill being taught can have protective (risk-reducing) abilities in a variety of life contexts. Prevention can also be emphasized at the close of treatment, with a summation of key points made and key skills learned and how they can be proactively used.

The following is a transcript of a hypnosis session that can serve as an example of a prevention-focused session. It is the final session of the *Focusing on Feeling Good* program (See Appendix B):

Introduction

I want to address directly what I consider to be some of the most important implications of everything that I've talked about, both during the hypnosis sessions as well as the introductions to each of them. One of the unfortunate things about my job as a clinical psychologist is that most often I am doing work that can only be described as "mop-up." So often by the time people come to see me for therapy, they have already experienced bad times, hard times, trauma, neglect, abuse, and all the other countless evils of the world we live in that can negatively affect individual lives. The fact that bad things or bad times have already happened often lead people into therapy in order to try to come to terms in some way with what has happened. That is undoubtedly an appropriate and good use of therapy, but that is still a "mop-up" process. To me, one of the most important aspects of knowing everything that I have learned about depression over the last quarter century is that depression experts now know what the major risk factors are for depression. We know a lot about who is likely to get depressed and under what circumstances. Here is an opportunity for you to learn something about *prevention*.

The truth of the matter is, bad times happen to *everyone*. But, not everyone sinks into depression as a result. Through these tapes and, hopefully, through my writings, you've now been exposed to a comprehensive set of tools for understanding your own patterns for responding to life experiences and the vulnerabilities associated with those patterns. From the insights that you have hopefully gained from reading *Breaking the Patterns of Depression* and listening to these tapes, you've had many opportunities to realize that you can actually take steps, *significant* steps, in the direction of prevention of later episodes. If I had my way, I wouldn't want you to ever experience depression again. Although I can't stop bad or hurtful things from happening in people's lives, I can certainly strive to make sure, and so can you, that you're better equipped to deal with the difficulties that life throws at each of us. I can try to encourage you to be more critical as a thinker, and I can attempt to help you recognize the nasty trap of just believing whatever happens to fly through your mind. You're capable of having all kinds of thoughts, but not all of them are going to be sensible and rational, or well-thought out. Some of them can be quite distorted, and even depressing. That is true for you, me, and *everyone*. And, if you've learned *anything* from reading my book and listening to these tapes, it's that you will have the life-long obligation to yourself to continually monitor your thoughts, correct them when they are distorted—which means first recognizing that they are distorted—and, beyond thinking more clearly, it also means using clear thinking to have a better sense of who you are as a person and what your contribution is to the ongoing network of people that you are involved with—be it your family, your friends, or co-workers at your job. Being aware of yourself means defining and *accepting* the different dimensions of who you are and what your life is about, being aware that your feelings are just one part of you. You're more than your mood, you're more than your depression, you're more than your job, you're more than your history, you're more than your marriage. You're more than *any* one part of you. And what more are you, but the ability to think ahead, and to create life circumstances in your future that can bring out the best in you in the years to come? I hope you are becoming more able to recognize that the things that you think and feel may actually have little bearing on what is really objectively true. I also hope you now recognize how important it is to be a good problem-solver, because as one realist put it, "Life is one damn thing after another." We *all* smile through our tears, and often wonder how we can make it through the next five minutes.

It's the goal of this session to help you integrate at a deep level all that you've learned, and make good sense of all that you will continue to learn through new experiences, new places that you will go and new people you will meet, things that you will read, and things that you will hear. I hope you'll always strive to seek out new growth experiences, and continually challenge yourself to grow in new and meaningful ways. There is *so* much that is possible in life. Keep the goals in mind of learning to think preventively and learning to eventually master the vulnerabilities of having a human body and a human mind, with all its strengths and weaknesses and all its remarkable potentials.

Hypnosis session

And so, I'd like you to arrange yourself in a position that is comfortable . . . that you can sit in for a while . . . easily . . . and effortlessly . . . one in which you can be comfortable and yet still remain alert enough . . . to focus on the meaningful things that I'm talking about . . . to absorb their deeper meaning . . . and their deeper value . . . in terms of your overall life experience . . . And when you're ready to begin to focus yourself . . . you can begin by taking in a few deep, relaxing breaths . . . breathing slowly . . . feeling the rise of your chest . . . as you inhale . . . slowly . . . and deeply . . . and feeling it gently fall . . . as you gradually . . . exhale . . . and each breath . . . in . . . and out . . . can relax you . . . calm you . . . reacquaint you . . . with the deeper parts of yourself . . . that you sometimes get too busy to notice . . . You know . . . and I know . . . it's very easy . . . to get caught up in day-to-day living . . . there is always so much to do . . . so many obligations to attend to . . . But, certainly . . . one of the things that you've now learned . . . is that unless you deliberately take the time for yourself . . . stress can build . . . and demands can be burdensome . . . and life can seem overwhelming . . . but now you have acquired a solution . . . many solutions, actually . . . Many different strategies for managing your life well . . . that you've learned along the way now . . . You've learned that you can take time . . . quiet time . . . to be with yourself in a way . . . through your thoughts . . . that's helpful . . . and focused on . . . solutions . . . not just problems . . . And you've also learned that you don't have to go dredging up the past . . . in order to move forward into the future . . . you've learned a lot about learning to think . . . in terms of what you *want* to have happen . . . and what the steps are . . . that you can take to bring those good and important things about. You've learned that taking action is vital . . . *Action* . . . not just thinking . . . not just contemplating . . . not just analyzing . . . because many times a day . . . you come to a fork in the road . . . and now you . . . can find it so much more automatic to . . . experiment with behavior and try something new . . . not just anything . . . but something well-thought out and planned . . . perhaps something you've observed in others that works well . . . and so you continue to train yourself to think in terms of what is possible . . . and what is realistic . . . solutions. And so, day-by-day . . . all the things that you've learned . . . about the differences between . . . what is really true . . . versus your own subjective interpretations . . . that has led you to be more skilled at looking for evidence . . . and asking questions . . . and gathering relevant information . . . and making forward-looking decisions. *These* are many of the skills that you need to live life well . . . and you're learning them and mastering them . . . and you can feel good about that. What you've been learning . . . are skills in thinking . . . skills that are important for relating to others . . . skills in knowing yourself . . . and appreciating yourself. You're made up of so many different parts . . . and what I think you're now in a comfortable position to appreciate . . . is that each part of you . . . is valuable some place. And with an eye on prevention . . . it's important to know all your different parts . . . the parts that like to work and those that like to play . . . those that like to be alone and like to be with others . . . the parts that like to be passive and the parts that like to be active . . . thinking parts and feeling parts . . . parts that like things to be simple and parts that enjoy when things are a little bit complicated . . . parts that think about the past and parts that think about the future . . . I can name dozens . . . maybe hundreds of parts of you. And what you've learned . . . is that to live life well . . . it's a matter of using the right part for the job. To be able to tap into and make good use of the part of you that likes to work . . . when it's time to work . . . is a powerful match . . . and to be able to set aside work and get in touch with the part of you that likes to play when it's a day off . . . can allow for some wonderful relaxation and recreation. And to be able to tap into the social part of you when you're with friends or family or colleagues . . . can lead you to genuinely enjoy others . . . and they'll know that simply by being with you. Or, to be able to tap into the part of you that enjoys being alone . . . when you have time to yourself where you can feel comfortable . . . just by yourself. And so what does it take to live well and happily? . . . I think it takes being able to move from . . . situation to situation . . . knowing your parts . . . and using your parts . . . skillfully . . . always having the question in the background . . . of 'what am I wanting to experience?' And to be able to think preventively . . . you can use your ability that is ever-growing in sophistication . . . of being able to think ahead . . . and to choose paths . . . that take you where you want to go in the long-run . . . and not just the path that is easy and familiar . . . but eventually takes you to someplace you really don't want to go . . . And it can really be quite comforting . . . to realize . . . at a very deep level within yourself . . . that you can be so . . . tuned in . . . to life . . . and what allows you to experience life as a . . . wonderful adventure. And to carry with you . . . a strong, enduring sense of optimism . . . that can insulate you against temporary hard times . . . a deep recognition that . . . hard times don't last . . . but *you* will. And to continually seek out new growth experiences . . . you can continue learning . . . continue experiencing . . . continue observing . . . and all the principles of effective living . . . come down to . . . you knowing . . . what it means to be powerful . . . in your ability to choose. You have the ability to choose . . . *you* get to choose . . . so much of what happens . . . like where you are and what you are doing. And one of the preventive tools that you have now acquired . . . is being able to recognize ever more efficiently . . . what you are in control of . . . and what you are responsible for . . . and likewise . . . what you're not. That's really quite a relief . . . to be able to keep moving forward with your life . . . seeking out new challenges . . . rising to them . . . always bringing out the best . . . of your deeper self . . . through the life that you lead. And so, as you move into the future . . . you can take great comfort in knowing . . . that you carry with you . . . many wonderful skills and resources . . . the things that you've learned and experienced. Use these resources . . . to your own best advantage . . . use your power. And so . . . take whatever time you want to process your thoughts and feelings . . . and integrate deeply whatever you need to or want to in order to start to bring this experience to a close. And then when you're ready . . . you can start the process of slowly reorienting yourself . . . at a rate that is gradual and comfortable . . . so that when you're ready . . . you can reorient yourself fully . . . and open your eyes . . . fully alert and refreshed . . . feeling good . . . feeling good. And for all your life, keep focusing on feeling good . . .

Discussion of the session

The introduction to the formal hypnosis session draws the client's attention to key points developed throughout the therapy, reinforcing them. The goal of the session is clearly defined as "integration." Perhaps the most important part of the session, though, is the emphasis on recognizing the value of all of one's "parts." It is respectful and validating to affirm that each person is comprised of many different components, namely, facets to one's being. I have often emphasized in this book that so often the problems people experience are problems in finding and matching the "best part" for the demands of the context. So, as examples, people focus internally when they'd do better to notice more of what's going on around them; they focus on their own personal needs when they'd do better to notice and fulfill their obligations to others; and they focus on their feelings when they'd do better to respond rationally. This session provides the preventive reminder that "you are more than any one part of yourself, and all of your parts are valuable someplace, some time." The opportunity for prevention comes with the ability to choose wisely which aspects of Self to engage with from context to context.

Prevention at the interpersonal (social) level

I know that most of the individuals reading this book will do so for the hypnotic strategies presented here for treating individuals, and not because they either want to or have time to be social activists rallying against depression. But, I can't resist offering just a few ideas of things almost any clinician can do that can help nip depression in the bud well before someone becomes a distressed therapy client.

Teach foresight

The very antithesis of the popular, "Be fully present in the moment" philosophy involves first modifying the message slightly to encourage discrimination skills by saying, "Be fully present in the moment *sometimes*." Next, the emphasis on teaching cause–effect thinking is critical in therapy, in families, in schools, and in communities. So much misery could be prevented with simple foresight, and the increased discipline that can come from "knowing where it leads and if you don't like it making sure you don't go there."

Treat spouses and families

The statistics on distressed marriages, divorce, children of divorce, and higher risks for depression in children of depressed parents highlight several key recommendations. First, if you see a depressed adult, and this person is married and/or has children, please at least *consider seeing the spouse and children*. They are highly likely to be suffering, too, and can be helped *before* the contagion of depression engulfs them. Second, *if you really want to help children, help their parents*. A depressed parent (or two) so significantly increases the risk for depression in his/her/their children that just treating the child alone in such cases is probably not enough.

A preventive opportunity exists even when you don't see the family as clients when you simply take family members into account in your individual therapies. Knowing there are others that the individual client regularly interacts with and influences provides a chance to keep the contagion of depression in check.

Teach children

The ability to prevent depression on a bigger scale has been well demonstrated. Martin Seligman's book *The Optimistic Child*, and John Gottman's book *Raising an Emotionally Intelligent Child* both represent research-based, clinically relevant implementations of preventive programs. Teaching children in school settings, since we can't yet rely on families to do it, how to think and problem solve holds the best potential of all for preventing making other life-ruining, depressing mistakes. But, we can't do that if we're simply going to run schools as drug screening centers. Peter Breggin, M.D., was quite right when he wrote in *Reclaiming Our Children*, that, "Schools are already comparable to mental hospitals in which the staff keeps a constant eye out for children who need medication . . . We end up sweeping them under the drug rug, rather than attending to their individual needs . . . We have turned to medicating them into silence so that we don't have to deal with their pain" (Breggin, 1999, p. 38). Paying more and better attention to our kids can go a long way.

The United States consumes 75% of the world's Prozac, and 90% of the world's Ritalin. How can we justify striving to help people chemically adjust themselves to often crazy circumstances instead of encouraging them to be social activists in changing their own lives? James Hillman and Michael Ventura make the point convincingly in their excellent book, *We've Had a Hundred Years of Psychotherapy, and the World's Getting Worse.*

Teach people

The campaigns to educate people aren't working very well. Telling people the seemingly optimistic message, "We can cure the disease of depression so go get the help you need" isn't very effective in getting more people the help they need. Depressed people are still going largely untreated. Why? I think it's partly because people don't buy the viewpoint and see themselves as "diseased." I think they see themselves as overworked, stressed, harried, rushed, and hassled, but *not* as diseased. Feeling overwhelmed just doesn't strike most people as a basis for taking medications or talking to a therapist. We need more clinicians going on television, writing internet postings and newspaper and magazine articles about practical ways of meeting life's demands without succumbing to harmful states of mind. We need clinicians talking publicly in every visible place about people feeling overwhelmed and where those feelings can lead if they aren't well addressed. We need them talking sensibly about things people can actively do to help themselves that can forestall matters going from bad to worse. We need repeated media exposure to share insights about depression with the millions of people who most need the information who will never see the inside of a clinician's office.

Final thoughts

The growing problem of depression, a highly treatable disorder, is telling us we're doing something wrong. We clearly need to do something different.

The clinical hypnosis community—the researchers and clinicians—can have much more *to* say and also much more of *a* say about the future direction of both treatment and prevention. But, the voice of the hypnosis community has been strangely silent. (In fact, the first formal research study involving hypnosis in the treatment of depression I am aware of is about to get underway as I write this (Spiegel & Butler, in progress). Obviously, much more research needs to be done.) Experts in hypnosis already understand the power of communication, the power of metaphor, and the power of information. What do we want to tell people? What must we use our skills with words to go out and do in order to make a positive difference?

Above all else, I believe we have to encourage people to develop a sense of *vision*. We have to emphasize longer term thinking and planning over merely "living in the moment." We have to emphasize the *optimism* that comes from our knowing that people can change for the better. We have to catalyze an awareness that depression is about more than biochemistry—that it involves our relationships with our Self and others. We have to curtail the luxury of arguing over whose style of hypnosis is best or whose notion of the unconscious is more appealing and start better addressing the needs of all those who are suffering at this very moment.

Our work is cut out for us.

References

Ablon, J., & Jones, E. (1999). Psychotherapy process in the National Institute of Mental Health treatment of depression collaborative research program. *Journal of Consulting and Clinical Psychology, 67,* 64–75.

Abramson, L., Seligman, M., & Teasdale, J. (1985). Learned helplessness in humans: Critique and reformulation. In J. Coyne (Ed.), *Essential papers on depression* (pp. 259–301). New York: New York University Press.

Altamura, A., & Percudani, M. (1993). The use of antidepressants for long-term treatment of recurrent depression: Rationale, current methodologies, and future directions. *Journal of Clinical Psychiatry, 54*(Suppl. 8), 1–23.

American Psychiatric Association. (1994). *Diagnostic and statistical manual of mental disorders (4th ed.).* Washington, DC: American Psychiatric Association.

American Psychiatric Association. (1993). Practice guidelines for major depressive disorder in adults. Washington, DC: American Psychiatric Association Press.

American Psychological Association, Division of Psychological Hypnosis. (1993). Hypnosis. *Psychological Hypnosis, 2,* 3.

American Psychological Association, Division of Psychological Hypnosis. (1985). *A general definition of hypnosis and a statement concerning its application and efficacy* (Report). Washington, DC: American Psychological Association.

American Psychological Association, Division of Psychological Hypnosis. (1999). *Policy and Procedures Manual, 4–5.* Washington, DC: American Psychological Association.

Antonuccio, D., Danton, W., & DeNelsky, G. (1994). Psychotherapy for depression: No stronger medicine. *Scientist Practitioner, 4,* 2–18.

Antonuccio, D., Danton, W., & DeNelsky, G. (1995). Psychotherapy versus medication for depression: Challenging the conventional wisdom with data. *Professional Psychology: Research and Practice, 26,* 574–585.

Aronson, E. (1999). *The social animal* (8th ed.). San Francisco: W. H. Freeman.

Azar, B. (1997a). Environment is key to serotonin levels. *APA Monitor, 28,* 26–29.

Azar, B. (1997b). Nature, nurture: Not mutually exclusive. *APA Monitor, 28,* 1–28.

Barber, J. (1991). The locksmith model: Accessing hypnotic responsiveness. In S. Lynn & J. Rhue (Eds.), *Theories of hypnosis: Current models and perspectives* (pp. 241–274). New York: Guilford.

Barber, T. (2000). A deeper understanding of hypnosis: Its secrets, its nature, its essence. *American Journal of Clinical Hypnosis, 42,* 208–272.

Basco, M. (1999). *Never good enough: Freeing yourself from the chains of perfectionism.* New York: Simon & Schuster.

Beach, S., Sandeen, E., & O'Leary, K. (1990). *Depression in marriage.* New York: Guilford.

Beach, S., Whisman, M., O'Leary, K. (1994). Marital therapy for depression: Theoretical foundations, current status, and future directions. *Behavior Therapy, 25*, 345–371.

Beck, A. (1987). Cognitive therapy. In J. Zeig (Ed.), *The evolution of psychotherapy* (pp. 149–163). New York: Brunner/Mazel.

Beck, A. (1997). Cognitive therapy: Reflections. In J. Zeig (Ed.), *The evolution of psychotherapy: The third conference* (pp. 55–64). New York: Brunner/Mazel.

Beck, A., Brown, G., Berchick, R., Stewart, B., & Steer, R. (1990). Relationship between hopelessness and ultimate suicide: A replication with psychiatric outpatients. *American Journal of Psychiatry, 147*, 190–195.

Beck, A., Rush, A., Shaw, B., & Emery, G. (1979). *Cognitive therapy of depression.* New York: Guilford.

Begley, S. (1996, October 14). Born happy? *Newsweek,* vol. CXXXII, 78–80.

Bell, A. (1997). *The quickening.* New Orleans, LA: Paper Chase Press.

Billings, A., & Moos, R. (1985). Psychosocial theory and research on depression: An integrative framework. In J. Coyne (Ed.), *Essential papers on depression* (pp. 331–365). New York: New York University Press.

Blatt, S., Zuroff, D., Bondi, C., Sanislow III, C., & Pikonis, P. (1998). When and how perfectionism impedes the brief treatment of depression: Further analyses of the National Institute of Mental Health Treatment of Depression Collaborative Research program. *Journal of Consulting and Clinical Psychology, 66*, 423–428.

Blumenthal, S. J., & Kupfer, D. J. (Eds.). (1990). *Suicide over the life cycle.* Washington, DC: American Psychiatric Press,

Breggin, P. (1999). *Reclaiming our children: A healing plan for a nation in crisis.* Cambridge, MA: Perseus Publishing.

Brown, D. (1992). Clinical hypnosis research since 1986. In E. Fromm & M. Nash (Eds.), *Contemporary hypnosis research* (pp. 427–458). New York: Guilford.

Buchanan, G., Rubenstein, C., & Seligman, M. (1999, December 21). Physical health following a cognitive-behavioral intervention. [On-line]. *Prevention & Treatment, 2*, Article 10. Available: http://journals.apa.org/prevention/volume2/pre0020010a.html

Chaves, J. (1993). Hypnosis in pain management. In J. Rhue, S. Lynn, & I. Kirsch (Eds.), *Handbook of clinical hypnosis* (pp. 511–532). Washington, DC: American Psychological Association.

Cheek, D., & Lecron, L. (1968). *Clinical hypnotherapy.* New York: Grune & Stratton.

Clarkin, J., Pilkonis, P., & Magrude, K. (1996). Psychotherapy of depression. *Archives of General Psychiatry, 53*, 717–723.

Coe, W. (1993). Expectations and hypnotherapy. In J. Rhue, S. Lynn, & I. Kirsch (Eds.), *Handbook of clinical hypnosis* (pp. 73–93). Washington, DC: American Psychological Association.

Coe, W. & Sarbin, T. (1991). Role theory: Hypnosis from a dramaturgical and narrational perspective. In S. Lynn & J. Rhue (Eds.), *Theories of hypnosis: Current models and perspectives* (pp. 303–323). New York: Guilford.

Cohen, D. (1994). *Out of the blue: Depression and human nature.* New York: Norton.

Crasilneck, H., & Hall, J. (1985). *Clinical hypnosis: Principles and applications* (2nd ed.). New York: Grune & Stratton.

Crawford, H., & Barabasz, A. (1993). Phobias and intense fears: Facilitating their treatment with hypnosis. In J. Rhue, S. Lynn, & I. Kirsch (Eds.), *Handbook of clinical hypnosis* (pp. 311–338). Washington, DC: American Psychological Association.

Cronkite, R., & Moos, R. (1995). Life context, coping processes, and depression. In E. Beckham & W. Leber (Eds.), *Handbook of depression* (pp. 569–587). New York: Guilford.

Culbertson, F. (1997). Depression and gender. *American Psychologist, 52,* 25–31.

de Shazer, S. (1985). *Keys to solutions in brief therapy.* New York: Norton.

de Shazer, S. (1991). *Putting difference to work.* New York: Norton.

de Shazer, S., & Yapko, M. (1998, August). *Conversation Hour on Brief Therapy.* Paper presented at the Brief Therapy: Lasting Impressions Conference. New York, NY.

DeBattista, C., & Schatzberg, A. (1995). Somatic therapy. In I. Glick (Ed.), *Treating depression* (pp. 153–181). San Francisco: Jossey-Bass.

DeLeon, P., & Wiggins, J. (1996). Prescription privileges for psychologists. *American Psychologist, 51,* 225–229.

Depression Guideline Panel. (1993). *Clinical practice guideline number 5: Depression in primary care. Volume 2: Treatment of major depression.* (AHCPR Publication 93-0550). Rockville, MD: U.S. Dept. of Health and Human Services, Agency for Health Care Policy and Research.

Dobson, K. (1989). A meta-analysis of the efficacy of cognitive therapy for depression. *Journal of Consulting and Clinical Psychology, 57,* 414–419.

Dubovsky, S. (1997). *Mind-body deceptions: The psychosomatics of everyday life.* New York: Norton.

Eimer, B. (2000). Clinical applications of hypnosis for brief and efficient pain management psychotherapy. *American Journal of Clinical Hypnosis, 43,* 17–40.

Ellis, A. (1994). *Reason and emotion in psychotherapy.* New York: Birch Lane Press.

Ellis, A. (1997). The evolution of Albert Ellis and Rational Emotive Behavior Therapy. In J. Zeig (Ed.), *The evolution of psychotherapy: The third conference* (pp. 69–78). New York: Brunner/Mazel.

Erickson, M., & Rossi, E. (1979). *Hypnotherapy: An exploratory casebook.* New York: Irvington Publishers.

Erickson, M., & Rossi, E. (1981). *Experiencing hypnosis: Therapeutic approaches to altered states.* New York: Irvington.

Evans, F. (2000). The domain of hypnosis: A multifactorial model. *American Journal of Clinical Hypnosis, 43,* 1–16.

Everson, S., Goldberg, D., Kaplan, G., Cohen, R., Pukkala, E., Tuomilehto, J., & Salonen, J. (1996). Hopelessness and risk of mortality and incidence of myocardial infarction and cancer. *Psychosomatic Medicine, 58,* 113–121.

Fava, G., Rafanelli, C., Grandi, S., Conti, S., & Belluardo, P. (1998). Prevention of recurrent depression with cognitive behavioral therapy. *Archives of General Psychiatry, 55,* 816–820.

Frankl, V. (1971). Determinism and humanism. *Humanitas, 7,* 23–36.

Frasure-Smith, N., Lesperance, F., & Talajic, M. (1993). Depression following myocardial infarction: Impact on 6 month survival. *Journal of the American Medical Association, 270,* 1819–1825.

Frauman, D., Lynn, S., & Brentar, J. (1993). Prevention and therapeutic management of "negative effects" in hypnotherapy. In J. Rhue, S. Lynn, & I. Kirsch (Eds.), *Handbook of clinical hypnosis* (pp. 95–120). Washington, DC: American Psychological Association.

Frischholz, E. (1998). Editorial. *American Journal of Clinical Hypnosis, 40,* 271–272.

Gabbard, G. (1998). The cost effectiveness of treating depression. *Psychiatric Annals, 28,* 98–103.

Giesler, R., & Swann, W. (1999). Striving for confirmation: The role of self-verification in depression. In T. Joiner & J. Coyne (Eds.), *The interactional nature of depression: Advances in interpersonal approaches* (pp. 189–217). Washington, DC: American Psychological Association.

Giles, T. (1993). *Handbook of effective psychotherapy*. New York: Plenum Press.

Gilligan, S. (1987). *Therapeutic trances: The cooperation principle in Ericksonian hypnotherapy*. New York: Brunner/Mazel.

Glass, R. (1999). Treating depression as a recurrent or chronic disease. *Journal of the American Medical Association, 281,* 1, 83–84.

Glassman, A., & Shapiro, P. (1998). Depression and the course of coronary artery disease. *American Journal of Psychiatry, 155,* 4–11.

Greenberg, P., Stiglin, L., Finkelstein, S., & Berndt, E. (1993). The economic burden of depression in 1990. *Journal of Clinical Psychiatry, 54,* 405–426.

Greenberger, D., & Padesky, C. (1995). *Mind over mood*. New York: Guilford.

Grinder, J., & Bandler, R. (1981). *Trance-formations: Neuro-Linguistic Programming and the structure of hypnosis*. Moab, UT: Real People Press.

Haley, J. (1973). *Uncommon therapy: The psychiatric techniques of Milton H. Erickson, M.D.* New York: Norton.

Hammen, C. (1999). The emergence of an interpersonal approach to depression. In T. Joiner & J. Coyne (Eds.), *The interactional nature of depression: Advances in interpersonal approaches* (pp. 21–35). Washington, DC: American Psychological Association.

Heim, S., & Snyder, D. (1991). Predicting depression from marital distress and attributional processes. *Journal of Marital and Family therapy, 17,* 67–72.

Hetherington, E., Bridges, M., & Insabella, G. (1998). What matters? What does not? Five perspectives on the association between marital transitions and children's adjustment. *American Psychologist, 53,* 167–184.

Hilgard, E. (1965). *Hypnotic susceptibility*. New York: Harcourt, Brace & World.

Hilgard, E. (1991). A neodissociation interpretation of hypnosis. In S. Lynn & J. Rhue (Eds.), *Theories of hypnosis: Current models and perspectives* (pp. 83–104). New York: Guilford.

Hirschfeld, R., Keller, M., Panico, S., Arons, B., Barlow, D., Davidoff, F., Endicott, J., Froom, J., Goldstein, M., Gorman, J., Guthrie, D., Marek, R., Maurer, T., Meyer, R., Phillips, K., Ross, J., Schwenk, T., Sharfstein, S., Thase, M., & Wyatt, R. (1997). The National Depressive and Manic-Depressive Association consensus statement on the undertreatment of depression. *Journal of the American Medical Association, 277,* 333–340.

Holahan, C., Moos, R., & Bonin, L. (1999). Social context and depression: An integrative stress and coping framework. In T. Joiner & J. Coyne (Eds.), *The interactional nature of depression: Advances in interpersonal approaches* (pp. 39–63). Washington, DC: American Psychological Association.

Jack, D. (1999). Silencing the self: Inner dialogues and outer realities. In T. Joiner & J. Coyne (Eds.), *The interactional nature of depression: Advances in interpersonal approaches* (pp. 221–246). Washington, DC: American Psychological Association.

Joiner, T., Coyne, J., & Blalock, J. (1999). On the interpersonal nature of depression: Overview and synthesis. In T. Joiner & J. Coyne (Eds.), *The interactional nature of depression: Advances in interpersonal approaches* (pp. 3–19). Washington, DC: American Psychological Association.

Just, N., & Alloy, L. (1997). The response styles theory of depression: Tests and an extension of the theory. *Journal of Abnormal Psychology, 106,* 221–229.

Kaelber, C., Moul, D., & Farmer, M. (1995). Epidemiology of depression. In E. Beckham & W. Leber (Eds.), *Handbook of depression* (pp. 3–35). New York: Guilford.

Kaminer, W. (1993). *I'm dysfunctional, you're dysfunctional.* New York: Vintage Books.

Kihlstrom, J. (1997). Convergence in understanding hypnosis? Perhaps, but not so fast. *International Journal of Clinical and Experimental Hypnosis, 45,* 324–332.

Kirsch, I. (1996). Hypnosis in psychotherapy: Efficacy and mechanisms. *Contemporary Hypnosis, 13,* 109–114.

Kirsch, I. (1997). Suggestibility or hypnosis: What do our scales really measure? *International Journal of Clinical and Experimental Hypnosis, 45,* 212–225.

Kirsch, I. (2000a, Spring). The placebo effect in antidepressant medication. *The Milton H. Erickson Foundation Newsletter, 20,* 12–13.

Kirsch, I. (2000b). The response set theory of hypnosis. *American Journal of Clinical Hypnosis, 42,* 274–293.

Kirsch, I., Montgomery, G., & Sapirstein, G. (1995). Hypnosis as an adjunct to cognitive-behavioral psychotherapy: A meta-analysis. *Journal of Consulting and Clinical Psychology, 63,* 214–220.

Kirsch, I., & Sapirstein, G. (1999). Listening to Prozac but hearing placebo: A meta-analysis of antidepressant medication. In I. Kirsch (Ed.), *How expectancies shape behavior* (pp. 303–320). Washington, DC: American Psychological Association.

Klerman, G., & Weissman, M. (1989). Increasing rates of depression. *Journal of the American Medical Association, 261,* 2229–2235.

Kornstein, S. (1997). Gender differences in depression: Implications for treatment. *Journal of Clinical Psychiatry, 58*(Suppl. 15), 12–18.

Kovacs, M., & Beck, A. (1985). Maladaptive cognitive structures in depression. In J. Coyne (Ed.), *Essential papers on depression* (pp. 240–258). New York: University Press.

Kramer, P. (1993). *Listening to Prozac.* New York: Penguin.

Kramer, P. (1997). *Should you leave?* New York: Scribner.

Kravitz, H., & Newman, A. (1995). Medical diagnostic procedures for depression: An update from a decade of promise. In E. Beckham & W. Leber (Eds.), *Handbook of depression* (pp. 302–326). New York: Guilford.

Kroger, W. (1977). *Clinical and experimental hypnosis* (2nd ed.). Philadelphia: Lippincott.

Lankton, S., & Lankton, C. (1983). *The answer within: A clinical framework of Ericksonian hypnotherapy.* New York: Brunner/Mazel.

Lewinsohn, P., Munos, R., Youngren, M., & Zeiss, A. (1986). *Control your depression.* New York: Prentice Hall.

Lynch, D. (1999) Empowering the patient: Hypnosis in the management of cancer, surgical disease and chronic pain. *American Journal of Clinical Hypnosis, 42,* 122–131.

Lynn, S., & Sherman, S. (2000). The clinical importance of sociocognitive models of hypnosis: Response set theory and Milton Erickson's strategic interventions. *American Journal of Clinical Hypnosis, 42,* 294–315.

Lynn, S., Kirsch, I., Barabasz, A., Cardena, E., & Patterson, D. (2000). Hypnosis as an empirically supported clinical intervention: The state of the evidence and a look to the future. *International Journal of Clinical and Experimental Hypnosis, 48,* 239–259.

Lynn, S., Kirsch, I., Neufeld, J., & Rhue, J. (1996). Clinical hypnosis: Assessment, applications, and treatment considerations. In S. Lynn, I. Kirsch, & J. Rhue (Eds.), *Casebook of clinical hypnosis* (pp. 3–30). Washington, DC: American Psychological Association.

MacHovec, F. (1986). *Hypnosis complications: Prevention and risk management.* Springfield, IL: C. C. Thomas.

McGrath, E., Keita, G., Strickland, B., & Russo, N. (Eds.). (1990). *Women and depression: Risk factors and treatment issues.* Washington, DC: American Psychological Association.

Miller, S., Hubble, M., & Duncan, B. (1997). *Escape from Babel: Toward a unifying language for psychotherapy practice.* New York: Norton.

Mondimore, F. (1993). *Depression: The mood disease.* Baltimore: The Johns Hopkins University Press.

Montgomery, G., DuHamel, K., & Redd, W. (2000). A meta-analysis of hypnotically induced analgesia: How effective is hypnosis? *International Journal of Clinical and Experimental Hypnosis, 48,* 134–149.

Moore, K., & Burrows, G. (1991). Hypnosis in the treatment of obsessive-compulsive disorder. *Australian Journal of Clinical and Experimental Hypnosis, 19,* 63–75.

Murray, C., & Lopez, A. (1997). Global mortality, disability, and the contribution of risk factors: Global burden of disease study. *Lancet, 349,* 1436–1442.

Myers, D. (2000). The funds, friends, and faith of happy people. *American Psychologist, 55,* 56–67.

National Institute of Mental Health (1999, June 1). Depression: The invisible disease. [On-line]. Available: http://www.nimh.nih.gov/publicat/invisible.ctm

NewsRx.com (2000, July 5). Survey finds 103 medicines in development for mental illnesses. [On-line]. *Drug Week.* Available: http://www.psycport.com/2000/07/05/eng-newsrx/eng-newsrx_101417_137_708142497577.html

Nolen-Hoeksema, S., Grayson, C., & Larson, J. (1999). Explaining the gender difference in depressive symptoms. *Journal of Personality and Social Psychology, 77,* 1061–1072.

O'Leary, K., Christian, J., & Mendell, N. (1993). A closer look at the link between marital discord and depressive symptomatology. *Journal of Social and Clinical Psychology, 13,* 31–41.

Persons, J., Thase, M., & Christoph, P. (1996). The role of psychotherapy in the treatment of depression: Review of two practice guidelines. *Archives of General Psychiatry, 53,* 283–290.

Peterson, C. (2000). The future of optimism. *American Psychologist, 55,* 44–55.

Peterson, C., Maier, S., & Seligman, M. (1993). *Learned helplessness: A theory for the age of personal control.* New York: Oxford University Press.

Philipchalk, R., & McConnell, J. (1994). *Understanding human behavior* (8th ed.). New York: Holt, Rinehart & Winston.

Real, T. (1997). *I don't want to talk about it: Overcoming the secret legacy of male depression.* New York: Scribner.

Reuters Health Information (1999, November 30). Few patients satisfied with antidepressants. [On-line]. Available: http://www.drkoop.com/news/stories/november/antidepressant_unhappy.html

Rothbaum, F., Weisz, J., & Snyder, F. (1982). Changing the world and changing the self: A 2 process model of perceived control. *Journal of Personality and Social Psychology, 42*, 5–37.

Sacco, W., & Beck, A. (1995). Cognitive theory and therapy. In E. Beckham & W. Leber (Eds.), *Handbook of psychotherapy* (pp. 329–351). New York: Guilford.

Satcher, D. (1999, December 13). Mental health: A report of the Surgeon General. [On-line]. *The Virtual Office of the Surgeon General.* Available: www.surgeongeneral.gov

Schoenberger, N. (2000). Research on hypnosis as an adjunct to cognitive-behavioral psychotherapy. *International Journal of Clinical and Experimental Hypnosis, 48*, 154–169.

Schoenberger, N., Kirsch, I., Gearan, P., Montgomery, G., & Pastyrnak, S. (1997). Hypnotic enhancement of a cognitive behavioral treatment for public speaking anxiety. *Behavior Therapy, 28*, 127–140.

Schrof, J., & Schultz, S. (1999, March 8). An age of melancholy. *U.S. News & World Report, 127*, 55–63.

Schulberg, H., Katon, W., Simon, G., & Rush, A. (1998). Treating major depression in primary care practice. *Archives of General Psychiatry, 55*, 1121–1127.

Schulberg, H., & Rush, A. (1994). Clinical practice guidelines for managing major depression in primary care practice: Implications for psychologists. *American Psychologist, 49*, 34–41.

Schuyler, D. (1998). *Taming the tyrant: Treating depressed adults.* New York: Norton.

Schwartz, J. (1996). *Brain lock.* New York: Regan Books.

Seligman, M. (1989). Explanatory style: Predicting depression, achievement, and health. In M. Yapko (Ed.), *Brief therapy approaches to treating anxiety and depression* (pp. 5–32). New York: Brunner/Mazel.

Seligman, M. (1990). *Learned optimism.* New York: Alfred A. Knopf.

Seligman, M. (1993). *What you can change and what you can't.* New York: Alfred A. Knopf.

Seligman, M. (1995). The effectiveness of psychotherapy: The "Consumer Reports" study. *American Psychologist, 50*, 965–974.

Seligman, M. E. P. (2000). *American Psychologist: Special Issue on Happiness, Excellence and Optimal Human Functioning, 55*, 1, 5–183 .

Seligman, M., & Csikszentmihalyi, M. (2000). Positive psychology: An introduction. *American Psychologist, 55*, 5–14.

Siever, L., & Frucht, W. (1997). *The new view of self.* New York: Macmillan.

Spanos, N. (1991). A sociocognitive approach to hypnosis. In S. Lynn & J. Rhue (Eds.), *Theories of hypnosis: Current models and perspectives* (pp. 324–361). New York: Guilford.

Spanos, N., & Chaves, J. (Eds.). (1989). *Hynosis: The cognitive-behavioral perspective.* New York: Prometheus Books.

Spanos, N., & Chaves, J. (1991). History and historiography of hypnosis. In S. Lynn & J. Rhue (Eds.), *Theories of hypnosis: Current models and perspectives* (pp. 43–78). New York: Guilford.

Spanos, N., & Coe, W. (1992). A social-psychological approach to hypnosis. In E. Fromm & M. Nash (Eds.), *Contemporary hypnosis research* (pp. 102–130). New York: Guilford.

Spiegel, D., & Butler, L. (in progress). *Alternative treatments for long term depressed mood: Use of meditation and hypnosis for dysthymia.* Unpublished manuscript, Stanford University School of Medicine, Department of Psychiatry and Behavioral Sciences.

Spiegel, H., & Spiegel, D. (1987). *Trance and treatment: Clinical uses of hypnosis.* Washington, DC: American Psychiatric Press.

Stevens, D., Merikangas, K., & Merikangas, J. (1995). Comorbidity of depression and other medical conditions. In E. Beckham & W. Leber (Eds.), *Handbook of depression* (pp. 147–199). New York: Guilford.

Strauss, B. (1993). Operator variables in hypnotherapy. In J. Rhue, S. Lynn, & I. Kirsch (Eds.), *Handbook of clinical hypnosis* (pp. 55–72). Washington, DC: American Psychological Association.

Swindle, R., Heller, K., Pescosolido, B., & Kikuzawa, S. (2000). Responses to nervous breakdowns in America over a 40 year period: Mental health policy implications. *American Psychologist, 55,* 740–749.

Thase, M., & Glick, I. (1995). Combined treatment. In I. Glick (Ed.), *Treating depression* (pp. 183–208). San Francisco: Jossey-Bass.

Thase, M., & Howland, R. (1995). Biological processes in depression: An updated review and integration. In E. Beckham & W. Leber (Eds.), *Handbook of depression* (pp. 213–279). New York: Guilford.

Tolman, A. (1995). *Major depressive disorder: The latest assessment and treatment strategies.* Kansas City, MO: Compact Clinicals.

Valenstein, E. (1998). *Blaming the brain: The truth about drugs and mental health.* New York: Free Press.

Wagstaff, G. (1991). Compliance, belief, and semantics in hypnosis: A nonstate, sociocognitive perspective. In S. Lynn & J. Rhue (Eds.), *Theories of hypnosis: Current models and perspectives* (pp. 324–361). New York: Guilford.

Watkins, J. (1987). *Hypnotherapeutic techniques.* New York: Irvington Publishers.

Watzlawick, P. (1978). *The language of change.* New York: Basic Books.

Weissbourd, R. (1996). *The vulnerable child: What really hurts America's children and what we can do about it.* Reading, PA: Addison-Wesley.

Weissman, M. (1987). Advances in psychiatric epidemiology: Rates and risks for major depression. *American Journal of Public Health, 77,* 445–451.

Weissman, M., Bland, R., Canino, G., Faravelli, C., Greenwald, S., Hwu, H.-G., Joyce, P., Karam, E., Lee, C.-K., Lellouch, J., Lepine, J.-P., Newman, S., Rubio-Stipec, M., Wells, E., Wickramaratne, P., Wittchen, H.-U., & Yeh, E.-K. (1996). Cross-national epidemiology of major depression and bipolar disorder. *Journal of the American Medical Association, 276,* 293–299.

Weissman, M., Warner, V., Wickramaratne, P., Moreau, D., & Olfston, M. (1997). Offspring of depressed parents: 10 years later. *Archives of General Psychiatry, 54,* 932–940.

Weitzenhoffer, A. (1989). *The practice of hypnotism* (Vols. 1, 2). New York: Wiley.

The White House (1999, June 7). The White House remarks at the White House conference on mental health. [On-line]. Available: http://www.whitehouse.gov/WH/New/html/19990607.html

Yapko, M. (1987, Winter). An interview with William Kroger. *The Milton H. Erickson Foundation Newsletter, 7,* 1–4.

Yapko, M. (1988a, Winter). An interview with Martin E. P. Seligman, Ph.D. *The Milton H. Erickson Foundation Newsletter, 9,* 1–14.

Yapko, M. (1988b). *When living hurts: Directives for treating depression.* New York: Brunner/Mazel.

Yapko, M. (1989). Disturbances of temporal orientation as a feature of depression. In M. Yapko (Ed.), *Brief therapy approaches to treating anxiety and depression* (pp. 106–118). New York: Brunner/Mazel.

Yapko, M. (1990). *Trancework: An introduction to the practice of clinical hypnosis* (2nd ed.). New York: Brunner/Mazel.

Yapko, M. (1992). *Hypnosis and the treatment of depressions: Strategies for change.* New York: Brunner/Mazel.

Yapko, M. (1993). Hypnosis and depression. In J. Rhue, S. Lynn, & I. Kirsch (Eds.), *Handbook of clinical hypnosis* (pp. 339–355). Washington, DC: American Psychological Association.

Yapko, M. (1994). *Suggestions of abuse: True and false memories of childhood sexual trauma.* New York: Simon & Schuster.

Yapko, M. (1995). *Essentials of hypnosis.* New York: Brunner/Mazel.

Yapko, M. (1996). Depression: Perspectives and treatments. *Encyclopedia Britannica: 1997 Medical and Health Annual,* 287–291.

Yapko, M. (1997). *Breaking the patterns of depression.* New York: Doubleday.

Yapko, M. (1999). *Hand-me-down blues: How to stop depression from spreading in families.* New York: St. Martins Griffin.

Zeig, J. (1980a). Symptom prescription techniques: Clinical applications using elements of communication. *American Journal of Clinical Hypnosis, 23,* 23–32.

Zeig, J. (Ed.). (1980b). *A teaching seminar with Milton H. Erickson, M.D.* New York: Brunner/Mazel.

Appendix A
Useful information on the Internet

Depression

Using the search words "depression" and "mental health" will lead you to more information and referrals than you can imagine. Listed below are some of the more useful websites.

Managing Depression Intelligently
www.managing-depression-intelligently.com

National Institute of Mental Health
www.nimh.nih.gov

National Mental Health Association
www.nmha.org

National Depressive and Manic-Depressive Association
www.ndmda.org

American Psychological Association (Consumer Help Center)
www.apa.org

Psych Central
www.grohol.com

American Association for Marriage and Family Therapy
www.aamft.org

Dr. Ivan's Depression Central
www.psycom.net/depression.central

All About Depression
www.AllAboutDepression.com

Self Help for Depression
www.self-help-for-depression.com

National Alliance for the Mentally Ill
www.nami.org

Hypnosis

Society for Clinical and Experimental Hypnosis
www.hypnosis-research.org

International Society of Hypnosis
www.ish.unimelb.edu.au

American Society of Clinical Hypnosis
www.asch.org

British Society of Medical Hypnosis
www.bsmdh.org

The Milton H. Erickson Foundation
www.erickson-foundation.org

Appendix B
Supplemental materials
From Michael D. Yapko, Ph.D.

Readers of this book may be interested in some of the audiotapes and videotapes featuring Dr. Yapko's clinical interventions. These are described below.

Videotapes

"The Case of Vicki: Patterns of Trancework with a Terminal Cancer Patient."
This clinical demonstration features Dr. Yapko's profoundly moving single-session intervention with a 42-year-old woman named Vicki who is dying of cancer. Vicki requests help in learning to manage pain without the use of medication so that she may remain clear-headed for the little time she has left to live. This session is transcribed with commentary and analysis in Dr. Yapko's hypnosis textbook, *Trancework: An Introduction to the Practice of Clinical Hypnosis.* (2 hours, $79.95)

"Breaking Patterns of Depression: Hypnosis and Building Resources."
Transcribed with commentary and analysis in Chapter 8 of this volume, this elaborate, professionally produced and edited demonstration shows a single session with a moderately depressed man named Mike who has a history of severe physical abuse. Includes discussion and follow-up. (90 minutes, $79.95)

"Hypnosis and Exploring Options."
Transcribed with commentary and analysis in Chapter 7 of this volume, this beautifully filmed session shows Dr. Yapko's hypnotic and strategic work with Consuelo, a psychologist from Italy, who experiences herself as "feeling stuck" in her inability to write. The teaching value of the session is enhanced by the addition of explanatory subtitles and commentary throughout the hypnotic intervention. Includes follow-up information. (60 minutes, $39.95)

"Hypnotically Generating Therapeutic Possibilities."

This session was described in Chapter 4 of this volume. It features Dr. Yapko's use of hypnosis with Bob, a therapist new to the field, who is feeling overwhelmed and insecure about his new career. Some emotionally powerful material emerges during hypnosis about his relationship with his father that is utilized in the therapy. Includes explanatory subtitles, commentary, and follow-up information. (60 minutes, $39.95)

Audiotapes/Compact Discs

"Focusing on Feeling Good"

Designed as an experiential supplement to Dr. Yapko's clinical writings on depression, this program is a professionally produced and innovative series of skill-building sessions involving the use of formal hypnosis. There are seven hypnosis sessions, each targeting a different issue or symptom commonly associated with depression. The topics are listed below. Each side (except the first) is approximately 25 minutes long and provides a brief discussion of the topic followed by a hypnosis session.

1. Depression as a Problem: Hypnosis as a Solution (Overcoming depression)
2. The Power of Vision (The value of goals)
3. Try Again . . . But Do Something Different (Developing flexibility)
4. Is It In Your Control? (Discriminating controllability)
5. You're the Border Patrol (Developing boundaries)
6. Presumed Innocent But Feeling Guilty (Resolving guilt)
7. Good Night . . . And Sleep Well (Enhancing sleep)
8. Prevention Whenever Possible (Thinking preventively)

The program also includes a 24-page informative manual (Audiotape program: $39.95; CD program: $49.95)

Ordering information

Any of the videotapes or the *Focusing on Feeling Good* program can be ordered online by visiting Dr. Yapko's website **www.self-help-for-depression.com**. Additional information about each item can also be obtained there.

Items can also be ordered by mail by sending a check or money order payable to "Dr. Yapko" for the amount of the product plus $6 shipping and handling for the first item and $3 for each additional item to:

Dr. Michael Yapko
P.O. Box 234268
Leucadia, CA 92023-4268

International shipping costs are extra.

Index